گر عشق نبودی و غم عشق نبودی
چندین سخن نغز که گفتی که شنودی

ور باد نبودی که سر زلف ربودی
رخساره معشوق بعاشق که نمودی

Were there no love nor pain of yearning for love
Who would speak and who would hear such lofty words?

Were there no wind to steal the curl of her lock
Who would unveil the face of the Beloved to her lover?

Suhrawardi and the School of Illumination

CURZON SUFI SERIES

Series editor: Ian Richard Netton

Professor of Arabic Studies,
University of Leeds

The Curzon Sufi Series attempts to provide short introductions to a variety of facets of the subject, which are accessible both to the general reader and the student and scholar in the field. Each book will be either a synthesis of existing knowledge or a distinct contribution to, and extension of, knowledge of the particular topic. The two major underlying principles of the Series are sound scholarship and readability.

BEYOND FAITH AND INFIDELITY
The Sufi Poetry and Teachings of Mahmud Shabistari
Leonard Lewisohn

AL-HALLAJ
Herbert W. Mason

RUZBIHAN BAQLI
Mysticism and the Rhetoric of Sainthood in Persian Sufism
Carl W. Ernst

ABDULLAH ANSARI OF HERAT
An Early Sufi Master
A.G. Ravan Farhadi

PERSIAN SUFI POETRY
An Introduction to the Mystical Use of Classical Persian Poetry
J.T.P. de Bruijn

THE CONCEPT OF SAINTHOOOD IN EARLY ISLAMIC MYSTICISM
Bernd Radtke and John O'Kane

Suhrawardi and the School of Illumination

by

Mehdi Amin Razavi

CURZON

First published in 1997
by Curzon Press
St John's Studios, Church Road, Richmond
Surrey, TW9 2QA

Typeset in Baskerville by LaserScript, Mitcham, Surrey

Printed in Great Britain by
Biddles Limited, Guildford and King's Lynn

British Library Cataloguing in Publication Data
A catalogue record for this book is available from the British Library

Library of Congress in Publication Data
A catalogue record for this book has been requested

ISBN 0–7007–0451–5 (hbk)
ISBN 0–7007–0412–4 (pbk)

To
Marylynn, Mitra and Arya

Contents

NOTE

1. All translations are mine unless otherwise stated.
2. Diacritic marks are not placed on the following words since they are repeated throughout the work: Suhrawardi, Ishraq, Sufi. Diacritic marks have not been placed on the name of cities, countries and dynasties.
3. All dates are given first in the Islamic calendar year followed by the common era.

Acknowledgements

I am indebted to Professor Seyyed Hossein Nasr for his comments and guidance and Ms. Jacqueline Bralove for reading the manuscript and providing me with editorial suggestions. I would also like to express my appreciation to Lee Joanna Harper and Jason Chipman for their assistance and Cindy Toomey and Harriet Brennan for their administrative support.

Introduction

This work discusses the mystical dimension of Shihāb al-Dīn Yaḥyā Suhrawardi, the philosopher-mystic and the founder of the School of Illumination (*ishraq*) in the tradition of Islamic philosophy.

Suhrawardi is one of the most influential figures in the history of Islamic philosophy, because of the significance of his intellectual contributions and because of the impact he had on his successors, in particular later Islamic philosophy which culminated in the "School of Isfahan".

Despite the existing diversity of intellectual inquiries within Islam which range from the rationalistic philosophy of the peripatetics (*mashshā'īs*) and the intellectual intuition of the illuminationists (*ishrāqiyyūn*) to the ascetic and inner journey of the Sufis, there have been few philosophers who have made an attempt to synthesize these diverse schools of thought into a unified philosophical paradigm.

Amīrak Muḥammad ibn Shihāb al-Dīn Suhrawardi, the Persian philosopher of the 6/12 century and an advocate of what he called "ancient wisdom" (*ḥikmat al-'atīq*), made an attempt to unify various schools of wisdom in order to demonstrate the universal truth that lies at the heart of all divinely revealed religions. Unlike earlier Sufis and gnostics in Islam, Suhrawardi maintained that philosophical discourse was a necessary training for those seeking to pursue the path of illumination. This was quite revolutionary since Sufis rejected rationalistic philosophy as exemplified by the Peripatetics who in turn rejected Sufism. The significance of Suhrawardi becomes more clear when he is viewed as a gnostic who advocates both philosophical discourse and asceticism as an essential part of the path of illumination. He also incorporates various elements from such traditions of wisdom as the Egyptians, Greeks and Persians in order to bring a rapprochement between rationalistic philosophy, intellectual intuition and practical wisdom.

The foremost difficulty in writing on Suhrawardi's school of illumination, as with any visionary mystic/philosopher, is to find the qualified person who can comment from an insider's point of view. The heart of the visionary's brand of mysticism, is to have an intuitive knowledge of or an inner experience of, truth. By definition, then, commentators and authors of such a work would be qualified to explain this inner experience if they can relate to this message on an experiential basis and therefore can speak as an insider.

The above poses a problem for this author since on one hand I am to comment on a philosopher/mystic whose thoughts have drawn and engaged me for a number of years, while on the other hand I do not stand within the illuminationist tradition of the luminous world of lights, angels, archetypes and the interconnected web of ideas that Suhrawardi puts forward. In fact, Suhrawardi goes so far as to tell us that unless one has fasted for forty days, he will not understand his major work, *Ḥikmat al-ishrāq (The Philosophy of Illumination)*. An insight of the luminous world of Suhrawardi therefore, is not a "live option" for me, to use William James' term.

This volume presents not so much a discussion concerning the validity or soundness of Suhrawardi's specific ideas but an exposition of the mystical dimension of his rather broad and varied school of thought. As an outsider to a school of thought whose thrust remains the attainment of truth through a special mode of cognition, all an author can do is to engage himself in a close textual analysis and attempt to put them in coherent and well defined concepts. It is towards this aim which I have embarked upon an exegesis of various symbols used in Suhrawardi's mystical narratives as well as the decoding of the dense language which he uses to keep the esoteric secrets from those who are not among the "brothers in purity".

The present work, therefore, undertakes a study of the mystical dimension of Suhrawardi's thought. It is imperative to note that while mysticism remains one of the salient features of Suhrawardi's philosophical school, he was not only a Sufi nor was his school of thought only mystical. Suhrawardi was a system builder and like many others of the same stature (i.e. Ibn Sīnā), he comments on various traditional philosophical topics, i.e. metaphysics, ontology, epistemology, logic, etc.

In recent years there has been a discussion among the scholars of Suhrawardi as to the true nature of his teachings and the nature of his specific contributions to Islamic philosophy. These discussions have led to the emergence of three distinct interpretations of Suhrawardian philosophy. Before embarking on an exposition and analysis of Suhrawardi's mystical ideas, it is necessary to briefly discuss these trends since it will enable us to place the mystical thoughts of Suhrawardi in an appropriate context.

I. SUHRAWARDI THE LOGICIAN:

This view, primarily held by H. Ziā'ī,[1] argues that the salient feature of Suhrawardi's philosophy is his Peripatetic writings and in particular his commentaries on logic and his critique of the peripatetic view of definition as a means of cognition. Ziā'ī, who considers the non-Peripatetic writings of Suhrawardi to be of secondary value hardly ever refers to his mystical narratives.

Ziā'ī's interpretation of Suhrawardi's thought is rather narrow and does not present the comprehensive nature of Suhrawardi's philosophy of illumination as one that is inclusive of rationalistic philosophy but is not limited to peripatetic philosophy. I do not wish to provide an extensive response to the above view but this much should suffice, that even a brief examination of the corpus of Suhrawardi's writings reveals the extent to which he went beyond the fashionable philosophical school of his time, namely the sort of logical analysis that was carried out by the Peripatetics. Furthermore, to ignore the vast body of Suhrawardi's mystical narratives also ignores the reason he wrote these mystical treatises. If Suhrawardi did not consider them to be necessary, he would not have composed them with such care or given repeated instructions to his companions to safeguard them. The mystical narratives of Suhrawardi should be regarded as part and parcel of the doctrine of illumination and it is in such treatises that he offers the second component of the *ishraqi* school of thought, namely practical wisdom, something that the above interpretation completely ignores.

II. SUHRAWARDI THE NEO-AVICENNIAN:

The view held by some of the prominent scholars of Islamic philosophy such as Mehdī Ḥā'irī and Sayyid Jalāl al-Dīn Āshtiyānī, regards Suhrawardi as a philosopher who remains essentially within the Ibn Sīnian philosophical domain despite his innovations and deviations from the Peripatetic view.

A neo-Ibn Sīnian reading of Suhrawardi takes a broader look at his philosophy and considers both Suhrawardi's commentaries on logic and metaphysics and his *ishraqi* writings to be of great philosophical significance. Suhrawardi accordingly is regarded as one who by drawing from various sources, interprets Ibn Sīnā from a Neoplatonic view point, thereby synthesizing Aristotle, Plato, Pythagoreans and Hermeticism.

The above view in my opinion is more valid than the previous one but it too lacks emphasis on the mystical writings of Suhrawardi. Such notions as the attainment of knowledge through mystical experience and Suhrawardi's explicit emphasis on asceticism as a necessary component of pursuing the wisdom of illumination is too often ignored by a neo-Ibn Sīnian interpretation of Suhrawardi. Proponents of this interpretation, too do not pay the attention that the Persian writings of Suhrawardi deserve, often regarding them only as fine works of literature. The mystical narratives of Suhrawardi present in a metaphorical language that which the language of rationalistic philosophy often fails to achieve. Even Ibn Sīnā himself relies on the use of a symbolic language in his visionary recitals to propogate certain philosophical notions that ordinary language of peripatetic philosophy can not convey.

III. SUHRAWARDI THE THEOSOPHIST:

This interpretation of Suhrawardi as a theosophist (*ḥakīm*) is also advocated by a number of prominent Suhrawardi scholars such as Seyyed Ḥossein Naṣr and Henry Corbin. The thrust of this interpretation is the multidimensional aspect of the Suhrawardian philosophy. According to this interpretation, rationalistic philosophy is prerequsite to the study of *ishraqi* philosophy and an integral component of it.

Unlike the former two interpretations, however, Naṣr and Corbin argue that the role of rationalistic philosophy is a limited one according to Suhrawardi because it demonstrates the limitations of reason to bring about knowledge of an existential nature. The intellect that yearns towards the absolute, transcends reason and through intellectual intuition (*dawq*) embraces the Divine truth. The faculty of intellectual intuition which exists potentially in man can be actualized if one is engaged in inner cleansing and purification which makes one receptive to divine wisdom. In one of his lengthiest treatises, Suhrawardi himself alludes to the practical as well as the theoretical dimension of *ḥikmah* and states:

> He [God] is *ḥikmah* in that *ḥikmah* is of two divisions: one is pure knowledge and the other one is practical. Knowledge is to conceptualize the reality of the existent beings but praxis is the structure of action emanating from the essence of the doer.[1]

In numerous places throughout his treatises, Suhrawardi explicitly addresses the role and place of the practical dimension of the *ishraqi* school by discussing in great detail specific Sufi rituals, components of an ascetic path and their spiritual consequence for the *sālik* (he who is on the path).

I adhere to the third interpretation since it does not negate or exclude the first two alternative interpretations but gives appropriate credit to Suhrawardi's mystical dimension as well. Since this study will focus on the Sufi aspects of Suhrawardi's school of illumination, emphasis is placed on the mystical elements of his thoughts.

It is obvious that Suhrawardi has written a variety of mystical narratives deliberately using the traditional Sufi symbolism and metaphors. Furthermore, the number of these treatises, the use of Sufi language and expressions, as well as explicit emphasis on such notions as the spiritual path, the need for a master and ascetic practices, all indicate one thing, namely Suhrawardi's desire to disclose the place and significance of the Sufi component of the school of *ishraq*.

It is therefore our view that disregarding the Sufi elements of the Suhrawardian thoughts leads to a misinterpretation of the school of *Ishraq* which is often followed by an attempt to place Suhrawardi in one of the traditional schools of Islamic philosophy i.e. peripatetics. It is the opinion of this author that Suhrawardi did not rely on one methodology for the understanding of truth but that he made full use of the possibilities that exist in the philosophical as well as the practical aspects of wisdom.

A more comprehensive study of Suhrawardi includes an extensive discussion of his ontology, epistemology, angelology and logic. Since this study will focus on the Sufi aspect of Suhrawardi and the school of illumination, our treatment of the peripatetic aspects of his thoughts are necessarily rather brief. However, certain aspects of his angelology and ontology that serve as the background for both practical and philosophical Sufism have been treated more extensively than others.

In the first chapter, the life and works of Suhrawardi have been discussed. Both Suhrawardi's philosophical and Sufi writings are briefly analyzed, particularly the structure of his philosophical works. In the second chapter, the intellectual context of Suhrawardi's thought in his historical period has been alluded to before a broad survey of the central themes and the essential components of his school of *ishraq* are discussed. Finally, we have presented the distinction Suhrawardi makes between philosophy in its rationalistic sense and *ḥikmah*. A thorough understanding of this distinction is crucial for placing the Suhrawardian thought in its proper context.

In the third chapter, Suhrawardi's views concerning practical wisdom are discussed. Sufism on a practical level remains an integral part of Suhrawardi's philosophy and he describes the various elements of the spiritual path in great detail. In this chapter such topics as mystical visions, the nature of man and carnal desires, the role of the Sufi master and the spiritual journey of the soul as well as the role of asceticism have been discussed. Finally, unity as the ultimate goal of Sufis has been treated as the final stage of the spiritual path.

In the fourth chapter, philosophical Sufism is extensively treated. The subject of emanation and the hierarchy of light and their relationship with one another as well as angelology, a derivative of Suhrawardi's ontology, have been discussed. Angelology in Suhrawardi represents an important aspect of his thought in that he introduces various elements from other traditions, in particular the Zoroastrian religion. Through angelology, Suhrawardi discusses the archetypal world as well as the imaginal world as realities that stand opposite to the world of imagination. Subsequently, Suhrawardi's theory of vision in its physical and spiritual sense as well as the relationship between knowledge, presence, light and self have been discussed.

At the heart of Suhrawardi's school of illumination is a particular theory of knowledge known as "knowledge by presence". To offer an exposition of this theory, a critique of the more conventional theories of knowledge such as knowledge by definition, sense perception and innate concepts has first been offered in the second part of this chapter. Having presented Suhrawardi's critique of the inadequacies of these modes of knowing, his theory of knowledge by presence has been discussed. The chapter concludes with a discussion concerning the practical consequences of this theory and a critique of knowledge by presence.

In the fifth chapter, the influence of Suhrawardi on Islamic philosophy in various parts of the Islamic world as well as the West has been presented. Among the topics discussed are the influence of Suhrawardi's *ishraqi* thought in bringing about such schools of philosophy as the "School of Isfahan". We have noted Suhrawardi's influence in India and Pakistan and the extent to which his ideas were instrumental in making the intellectual milieu of this region receptive to the philosophy of Mullā Ṣadrā. Finally, the possible influence of Suhrawardi in such regions as Syria and Turkey have been alluded to and the limited influence of Suhrawardi in the west, in particular in France, was briefly discussed.

I have brought the volume to a conclusion by examining a possible relationship between Suhrawardi and the Persian nationalistic movement known as Shu'ūbiyyah.

In the appendix, my translation into English of a partial commentary of a 7/13 Indian author on *The Chant of Gabriel's Wing*, one of the most important esoteric works of Suhrawardi has been included. This translation is important: first, it represents a sample of Suhrawardi's esoteric writing; second, the commentary elaborates on some of the more complex symbolism in this treatise; and finally, it signifies the historical importance of Suhra- wardi as it demonstrates how his writings have traveled from Syria to India only two centuries after him.

1

THE LIFE AND WORKS OF SUHRAWARDI

A. LIFE

Suhrawardi was born in a village near Zanjan, a northern Iranian city. His full name is Shihāb al-Dīn Yaḥyā ibn Ḥabash ibn Amīrak Abū'l-Futūḥ Suhrawardi, who also received the title "Shaykh al-ishraq" (the Master of Illumination) and "al-Maqtūl" (the Martyr).[1] The date of his birth is not certain but his most notable biographer, Shahrazūrī,[2] indicated that he was born in 545/ 1166 or 550/1171 while S.H. Nasr,[3] a notable scholar of Suhrawardi, has stated the date to be 549/1170.

At an early age Suhrawardi went to the city of Maraghah, where he studied *ḥikmat* with Majd al-Dīn Jīlī, and he then traveled to Isfahan, where he studied philosophy with Ẓahir al-Dīn al-Qārī and *The Observations* (*al-Baṣā'ir*) of 'Umar ibn Ṣalān al-Ṣāwī.[4] He journeyed through the Islamic lands to meet the Sufi masters while practicing asceticism and withdrawing for long spiritual retreats. He tells us that he had looked for a companion with spiritual insight equal to his, but he failed to find one.[5]

Having wandered through Anatolia and Syria on one of his journeys from Damascus to Alleppo, he met Malik Ẓāhir, the son of the famous Ṣalāḥ al-Dīn Ayyūbī (Ṣalādīn). Yāqūt ibn 'Abdallāh al-Ḥamawī[6] put the date of this journey to Syria at 579/1200. Shahrazūrī, his contemporary and bibliographer, writes:

> Malik liked the Shaykh and he liked him. The 'ulama of Syria gathered around the Shaykh and heard his words. In discussions he clarified the thoughts of the *ḥukamā'* and their validity and weakened the opinion of the opponents of the *ḥukamā'*.[7]

It is not known whether Suhrawardi did train a number of students or not, but it is known that he had a circle of close friends and companions on whose request he composed *The Philosophy of Illumination (Ḥikmat al-ishrāq)*. Towards the end of this book,[8] he refers to his companions as "his brothers" and asks them to preserve the book from the enemies of wisdom. This again alludes to the existence of a certain group of friends or followers who knew him personally.

Perhaps for political reasons Suhrawardi's friends found it difficult to write his biography.[9] Shahrazūrī is the only one who speaks of him in a manner that suggests he had met him personally, though this is highly unlikely because neither Suhrawardi nor any other biographer of him makes reference to this point. It is possible that Shahrazuri came to know of Suhrawardi through some individual who knew the master personally.

Suhrawardi's keen intelligence, his vast and profound knowledge and finally his openness to other traditions of wisdom as well as his esoteric orientation, brought about hostility and antagonized the doctors of law at Malik Ẓāhir's court. Yūsūf ibn Taqhribirdī in his book *al-Nujūm al-ẓāhirah fī mulūk miṣr wa'l-qāhirah,*[10] describes a meeting between himself and Suhrawardi in which he calls him a "man with vast knowledge and a small mind".[11]

In comparison to other Muslim philosophers, especially Ibn Sīnā, he ranked himself as equal and stated:

> In discursive sciences I am equal, if not superior, but in intellectual intuition (*dhawq*) I am superior.[12]

Having advocated a type of wisdom which was inconsistent with the views of the orthodox jurists, they finally asked Malik Ẓāhir to put Suhrawardi to death for believing in heretical ideas. When he refused they signed a petition and sent it to Ṣalādīn, who ordered his son to have him killed. Malik Ẓāhir reluctantly carried out his father's order and Suhrawardi was killed in the year 587/1208. Taqhribirdī indicated[13] that Suhrawardi's death took place on the Friday of the month of July (Dhu'l-ḥajjah). According to Shahrazurī, there are different accounts of how he died. Shahrazurī writes:

> . . . he was thrown in jail and eating and drinking was denied to him until he died. Some say he fasted until he joined with his Origin. Some are of the opinion that he was suffocated

> and yet others believe he was killed by the sword and there are those who say he was dropped from the wall of the fortress and then burned.[14]

Suhrawardi's death was as mysterious as his life. Except for a number of works, he did not leave much behind to shed light on his life. He shied away from people and only sought the companionship of learned men. His manner of dressing is said to have varied from day to day. One day he would dress in court style and the very next day he would dress modestly.

In order to understand Suhrawardi's philosophy, the sociopolitical conditions under which he lived must be understood. This is not to say that his philosophy is subject to historicity, but that some of the issues involved in his death as well as certain philosophical trends in his ideas may be further clarified if the circumstances under which he lived are better known. As S.H. Naṣr states:

> The causes for Suhrawardi's death can not be truly discovered until the situation of the region, historically, religiously, philosophically and socially is thoroughly investigated.[15]

Suhrawardi lived during a turbulent period when northern Syria was undergoing a major change from being a strong Shi'ite center to a Sunni dominated region. He came to Aleppo at a time when this transformation was taking place and when Ṣalādīn was seen as the last hope for Muslims as the strong man who could confront the Crusaders. In a situation such as this the more exoteric jurists were not in any mood to allow a young philosopher, perhaps with some Shi'ite tendencies, to "corrupt" Ṣaladin's son, Malik Ẓāhir, in whose court Suhrawardi lived.

In light of the above factors, one can view Suhrawardi as a Persian who inherited a rich culture with Zoroastrian elements in it, a philosopher well versed in Peripatetic philosophy, and a mystic who tried to demonstrate that at the heart of all the divinely revealed traditions of wisdom there is one universal truth. Perhaps his desire to demonstrate such a unity had to do with the apparent hostility of different religions to one another, in particular Christianity and Islam. At a time when Christians and Muslims were engaged in a bloody war, Suhrawardi's message of unity was perceived to be a dangerous and even a heretical doctrine.

There are several possible explanations for Suhrawardi's death which can be formulated as follows:

1. Suhrawardi was advocating a form of Persian nationalism[16] which is generally considered to be a reaction to the domination of Arabs over Persia. This view, which is often supported by the presence of Zoroastrian elements in his doctrine, is in my opinion incorrect since it is contrary to the spirit of his philosophy and because Suhrawardi must have understood that the court of Malik Ẓāhir, the center of the Arab world, was not the best place to advocate Persian nationalism.
2. In his article, "The Source and Nature of Political Authority in Suhrawardi's Philosophy of Illumination,"[17] H. Ziā'ī argues that Suhrawardi advocated a political doctrine which considered the "king philosopher" to be the rightful ruler. This must have been offensive to both the Caliph in Baghdad and Ṣalāḥ al-Dīn Ayyūbī. As he states:

   > While Suhrawardi's categories of Divine philosophers-sages include a wide range of types, the most general being composed of the type called Brethren of Abstraction *ikhwān al-tajrid*) which includes the perfect philosopher referred to as God's vicegerent (*khalifat Allāh*) who may be the actual ruler (*ra'is*) of an era.[18]

   Such an idea as advocated in the beginning of *Ḥikmat al-ishrāq* must have been rather alarming to the more orthodox elements in Malik Ẓāhir's court.
3. It has been argued by some, including Shahrazurī, that some of Suhrawardi's companions called him "a prophet of God" (Abū'l-Futūḥ Rasūl Allāh).[19] If the above is true, then it may have been the likely cause of Suhrawardi's execution. One can make a case for this by arguing that since Suhrawardi believed that he was the unifier of two branches of wisdom, he must have assumed a role for himself which was above and beyond that of a philosopher and mystic. The argument becomes stronger when Suhrawardi tells us that wisdom as such began by the prophet Hermes and then was divided into two branches. Suhrawardi then implicitly argued that he was at least at the same rank as Hermes.

B. INTELLECTUAL CONTEXT

Suhrawardi lived at a time when the influence and power of the Mu'tazilite's theology had been substantially curtailed by the

Ash'rites. The result of the Mu'tazilite's rationalization was the Ash'arite *Kalām*, which paved the way for a more literary and exoteric interpretation of Islam. While the debate among the advocates of intellectual sciences continued, philosophical and theological schools were also challenged by the more experiential school of the Sufis, whose epistemological methodology questioned the very foundation upon which intellectually oriented schools had established their theories of knowledge. Such Sufi sages as Bāyazid and Ḥallāj, who influenced Suhrawardi, were instrumental in the development of his mystical thought. Their reliance upon purification and asceticism was an alternative to the more philosophically oriented epistemological paradigms.

At this historical juncture, Ghazzālī, as the most prestigious master of *Kalam* and learned man in the religious sciences, attacked the philosophers for their reliance solely upon reason for the attainment of certainty. Ghazzālī's attempt to demonstrate the above as exemplified in the *Tahāfut al-falāsifah*[20] paved the way for Sufism to challenge the more philosophically oriented schools of thought. Sufism, as a result of Ghazzālī's attack on philosophy, came to be viewed in a different light as a school whose intellectual merit had to be recognized and was not limited to outbursts of emotions embodied in lyrics, poetry and the practice of asceticism. Considering the apparent polarization between the Peripatetics and Sufis, the question on the intellectual horizon of the time may have been whether it was possible to bring about a rapprochement between these two opposing schools. Suhrawardi, as we will see, demonstrated that such a synthesis was not only possible but necessary and that a thorough familiarity with the Peripatetic philosophy was the prerequisite for the understanding of the philosophy of illumination. This attempt to create a bridge between the rationalistic tradition in Islamic philosophy and a gnostic view of knowledge dominated philosophical activities in Persia for several centuries.

At the center of these controversies stood Ibn Sīnā with his all-encompassing philosophical system. Ibn Sīnā's philosophy by the time of Suhrawardi had been interpreted in different ways and this brought about a number of schools which were essentially Ibn Sīnian but each one emphasised certain aspects of his ideas.

First, there were those sections of Ibn Sīnā's philosophy which were purely Aristotelian in nature and can be categorized as Peripatetic philosophy. The peripatetic tradition flourished and it was this interpretation of Ibn Sīnā which was mainly opposed to

Sufism. There were also those such as the exponents of *Kalām* who found Ibn Sīnā's logic and metaphysics to be a useful means of analysis and therefore adopted them. Such a trend reached its climax in the works of Fakhr al-Dīn Rāzī who applied Ibn Sīnian logic and metaphysics to solve various problems in *Kalām.* Finally, there was the mystical aspect of Ibn Sīnā which received less attention than his rationalistic writings. In these types of writings such as *Ḥayy ibn Yaqẓān* and the final chapter of the *Ishārāt,* the Neoplatonic aspect of Ibn Sīnā's philosophy is most apparent. Suhrawardi was well aware of such writings. For example, in his work *al-Ghurbat al-qharbiyyah* (*The Occidental Exile*), he continues Ibn Sīnā's story using some of the same metaphors.

Suhrawardi therefore appeared on the intellectual scene at a time when various interpretations of Ibn Sīnā had resulted in the emergence of different schools which often were antegnostic to one another.

To the existing differences between various interpretations of Ibn Sīnā must be added the influx of foreign ideas and philosophies. This intellectual diversity was the result of the translation of Greek texts and the interaction of the learned masters of such traditions as Neoplatonism, Pythagoreans, Hermeticism and Greek philosophy within the Muslim intellectual circles. Suhrawardi, who saw himself as the reviver of *Sophia Perennis,* also synthesized rationalistic philosophy of the Peripatetics, the practical wisdom of the Sufis and intellectual intuition of the *ishraqis.*

Suhrawardi's ideas permeated the tradition of Islamic philosophy and provided the Shi'ite philosophers with the means to offer a more intellectually justifiable explanation for the more esoteric aspects of Islam, in contrast to the more scriptual or exoteric interpretation of Islam. Suhrawardi, as a thinker who was to reconcile rationalism and mysticism within one single philosophical system, bridged the deep division between two interpretations or approaches to the message of Islam. The type of wisdom that Suhrawardi developed, known as *al-Ḥikmat al-ilāhiyyah,* (transcendental theosophy), encompasses rationalism and yet goes beyond it by basing itself on a direct vision of the truth.

Suhrawardi carried out an ecumenical analysis with Zoroastrian religion, Pythagorianism and Hermeticism on an existential and esoteric level. Perhaps his major achievement is that he pioneered what H. Corbin calls "Spiritual Hermeneutics," which maintains ecumenical work has to be carried out by those who speak from within a tradition and that their very being has become the manifestation of the truth of the tradition in question.

C. A SURVEY OF SUHRAWARDI'S WORKS

Suhrawardi's writings are diverse and dynamic and he often moves from the exposition of a purely philosophical argument to a profoundly mystical narrative. His works are written in different styles, i.e. Peripatetic, mystical, and *ishraqi*. In the last few decades, although many of Suhrawardi's works were introduced to the public by S.H. Naṣr and H. Corbin,[21] a number of Suhrawardi's works remain unpublished. Among the unpublished works of Suhrawardi we can mention his writings on the natural sciences, mathematics and logic that are included in the two major books *al-Muṭāraḥāt* (*The Book of Conversations*) and *al-Muqāwamāt (The Book of Opposites)* as well as *al-Talwīḥāt (The Book of Intimations)*. Also, the complete Arabic texts of *Alwāḥ 'imādī (The Tablets of 'Imād al-Dīn)*, *al-Lamaḥāt* (*The Flashes of Light*) and *al-Wāridāt wa'l-Taqdīsāt* (*Invocations and Prayers*) are not available.

H. Corbin in his *l'Archange empourprée* has translated large sections of the Persian works of Suhrawardi. Also, Corbin's translation of all but the logic of the *Ḥikmat al-ishrāq*,[22] along with much of Qūṭb al-Dīn Shirāzī and Mullā Ṣadrā's commentary upon the *Ḥikmat al-ishrāq*, provides an excellent source for the students of Suhrawardi. W.M. Thackston[23] in the *Mystical and Visionary Treatises of Shihabuddin Yaḥyā Suhrawardi* has also translated some of the Persian mystical narratives of Suhrawardi.[24]

Several attempts have been made to offer a classification of Suhrawardi's works. L. Massignon's classification of Suhrawardi's works based on the period when he composed them is as follows:[25]

1 Writings of Suhrawardi in his youth (early works).
2 Peripatetic writings.
3 Writings which represent a synthesis of Ibn Sīnā and Plotinus.

The problem which this classification poses is that Suhrawardi did not live a long life, and most of his works were composed when he was quite young. Also, how do we account for such works as *Alwāḥ 'imādī*, which is one of his early writings and yet contains strong *ishraqi* elements? This work is dedicated to Prince 'Imād who ruled in 581/1181, and considering that Suhrawardi was killed in 587/

1181 he must have written this book at roughly the same time as *The Philosophy of Illumination.*

S.H. Nasr and H. Corbin have by and large agreed to a structural classification of Suhrawardi's works, which is as follows:[26]

1. Suhrawardi wrote four large treatises that were of doctrinal nature: *al-Talwīḥāt (The Book of Intimation), al-Muqāwamāt (The Book of Opposites), al-Muṭārahat (The Book of Conversations)* and finally *Ḥikmat al-ishrāq (The Philosophy of Illumination).* The first three of these works are written in the tradition of the Peripatetics although there are criticisms of certain concepts of the Peripatetics in them.
2. There are shorter works, some of which are also of a doctrinal significance but should be viewed as further explanations of the larger doctrinal treatises. These books are: *Hayākil al-nūr (Luminous Bodies), Alwāh 'Imadī (The Tablets of 'Imād al-Dīn), Partaw nāmah (Treatise on Illumination), I'tiqād fi'l-ḥukamā (On the Faith of the Theosophers), al-Lamaḥāt (The Flashes of Light), Yazdān shinākht (Knowledge of the Divine), and Bustān al-qulūb (The Garden of the Heart).* Some of these works are in Arabic and some in Persian. His works in Persian are among the finest literary writings in the Persian language. Suhrawardi himself may have translated some of these treatises from Arabic into Persian.[27]
3. Suhrawardi wrote a number of treatises of a esoteric nature in Persian. These initiatory narratives contain highly symbolic language and incorporate Zoroastrian and Hermetic symbols as well as Islamic ones. These treatises include:
   'Aql-i surkh (Red Intellect), Āwāz-i par-i Jibrā'il (The Chant of Gabriel's Wing), Qiṣṣat al-ghurbat al-gharbiyyah (Story of the Occidental Exile), Lughat-i mūrān (Language of the Termites), Risālah fī ḥālat al-ṭufūliyyah (Treatise on the State of Childhood), Rūzī bā jamā'at-i sufiyān (A Day Among the Sufis), Ṣafīr-i sīmūrg (The Sound of the Griffin), Risālah fi'l-mi'rāj (Treatise on the Nocturnal Ascent), Partaw-nāmah (Treatise on Illumination). These treatises are intended to demonstrate the journey of the soul toward unity with God and the inherent yearning of man toward gnosis (*ma'rifah*).
4. There are also a number of treatises of a philosophic and initiatic nature. These include his translation of *Risalat al-tayr (Treatise of the Birds)* of Ibn Sīnā and the commentary in Persian upon Ibn Sīnā's *Ishārāt wa'l-tanbihāt.* There are also his treatise *Risālah fī ḥaqiqat al-'ishq* (*Treatise on the Reality of Love*), which is

based on Ibn Sīnā's *Risālah fi'l-'ishq (Treatise on Love)*, and his commentaries on verses of the Quran and the *Ḥadīth* . . .

Also, it is said that Suhrawardi may have written a commentary upon the *Fuṣūṣ* of Fārābī, which has been lost.[28]

5. Finally, there is the category of his liturgical writings, namely prayers, invocations and litanies. Shahrazurī[29] calls them *al-Waridāt wa'l-taqdisāt* (*Invocations and Prayers*).[30]

These important writings of Suhrawardi, despite the extracts which appear in translation of H. Corbin's *l'Archang empourprée*, have received the least amount of attention.

In what follows, I have offered a brief discussion of Suhrawardi's works. Emphasis has been placed on Suhrawardi's mystical narratives, their significance and place in the school of *ishraq*, since this volume undertakes a disccusion of Suhrawardi's Sufi and mystical views and not his Peripatetic writings.

1. *AL-TALWĪḤĀT (INTIMATIONS)*

Suhrawardi wrote this book in the tradition of the Peripatetics as a first step in establishing the cornerstone of his philosophy of illumination. As he states:

> . . . and I, before writing this book (*Ḥikmat al-ishrāq*) and while doing this, when obstacles prevented me from proceeding with this, wrote books for you in the tradition of Peripatetics, and their philosophical principles have been summarized in those books. Among them there is a short work known as *al-Talwīḥāt al-lawḥiyyah al-'arshiyyah*, which consists of many principles, and, despite its small volume, all the philosophical principles of the Peripatetics have been summarized, and in the order of ranks it comes after the book *al-Lamaḥāt*.[31]

In this work, Suhrawardi reinterprets the categories of Aristotelian logic by reducing them from ten to four and introduces motion as a new category while arguing that it was not Aristotle who discovered them but a Pythagorean named Akhutas (Archytas).[32] Arguing that quantity can be reduced to quality, (i.e. a short line is "weaker" than a long one), Suhrawardi reduces quantitative differences into qualitative ones.[33]

Among other topics of discussion in the *al-Talwiḥāt* are universals and particulars, the real and the conceptual, and "being" (*wujūd*) and "essence" (*māhiyyah*). Instead of supporting the principality of existence as Ibn Sīnā did, Suhrawardi supports the principality of "essence".[34] Also, the existence of necessary beings and Ibn Sīnā's proofs for the existence of the Necessary Being (*wājib al-wujūd*)[35] as well as offering an *ishraqi* reading of Aristotle are among the topics discussed.

In the *al-Talwiḥāt*, Suhrawardi offers an account of his vision of whom he perceived to be the first teacher, Aristotle, and his conversations with him.[36] This encounter of Suhrawardi, which took place in a state between dreaming and being awake, had great influence on the development of his theory of the history of philosophy and the distinction that he makes between *ḥikmat* and philosophy in its discursive form.

The Aristotle to whom Suhrawardi alludes to is the Aristotle of the *Theologia*, who is actually Plotinus. Suhrawardi asked Aristotle if the Peripatetics like Fārābī and Ibn Sīnā were the true philosophers. Aristotle replied:

> Not a degree in a thousand. Rather, the Sufis Basṭāmī and Tustari are the real philosophers.[37]

Suhrawardi then discusses how *ḥikmat* and the "Science of Light" (*'ilm al-ishrāq*) originated with Hermes and passed on to such figures in the West as Pythagoras, Empedocles, Plato, Agathadaimons, Asclepius and so on until it reached him.[38] In the East this science was transmitted through two main channels, namely the ancient Persian priest kings such as Kayumarth, Faridūn, Kay Khūsraw, and such Sufis as Abū Yazīd al-Basṭāmī, Abū Ḥassan al-Kharraqānī and finally Manṣūr al-Ḥallāj, who deeply influenced Suhrawardi.[39]

> A person who needs it may find it necessary to know prior to *The Philosophy of Illumination* in the *Intimations* where I have stated the points on which I differ from the Master of discursive philosophy, Aristotle.[40]

2. *AL-MUQĀWAMĀT (OPPOSITES)*

Al-Muqāwamāt, which is written in the tradition of the Peripatetics and in the style of the *al-Talwiḥāt*, provides a much more specific explanation of *ishraqi* ideas. In the introduction to the *al-Muqāwamāt* Suhrawardi states:

> This is the summary of a book known as *al-Talwīḥāt* and in this, necessary corrections have been made in regard to what the ancients have said. The exposition of these materials, due to the necessity to be brief, was not done in this book and we have decided on the minimum amount of discourse . . . and for this reason we have called it *al-Muqāwamāt*, and on God I rely and seek help.[41]

al-Muqāwamāt should be regarded as an addendum to the *al-Talwīḥāt* although it is less expository in nature and more argumentative. Suhrawardi alludes to the fact that *al-Muqāwamāt* is a guide to a better understanding of *al-Talwīḥāt*,[42] and the Peripatetic doctrines are analyzed more fully therein.

3. *AL-MASHĀRI' WA'L-MUṬĀRAḤĀT (THE PATHS AND THE CONVERSATIONS)*

This is one of the more important works of Suhrawardi and his lengthiest work, which contains a mixture of discursive and illuminationist arguments. In the introductory section, he recommends this book to all those who have not attained mastery of the discursive sciences and therefore have their path towards understanding of the higher wisdom of illumination obstructed.

The introduction to this book is of great importance since it explains the purpose and the place of this work among other works of Suhrawardi and also alludes to the existence of a circle of spiritual companions to Suhrawardi. As he states:

> This book consists of three sciences that I have written in accordance with the request of you brothers and I have placed in them arguments and criteria. These arguments and criteria cannot be found in other texts and are truly beneficial and useful. They are the result of the inferences and experiences of my own intellect. However, in these criteria I did not deviate from the sources of the Peripatetics, and if I had put fine points and litanies in them, they are from the honorable principles of *ishraqi* wisdom which undoubtedly is superior to what the Peripatetics have brought. Anyone who would strive and be unbiased, after meditating upon the

> works of the Peripatetics, will arrive at the same conclusion that others have reached. Anyone who has not attained the mastery of discursive sciences, his path to the understanding of *ishraqi* wisdom is blocked and it is necessary that this book be studied before *The Philosophy of Illumination* and after a short work called *Intimations.* It should be known that I, in this book, have not compiled (the issues) chronologically, but the intention in this work is argumentation although we may end up with (the discussion of miscellaneous) sciences. When the person who desires discursive philosophy has properly understood this section and established his knowledge in this regard, then it is permissible for him to set foot in ascetic practices and enter *ishraq* so he can see certain principles of illumination. The three forms of illuminationist wisdom are as follows:  and knowledge of them comes only after illumination. The beginning of illumination is detachment from the world; the middle way is the observation of divine light; and the end is limitless. I have called this book *The Path and the Conversations.*[43]

From the above, it is apparent that this work of Suhrawardi is not only written in the tradition of the Peripatetics, but that it also contains some of his mystical experiences.

In section seven of this work,[44] he leaves the discursive method to elaborate on such topics as life after death, necessary beings, etc. The metaphysical and epistemological issues which he deals with are elaborated on to a great extent in his *Magnum Opus,* the *Ḥikmat al-ishraq.* On the significance of the *al-Muqāwamāt* he states:

> I recommend to you my brothers to detach yourselves from everything and meditate upon God continuously, and the key to this idea is in *The Philosophy of Illumination.* These issues which we have mentioned have not been discussed elsewhere and to set foot on this path we have prescribed a plan without revealing the secret.[45]

al-Mashāri' wa'l-muṭāraḥāt is one of the few places where Suhrawardi treats the subject of the language of illumination, and is crucial for the understanding of *The Philosophy of Illumination* and "the language of illumination" (*lisān al-ishrāq*).[46] In light of such analysis which is carried out within the context of light and darkness, Suhrawardi goes so far as to evaluate his mystical experiences.

4. *ḤIKMAT AL-ISHRAQ (THE PHILOSOPHY OF ILLUMINATION)*

This is the fourth doctrinal work and the *Magnum opus* of Suhrawardi. It brings together different elements of *ishraqi* tradition and was composed in the period of a few months in 582/1182. Suhrawardi maintains that the content of this book was revealed to him by the divine spirit. "These truths and secrets were revealed to me at once by the spirit on a Strange day . . . in only a few days."[47]

The philosophical and theosophical doctrines that are discussed in this book laid the foundation for future developments in the field of "philosophical gnosis," not to mention their profound influence upon the formulation of the esoteric aspect of Shi'ism.[48]

Despite numerous commentaries on the *The Philosophy of Illumination*, such as those of Quṭb al-Dīn Shirāzī and Aḥmad Ibn al-Harawī,[49] Suhrawardi's own introduction to his work is perhaps the most elucidating one. There he states:

> And this book of ours belongs to those who seek knowledge of both an initiatic and discursive nature. Those who only seek discursive reasoning and are neither divine nor desire to be, have no place in this book. We shall not discuss this book or its secrets except with those who are theosophists or seek divine knowledge.[50]

The Philosophy of Illumination can roughly be divided into two parts, the first being a discussion of Peripatetic philosophy, logic and other related issues which have been regarded by many as less significant than the second part. The second part consists of his *ishraqi* writings which are written in a peculiar language and are unique in the history of Islamic philosophy. In this work Suhrawardi provides a philosophical exposition of the journey of the soul beginning with purification and ending with illumination. This part of the book which is nevertheless discursive, disscusses many of the traditional problems of philosophy in a language other than that employed by peripatetics.

Suhrawardi begins the second part of *The Philosophy of Illumination* with a description of the axiomatic nature of light and the classification of different beings in terms of their transparency and the division of light into many different types, i.e. necessary and contingent. Suhrawardi also tells us in this section about the source of wisdom as that light which has illuminated various traditions of wisdom and which ancient Persians called Bahman. Having discussed the longtitudinal and latitudinal angelic orders, Suhrawardi then offers an *ishraqi* analysis of vision and sight, the role of light and their relationship to illumination.

In *The Philosophy of Illumination*, Suhrawardi is not consistent in that he often goes from subject to subject treating the same topic in many places. For instance, different types of lights and their relationships to one another often are elaborated upon in numerous places throughout the book. Using an illuminationist scheme, Suhrawardi discusses cosmology, in particular, movements of the heavenly bodies and their relationship to light, sense perception and the faculties that make up the human psyche.

Among the most important issues disscussed in this section are the *ishraqi* epistemology known as knowledge by presence, inner purification and asceticism. Suhrawardi, who dismisses this in numerous places, offers an analysis of how it is that the self comes to know of itself and how we can account for the direct and unmediated nature of this knowledge. Towards the end of this book, Suhrawardi reminds us that becoming recipient of this knowledge requires practicing asceticism.

We shall now turn to a summary treatment of his works in Persian that are not only crucial to the understanding of Suhrawardi's mysticism but also are amongst the finest examples of Persian Sufi literature.

5. *PARTAW NĀMAH (TREATISE ON ILLUMINATION)*

This work encompasses a complete survey of major philosophical issues beginning with such subjects as time, space, and motion and offers an argument which is strikingly similar to Descartes "*Cogito*" or Ibn Sīnā's "suspended man."[51]

Suhrawardi's philosophical views in *Partaw nāmah* are generally analogous to those of Ibn Sīnā. Having argued for the existence of the Necessary Being and the hierarchical structure of existence and the relationship between ontology and the moral worth of beings, Suhrawardi goes on to discuss the problem of evil, free will and determinism within an *ishraqi* context.

> Since the Necessary Being is Pure Goodness and its nature is the most complete and most intelligent of all beings, therefore, from Him emanates only pure benevolence. If there occurs evil its good exceeds its evil.[52]

Suhrawardi argues for the immortality of the soul, pleasure and pain, and their relationship with the state of the soul after it departs the body. Finally, *Partaw-nāmah* deals with prophets and prophecy, miracles and events of an unusual nature. This section is written in the style of his *ishraqi* writings and is different from the other chapters in that he makes extensive use of Zoroastrian symbolism.

6. *HAYĀKIL AL-NŪR (LUMINOUS BODIES)*[53]

This is one of his most important and well known treatises in Persian. Some of Suhrawardi's commentators have suggested that extensive use of the word *haykal* is an indication that Suhrawardi may have been influenced by Ismā'īlīs.[54]

In the first section of *Hayākil al-nūr,*[55] he offers a definition of what an object is. In the second chapter he discusses the mind–body problem, their interaction and the nature of "I", which is distinct from the body. He also pays attention to the problem of "personal identity" and argues as to what it is that constitutes the identity of a person. In the third chapter he discusses different concepts of Being such as necessary and contingent. It is in the fourth chapter, however, that Suhrawardi's philosophical views are discussed with a much greater depth and length.

He then goes on to discuss the problem of eternity (*qidam*) and the creation (*ḥudūth*) of the world in time and God's relation to it. Also, he investigates the relationship between the movement of the celestial bodies, the qualities he attributes to them, and the process of illumination. In the later part of *Hayākil al-nūr,* he investigates such issues as the immortality of the soul and its unification with the angelic world after it departs the human body.

7. *ALWĀḤ 'IMĀDĪ (TABLET OF 'IMĀD AL-DIN)*

In the introduction to this work Suhrawardi indicates that this book has been written in the style of the *ishraqis.*[56] He begins, however, by a discussion on semantics and then moves on to consider such issues as the soul, its powers and its relationship with the light of lights. The first part of the book discusses a number of philosophical issues such as the Necessary Being and its attributes, the problem of createdness and eternity of the world and motion. In so doing, he makes extensive references to *Quranic* verses and

Ḥadith. In the later part of the book Suhrawardi is engaged in an exegesis of the ancient Persian mythology and makes interpretations that are essential in the formulation of his theosophical epistemology. This is especially apparent towards the end of this work where the fate of the human soul is discussed in such a way that the similarity of Islamic eschatology and Zoroastrianism is demonstrated. Suhrawardi here argues that purification through asceticism is the necessary condition for illumination. As he states: "Once the soul is purified, it will be illuminated by divine light."[57]

Suhrawardi then tells us that asceticism and purification are like fire which, once applied to iron, illuminates the iron. The iron, in this case, being the soul or the "I", can become illuminated not only because of the dominant character of the light of lights but also because of the inner yearning of the human soul for perfection. The light that functions as the illuminator of the body and the soul for Suhrawardi is the incorporeal light which he calls *Kharrah.* It is the presence of this light in the human soul that enables man to have the inner yearning which is necessary for the pursuit of the spiritual path. Suhrawardi describes the human soul as a tree whose fruit is certainty, or a niche that, through divine fire, becomes illuminated.[58] In his writings Suhrawardi sees the encounter of Moses and the burning bush in this context and uses the story to substantiate his *ishraqi* claim that it is only the divine fire that can illuminate the human soul. Suhrawardi tells us that the reason for writing this book is to expose the "origin" and destination of man. He describes the origin as:

> The principles which are necessarily the case with regard to the knowledge of the origin of man's nature, are of eschatalogical nature. This is in accordance with the creed of the theosophists and the principles (laid down by) the learned men of theosophy.[59]

At the end Suhrawardi offers an esoteric reading of a story by Firdawsī, the Persian poet whose monumental work, *The Book of Kings,* is an encyclopedia of Persian mythology. A complete discussion of Suhrawardi's reading of such figures as Farīdūn, Ẓaḥḥāk and Kay Khusrūw is such that he sees them as the manifestations of divine light. On the significance of this work, S.H. Naṣr states:

> *Alwāḥ 'imādī* is one of the most brilliant works of Suhrawardi in which the tales of ancient Persia and the wisdom of gnosis

of antiquity in the context of the esoteric meaning of the Quran have been synthesized. Suhrawardi has made an interpretation of the destiny of the soul which Islamic theosophy and gnosis are in agreement with.[60]

8. *RISALĀT AL-ṬAYR (TREATISE OF THE BIRDS)*

This work was originally written by Ibn Sīnā and was translated and restated by Suhrawardi into Persian.[61] It discloses a number of esoteric doctrines through the language of the birds which Suhrawardi, 'Aṭṭār and Aḥmad Ghazzālī had also used before him. The story is about the fate of a group of birds, who, having fallen into the trap of hunters, describe how their attempt to free themselves is faced with a number of setbacks and how the birds overcome such obstacles. This work depicts the spiritual journey of man from his original abode into the world of form and how the attachments of the material world can obstruct one's desire to reunite with his spiritual origin.

In this work, Suhrawardi alludes to how human faculties that are directed to the sensible world obstruct the soul from its spiritual journey and the attainment of illumination. Suhrawardi describes the dangers of the mystical path as follows:

> Oh, brothers in truth, shed your skin as a snake does and walk as an ant walks so the sound of your footsteps cannot be heard. Be as a scorpion whose weapon is on his back since Satan comes from behind. Drink poison so you may be born. Fly continuously and do not choose a nest, for all birds are taken from their nests, and if you have no wings crawl on the ground. . . . Be like an ostrich who eats warm sand and vultures who eat hard bones. Like a salamander, be in the middle of fire so no harm can come upon you tomorrow. Be like a moth who remains hidden by day so he may remain safe from the enemy.[62]

Suhrawardi uses the above symbols to offer a set of practical instructions for those who are on the Sufi path. For example, the shedding of one's skin refers to the abandoning of one's ego, and walking like an ant alludes to the way one ought to walk on the path of truth so that no one will know it. Drinking poison symbolically indicates the endurance of the pains and frustrations which one is to experience on the spiritual path. By using the prophetic hadith "love death so you may live,"[63] Suhrawardi refers to the spiritual death. The Sufi concept of annihilation is the death and rebirth that Suhrawardi himself describes in a poem:

> If thou die before death.
> Thou hast placed thyself in eternal bliss.
> Thou who didst not set foot on this path.
> Shame be upon thee that broughtest suffering upon thyself.[64]

Suhrawardi illustrates various hardships of the path by alluding to them as the eating of hot sand by the ostrich or the eating of sharp bones by the vultures. Enduring such pain is necessary if one is to progress and achieve any station on the spiritual path. Suhrawardi's use of a salamander has different levels of interpretation. The Salamander is the symbol of gold in alchemy and gold is the symbol of Divine Intellect. He could be referring not only to Abraham who was thrown into fire, but also to the fire within man. The popular myth maintains that if a salamander goes through fire, and does not burn, it becomes resistant to everything. Therefore, those who are consumed by divine love, which burns like fire, have cast their impurities into the fire. They have swallowed this fire and become purified.

Finally, Suhrawardi tells us that we ought to be like a moth that flies at night and remains hidden by day. Night represents the esoteric, the hidden aspect, and day the exoteric. In this way Suhrawardi uses the symbols of traditional Sufi literature with night symbolizing the esoteric and the spiritual milieu, providing the sacred space which allows man to fly.

In the *Risālat al-ṭayr*[65] Suhrawardi describes the spiritual journey of man by recounting the tale of a number of birds who were "flying freely" but fell in the trap of the hunters. "Flying freely" here symbolizes the condition in which man lived in the eternal state prior to creation, and falling into the trap denotes coming into the domain of material existence. This change signifies the transition from the formless to the world of forms. Having become prisoners of the material world, often identified in Persian literature as the "prison of the body," those who are conscious of this imprisonment can begin their journey towards their origin.

The bird who finds himself a prisoner symbolizes the worldly man. However, because of the forgetfulness of human nature he becomes used to the attachments of the material world. This adaptation and the acceptance of the condition is the greatest danger in one's spiritual journey, according to Suhrawardi. In the language of the birds, Suhrawardi states:

> We focused our attention on how we could free ourselves. We were in that condition for a while until our first principle was forgotten (freedom) and settled with these chains, giving in to the tightness of the cage.[66]

Suhrawardi's description of the spiritual journey in the "Treatise of the Birds" continues with the flight of the birds when they free themselves from some of the bondages. To translate this into Sufi language, it can be said that men who have fallen into the world of forms can partly free themselves through their willpower; however, to remove all the chains of attachments they would need the guidance of a master. While the potentiality for man to become illuminated exists, the process will not take place without the inner yearning and the will to make the journey. This point becomes clear when the main character of the story begs the other birds to show him how they freed themselves.

Having pursued the path of asceticism and endured hardships, the birds arrive at different states and stations of the path where they think it is time to rest. Suhrawardi warns us against the desire to rest in one place, although the beauties of the path which he describes as the "attractions that remove the mind (*'Aql*) from the body" are extremely tempting.[67] Finally, their desire to stay is overcome by divine grace, exemplified as a voice calling upon them to continue. Suhrawardi then describes their encounter with God, whose presence he describes as a blinding light. The light of lights tells the birds that he who has placed the chains must remove them as well and God sends a messenger to oversee the removal of these chains.

The following principles can be inferred from the *Risālat al-ṭayr.*[68]

1. The earthly human state is a prison for the human soul.
2. There is a necessity for the soul to journey towards the Light of Lights.
3. The grace that is attained through such an experience helps the *Sālik* to remove the final attachments to this world.
4. The experience of the light of lights can be achieved if one is able to free himself from the prison of the material world.

It is important to treat Suhrawardi's narratives and their peculiar literary style as part and parcel of the *ishraqi* doctrine. Whereas in *The Philosophy of Illumination* he offers the doctrinal analysis of *ishraqi* thought, in his Persian writings he is disclosing the practical aspect of his *ishraqi* doctrine, without which his theosophical system would not be complete. Suhrawardi's epistemological system ultimately relies on the type of wisdom that is attained through practicing the *ishraqi* doctrine and that is precisely what he is trying to demonstrate in his mystical narratives. In fact, his instructions for the attainment of truth in some of his other works are even more direct and specific.

9. *ĀWĀZ-I PAR-I JIBRĀIL (THE CHANT OF GABRIEL'S WING)*

This highly esoteric work is about a seeker of truth who goes to a *khanāqah* (Sufi house) which has two doors, one facing the city and the other one the desert. Having gone to the desert, he meets ten spiritual masters and questions them with regard to the mystery of creation, the stations of the path, and the dangers therein.

The conversation which follows reveals the essential elements of the *ishraqi* doctrine and the initiation rite which is necessary if one is to understand the esoteric knowledge of the Quran. . . In the *Āwāz-i par-i Jibra'īl*, which has come to be known as a classical work of Persian literature,[69] Suhrawardi discusses the essential elements of his theosophical epistemology. There he states: "Most things that your sense perception observes are all from the chant of Gabriel's wings."[70]

In this most esoterically oriented treatise, he makes full use of the traditional symbolism of gnosisticism and a number of other symbols which are uniquely employed by him and cannot be found in the classical Persian Sufi literature. The thrust of the work is stated in the beginning:

> . . . Abū 'Alī Farmadī, peace be upon him, was asked, "How is it that those who are clothed in black call certain sounds the sound of Gabriel's wing?" He replied, "Know that most things that your faculties observe are from the sound of Gabriel's wing."[71]

One can say that Suhrawardi's theory of knowledge is discussed in this mystical tale. In metaphorical language Suhrawardi provides us with a map for developing a faculty within us that is capable of gaining knowledge directly and without mediation. Relying on the traditional symbolism of Sufi poetry and prose, Suhrawardi elaborates on the contention that exists between empiricism, rationalism and the gnostic mode of cognition.

10. *'AQL-I SURKH (THE RED INTELLECT)*

In *The Red Intellect*,[72] the story begins with the question of whether birds understand each other's language. The eagle, who initially says yes, is later captured by hunters and her eyes are closed, only to be opened gradually. The eagle meets a red-faced man who claims to be the first man who was created. He is old since he represents the perfect man who existed in the state of perfection before the creation,[73] the archetype of man, and he is young since ontologically he is far removed from God who is the eternal and therefore the oldest being.

Suhrawardi then uses the Zoroastrian symbolism of the Qāf mountain, the story of Zāl, Rustam and other epic heroes as exemplified in the *Shāh-nāmah*.[74] Qāf is the name of the mountain on whose peak Griffin (*Sīmūrgh*), the symbol of divine essence, resides. Zāl, who was born with white hair representing wisdom and purity, was left at the bottom of Qāf mountain. Simūrgh took Zāl to his nest and raised him until he grew up and married Tahminah from whom Rustam was born. Rustam, the hero of *Shāh-nāmah*, who often is perceived as the soul of epic Persia, is a man who has ultimately overcome his own ego. Whereas Firdawsī, the author of *Shāh-nāmah* emphasizes the epic and historical aspects of the Persian mythology, Suhrawardi focuses on its mystical and esoteric connotations.

In this work Suhrawardi's theory of knowledge is expressed in a symbolic language similar to that of *Āwāz-i par-i Jibrā'īl*. Using a new set of symbols, Suhrawardi brings forth some of the classical issues of Islamic philosophy and mysticism, such as the distinction between the rational faculty, which he calls the "particular intellect", (*'aql-i juz'ī*) and the Intellect which he calls "universal intellect," (*'aql-i kullī*). In doing so he relies heavily on Zoroastrian symbolism and sources from ancient Persia. It is precisely the interaction between the minor and major intellects that is the basis upon which one can gain knowledge. Like other works of a theosophical nature, Suhrawardi hides his theory of knowledge behind a maze of myth and symbols which can only be disclosed if one is familiar with the traditional Sufi symbolism.

11. *RŪZĪ BĀ JAMĀ'AT-I ṢUFIYAN (A DAY AMONG THE SUFIS)*

The story begins in a *khanaqāh,* where several disciples speak of the spiritual status of their masters and their views regarding the creation.[75] Suhrawardi, who speaks as a master, objects to such questions which merely seek to explain the nature of the universe and the structure of the heavens. Suhrawardi considers them to be shallow and maintains that there are those who see the appearance and those who understand the science of the heavens. Finally, there are those who attain the mastery of the celestial world, the true men of knowledge. Suhrawardi then goes on to give specific instructions which are essential in actualizing the power of the faculty which enables men to gain cognition without mediation. As he states:

> All that is dear to you, property, furniture and worldly pleasures and such things . . . (throw them away) . . . if this prescription is followed, then the vision will be illuminated.[76]

Amidst a mixture of myth, symbolism and traditional Islamic metaphysics, Suhrawardi continues to put emphasis on the relationship between pursuing the attainment of esoteric knowledge and the practicing of asceticism. Practicing asceticism will open the inner eye, which for Suhrawardi is the mode of cognition that is essential if one is to gain knowledge of the esoteric dimension of Islam. According to Suhrawardi, true knowledge is possible when empiricism and rationalism end. As he states:

> Once the inner eye opens, the exterior eye ought to be closed. Lips must be sealed and the five external senses should be silenced. Interior senses should begin to function so the person, if he attains anything, does so with the inner being (*Bāṭin*), and if he sees, he sees with the inner eye, and if he hears, he hears with the inner ear. . . . Therefore, when asked what one would see, (the answer of the inner self is that) it sees what it sees and what it ought to see.[77]

Therefore, closure of the five external senses for Suhrawardi is a necessary condition for the opening of the internal senses which are essential for the attainment of the truth. This work alludes to different states and stations of the spiritual path and how the spiritual elite can achieve purity of heart and clarity of vision. In this work, Suhrawardi describes his conversations with a group of Sufis and what their Masters have told them regarding the attainment of truth and how Suhrawardi's vision compares with theirs.

This brief work contains some important references to allegorical and metaphorical concepts and how different stages of the spiritual path can be described through them. In this highly symbolic work, the relationship between one's purity of heart and the degree to which one can gain knowledge, as well as the relationship between asceticism and epistemology, is discussed by using Sufi symbolism.

12. *RISĀLAH FI ḤĀLAT AL-ṬŪFULIYAH (ON THE STATE OF CHILDHOOD)*[78]

In this work, Suhrawardi describes having met a master who reveals the divine secret to him and he in turn discloses it to men of exoteric nature.

The master punishes him for "casting pearl before the swine."[79] Suhrawardi also alludes to the difficulty of communicating the esoteric message to those who stand outside of the tradition. Since *Sophia Perennis* is attained through other means than sense perception, it is difficult to communicate this mode of knowledge to those who may not be ready to receive it.

The Sālik, then, having repented, finds the master who tells him a number of secrets such as the ethics of the spiritual path and the rituals that are involved in the Sufi path such as *Samā'* (Sufi music and dancing). The exposition of many fine mystical points reveals Suhrawardi's thorough familiarity with the intricacies of the Sufi path. Suhrawardi expresses this in a symbolic conversation between a bat and a salamander whose passage through fire is supposed to have protected him against all harms. The bat is describing the pleasure of drinking cold water in the middle of winter, while the salamander is suffering from cold. Each one could provide a different interpretation of "cold water" in accordance to their experience.

So far, Suhrawardi has drawn an outline of the esoteric instructions needed for a seeker to pursue the path of spirituality, which begins by an inner yearning and continues with ascetic practices under the guidance of a master. This book intends to illustrate the spiritual path and the journey of the seeker *(sālik)* from its beginning, which Suhrawardi symbolically identifies as childhood. The significance of having a spiritual master to avoid the dangers on the path, as well as different stages of inner development, are among some of the issues that Suhrawardi elaborates upon. The core of the spiritual teachings of this book is a practical guide for pursuing the spiritual path.

13. *RISĀLAĪ FĪ ḤAQIQAT AL-'ISHQ (TREATISE ON THE REALITY OF LOVE)*

This work of Suhrawardi not only represents one of the most sublime examples of Persian literature, but it also contains some of his most profound philosophical views. He begins by quoting a verse from the Quran and then goes on to talk about knowledge and its relationship with the Intellect.

> Know that the first thing God, praise be upon him, created was a luminous pearl called Intellect (*'aql*). God first created Intellect and gave it three features: knowledge of God, knowledge of self and knowledge of that which was not and then was.[80]

This treatise reaches its climax when Suhrawardi offers a spiritual map of the universe in the sixth chapter. It has been argued that this work was written on the basis of Ibn Sīnā's *Risālat al-'ishq*.[81] However, it has to be noted that this work is different both in form and content from that work. Since the rest of Suhrawardi's works in Persian contain the same elements as the other works which we have considered, I will not expound upon them, although in our study of Suhrawardi's epistemology frequent references will be made to them. Such works include *Būstān al-qulūb* or *Rawḍat al-qulūb (Garden of the Heart)*[82] which is a more philosophically oriented work in which Suhrawardi addresses such issues as metaphysics, space, time and motion.

This work, along with *Yazdān shinākht (Knowing the Divine)* are both written in the style of the Peripatetics and not only contains a discussion of the classical problems of philosophy, but also occasional discussions regarding the theosophist's mode of knowing. Finally, in his book *Language of the Termites*[83] Suhrawardi describes the nature of the knowledge needed to come to know God. Self and the creation are among topics which "they [Peripatetics] all disagree upon as long as the veil is not removed and knowledge by presence is not attained."[84] Once this knowledge is attained, the "crystal ball" (*jām-i Jam*) is at your disposal and "whatever you want can be studied and you become conscious of the universe and the unseen world."[85]

14. *AL-WARIDĀT WA'L-TAQDISĀT (PRAYERS AND SUPPLICATIONS)*

These writings, due to their devotional nature, are distinct from other writings of Suhrawardi both in terms of form and content. Despite their significance for the formulation of Suhrawardi's angelology, they have not received the attention they deserve. In these writings Suhrawardi describes the relationship of the planets and their characteristics with that of the inner forces of man. His praise of the great "Luminous Being" (*al-Nayyir al-a'ẓam*), whose power and glory demand submission, addressing the heavenly sun *Hūrakhsh*, as well as the relationship between the Zoroastrian angels and spiritual entities, are among the issues that Suhrawardi discusses in these works. It is important for the reader of Suhrawardi not to view his writings as isolated and separated books, but rather as an interrelated and elaborate set of ideas in which every part can only be properly understood in regard to the whole while the whole derives its validity from its parts.

15. CONCLUSION

An extensive discussion of Suhrawardi's books requires a separate work. I will, however, consider some of these works at length in the forthcoming chapters.

In the foregoing discussion, a summary of Suhrawardi's doctrinal and the esoteric works has been presented. Suhrawardi wrote the majority of his works in a period of a few years and therefore the distinction of "early" and "later" works cannot be made. His thoughts, all of which form a paradigm, are not systematic if viewed individually. However, if they are viewed in their totality, they form a consistent and coherent philosophical system within which various truth claims become valid and meaningful. A close study of Suhrawardi's writings in Persian, with emphasis upon their epistemological aspect, reveals the existence of a theory of knowledge generally known as "Knowledge by Presence" (*al-'ilm al-ḥuḍūrī*). The intertwined and elaborate web of myth and symbolism in Suhrawardi's philosophy intends to articulate his theory of knowledge, an important and fundamental subject in the *ishraqi* school of thought. Suhrawardi, who claims to have first discovered the truth and then embarked on a path to find the rational basis of his experiential wisdom, represents a thinker who made an attempt to bring about a rapprochement between rational discourse and inner purification. Therefore, a comprehensive interpretation of Suhrawardi's school of *ishraq* should include the two distinct dimensions of his philosophical paradigm, the practical and the philosophical.

Notes

1 For more information concerning Suhrawardi's life and biography see Ibn Abī 'Uṣaybi'ah, *'Uyūn al-anba' fī ṭabaqāt al-aṭibbā'*, ed. Muller, (Koningsberg Press, 1884); Ibn Khallikan, *Wafayāt al-a'yān*, ed. I. 'Abbās, (Beirut: 1965); and Shams al-Dīn Shahrazūrī, *Nuzhat al-arwāḥ wa rawḍat al-afrāḥ fī tārīkh al-ḥukamā wa'l-falasifah*, ed. Khūrshid Aḥmad, vol. 2 (Haydarabad: 1976).
2 Hereafter I shall refer to this work as *Nuzhat al-arwāḥ*. Shahrazūrī, *Nuzhat al-arwāḥ wa rawḍat al-afrāḥ fī tārīkh al-ḥukamā' wa'l-falāsifah*, ed. S. Khūrshid (Aḥmad, 1976), 119–143.
3 Suhrawardi, *Opera Metaphysica et Mystical 3*, with an introduction by S.H. Nasr (Tehran: Institute d'Etudes et des Recherches culturelles, 1993, 12.
4 S.H. Nasr, *Three Muslim Sages* (Cambridge: Harvard University, 1964), 60.
5 Shahrazūrī, *Nuzhat al-arwāḥ*, 122.
6 Yāqūt al-Ḥamawī, *Mu'jam al-udabā'* vol.19, no 20, Ciro 626.
7 Shahrazūrī, *Nuzhat al-arwāḥ*, 125.
8 Suhrawardi, *Opera Metaphysica et Mystical* 2, with an intoduction by Henry Corbin (Istanbul: Maarif Matbaasi, 1945), 259.
9 The political reason might be the nature of his thoughts and openness to other traditions or perhaps because he may have claimed to be a prophet. See Shahrazūrī, *Nuzhat al-arwāḥ*, 126.
10 Ibn Taqhribirdī and Abū'l-Maḥāsin Yusūf, *al-Nujūm al-ẓāhirah fī mulūk miṣr wa'l-qahirah*, vol. 6 (Cairo, al-Mu'assasah al-Misr-iyah Press, 1963), 114.
11 Ibid., 115.
12 Ibid., 30.
13 Ibid., 114.
14 Shahrazūrī, *Nuzhat al-arwāḥ*, 126.
15 S.H. Nasr, "Suhrawardi: The Master of Illumination, Gnostic and Martyr,' trans. W.Chittick, *Journal of Regional Cultural Institute 2*, no. 4 (1969): 212.
16 Persian nationalism (*shu'ūbiyyah*) was a movement in the 3rd century A. H. During this period a movement by Persian intellectuals began as a protest against Arab domination. For more information see the conclusion of this work.
17 H. Ziā'ī, "The Source and Nature of Political Authority in Suhrawardi's Philosophy of Illumination", in *Political Aspects of Islamic Philosophy* (Cambridge: Harvard University Press, 1992) 304–344.
18 Ibid., 10.
19 Shahrazūrī, *Nuzhat al-arwāḥ*, 126.
20 Ghazzālī mentions twenty reasons for the fallacy of the philosopher's opinion. al-Ghazzālī, *Tahāfut al-falāsifah*, trans. S.A. Kamālī (Lahore: Pakistan Philosophical Congress, 1963), 11.
21 For more information see H. Corbin, *L'Archange empourprée* (Paris: Fayand, 1976).
22 For more information on this translation of Corbin see: Shihāboddin Yaḥyā Suhrawardi, *Le Livre de la sagesse orientale*, traduction et notes par by H. Corbin, (Paris: Verdier, 1986).

23 Thackston has also translated part of the 17th century Persian translation of the *Nuzhat al-arwāḥ* by 'Alī Tabrīzī into English. See: Thackston, *Mystical and Visionary Treatises of Suhrawardi* (London: the Octagon Press, 1982), 1–4.

24 Thackston's translation of Suhrawardi is generally criticized by the scholars of Suhrawardi. It is based on the text which is edited by Spies and this is a not a good edition of Suhrawardi. Also, the literary style of Thankston does not do justice to the beautiful mystical narratives of Suhrawardi in Persian.

25 For more information on L. Massignon's classification see *Recueil de textes inedits concernant l'histoire de la mystique en pays d'Islam* (Paris: 1929), 113.

26 For S.H. Naṣr's classification see *Three Muslim Sages,* 58. For H. Corbin's classification see the Prolgmena, *Opera* 1, 16ff.

27 S.H. Nasr argues that on the basis of the unity of style between the *Būstān al-qulūb* and his other works it can be concluded that this work does belong to Suhrawardi himself. For more discussion on this see M.M. Sharif, *A History of Muslim Philosophy* (Wiesbaden: Otto Harrassowitz, 1963), 375; and the introduction to Surawardi, *Opera* 3, 40.

28 Nasr, *Three Muslim Sages,* 150 no. 16.

29 Ibid., 58.

30 The invocations and prayers have been published in M. Mo'in, *Majala-yi āmūzish wa parwarish,* (Tehran: Ministry of Education Press, 1924), p.5ff. These writings represent Suhrawardi's angelology, relationship to the spiritual entities of the planets and their correspondence with the Zoroastrian archangels. For example, in the two most important prayers, the heavenly sun, Hūrakhsh, is being addressed. Also, Suhrawardi expounds upon the qualities of the Great Lumious Being (*al-Nayyir al-a'ẓm*), who is the incorporeal equivalent of an earthly king, and whose qualities are such that they demand submission.

31 Suhrawardi, *Opera Metaphysica et Mystical, 2,* with an introduction by H. Corbin (Istanbul: Maarif Matbassi, 1954), 10.

32 Suhrawardi, *Opera* 1, 12.

33 For a discussion on this see: Suhrawardi, *Opera* 2, 87, 88.

34 For more discussion on this see Sayyid Jalāl al-Dīn Āshtiyānī's commentary in Lāhījī, "Risālah Nūriyyah dar 'ālam-i mithāl," in *Majilla-yi ilāhiyyāt wa ma'ārif-i islām* (Iran: Mahhad University, 1972).

35 For more discussion on this see Suhrawardi, *Opera* 1, 34ff.

36 Suhrawardi, *Opera* 1, 70.

37 Ibid.

38 S.H. Nasr, *Three Muslim Sages,* 62.

39 For political significance of this claim concerning the transmission of knowledge see: H. Ziā'ī, "The Source and Nature of Political Authority in Suhrawardi's Philosophy of Illumination" in *The Political Aspects of Islamic Philosophy* (Cambridge: Harvard University Press, 1992), 304–344.

40 Suhrawardi, *Opera* 1, 484.

41 Ibid., 124.

42 Ibid., 192.

43 Ibid., 194–195.

44 Ibid., Sec.7.
45 Ibid., 505.
46 Ibid., 494.
47 Suhrawardi, *Opera* 2, 259.
48 S.H. Nasr "The Relationship Between Sufism and Philosophy in Persian Culture," *Hamdard Islamicus* 6, no.4 (1983): 33–47.
49 Harawī's commentary, *Anwāriyyah,* is particularly interesting since he has offered an *ishraqi* reading of cetain aspects of Hindu philosophy. The text represents one of the early examples of comparative philosophy. For more information see: M. Sh. al-Hirawī, *Anwāriyya,* ed. H. Ziā'ī (Tehran: Amir Kabir Press), 1358A.H.s.
50 Suhrawardi, *Opera* 2, 12–13.
51 Ibn Sīnā, *al-Shifā': kitāb al-nafs,* ch.6 and *al-Ishārāt wa'l-tanbīhāt,* final chapter.
52 Suhrawardi, *Opera* 3, 60–61.
53 For more information see: S.J. Sajjādī, *Shihāb al-Dīn Suhrawardi wa sayri dar falsafa-yi ishrāq* (Tehran: Falsafah Press, 1984).
54 For more information on Suhrawardi's emphasis on "seven bodies" and *hayākil* see above, 114–115.
55 Suhrawardi, *Opera* 3, 84.
56 Ibid., 110.
57 Ibid., 184.
58 Suhrawardi often refers to the famous Quranic verse that equates God with Light within a niche. See: Quran, XXIV: 35.
59 Suhrawardi, *Opera* 3, 110.
60 S.H. Nasr's Introduction to *Opera* 3, 45.
61 Suhrawardi, *Opera* 3, 198.
62 Ibid., 199.
63 This is a *ḥadith* by the Prophet of Islam. Suhrawardi has used this *ḥadith* in various places to argue for the doctrine that "spiritual death" is the necessary condition for "spiritual birth."
64 Suhrawardi, *Opera* 3, 395.
65 Ibid., 198.
66 Ibid., 200.
67 Ibid., 202.
68 Ibid., 198–205.
69 This work has gained widespread fame both for its literary style and the mystical symbolism in it. As early as the 15th century for example, one can find a commentary on this work written in Persian by an unknown Indian author. For more information on this com- mentary see: "Sharḥ-i āwāz-i par-i Jiba'īl," ed. M. Qasemī in *Ma'ārif* 1(March-May 1984).
70 Suhrawardi, *Opera* 3, 209.
71 Ibid., 208–209.
72 Ibid., 242.
73 Ibid., 228.
74 Suhrawardi has employed the symbolism that Firdawsī has used in the *Shāh-nāmah* to formulate his angelology. There are those who argue

that the *Shāh-nāmah* is a profoundly mystical work and make an esoteric reading of this book.

75 Suhrawardi, *Opera* 3, 242.

76 Ibid., 248.

77 Ibid., 249.

78 Ibid., 252.

79 This saying of Christ from an *ishraqi* point of view alludes to the esoteric knowledge that should not be revealed to the common people and to the fact that only initiates are allowed to know the secrets of the spiritual path.

80 Suhrawardi, *Opera* 3, 208–209.

81 Nasr, *Three Muslim Sages*, 59.

82 In his introduction (55) to *Opera 3*, Nasr indicates that this work has been attributed to a number of people such as Sayyīd Sharif Jurgānī, Ibn Sīnā, Khāwjah Naṣīr al-Dīn al-Ṭūṣī, Bābā Afḍal-i Kāshanī and finally 'Ayn al-Quḍāt Hamadānī. However, it is his opinion that, on the basis of the form and content of the book, it belongs to Suhrawardi.

83 Suhrawardi, *Opera* 3, 297–299.

84 Ibid., 297.

85 Ibid., 298.

2

CENTRAL THEMES

Suhrawardi has commented on numerous subjects, often making original contributions in each field. As to his predecessors and their influence upon him, he was influenced by Ghazzālī and his famous work *Mishkāt al-anwār* that was of such great significance in formulating the *ishraqi* doctrine. He was also influenced by Ḥallāj and Bāyazīd, whom he quoted so often, and who for Suhrawardi were the perfect representations of true philosophers. Finally, there was Ibn Sīnā, the master of Peripatetics, whom Suhrawardi criticized but nevertheless adhered to certain strands of his philosophical structure such as Ibn Sīnā's concept of hierarchy and emanation. Despite his own contributions Suhrawardi accepted the logic of the Peripatetics as a useful means of analysis. Let us elaborate on some of the areas where Suhrawardi's contributions are more substantial.

1. ONTOLOGY

Suhrawardi adhered to the traditional ontology as far as the hierarchical structure of reality is concerned. Within the context of levels of being, he sought to offer an exposition of various philosophical and mystical issues. He retained the notion of hierarchies of being but changed the matrix of this Ibn Sīnian ontology from one of "being" to one of "light." It was precisely this kind of fundamental change that allowed him to offer an exposition of mystical and esoteric doctrines as well as many of the traditional philosophical issues, in particular the relationship between essence and existence. According to Suhrawardi, the nature of light is axiomatic in that all things are known through it. Light is made up of an infinite succession of contingent dependent lights and each light is the existential cause of the light below it. The ultimate light, which is the same as the Necessary Being (*wājib al-wujūd*), is for Suhrawardi the light of lights (*nūr al-anwār*), which he regards as the ultimate cause of all things.

Although Suhrawardi's ontological scheme was later criticized by some of his successors, such as Mullā Ṣadrā and Ḥajjī Mullā Hādī Sabziwārī, it nevertheless provides a means by which ontological issues can be analyzed. As S.H. Naṣr puts it, for Suhrawardi:

> The ontological status of all beings, therefore, depends on the degree in which they approach the supreme light and are themselves illuminated.[1]

For Suhrawardi, just as light has degrees of intensity, so does darkness. Although he classifies light in accordance to the degree that it exists, by necessity his criterion for determining the ontological status of lights is whether or not they are conscious of themselves. Therefore, self-awareness becomes a criterion for higher ontological status, which in the *ishraqi* system means a more intense degree of light.

For Suhrawardi it is ultimately awareness of one's true nature that elevates a person's ontological status. To demonstrate this, he employs Zoroastrian symbols of light and darkness to depict the contradictions and the inner strife that exists within man. The key to the existential dilemma resulting from this inner struggle between the ego (*nafs*), which in the Zoroastrian *Weltanschauung* is darkness, and man's divine self, light, is knowledge or awareness of the reality of oneself.

Suhrawardi arrives at his ontology of light in two ways. First, he offers us philosophical arguments to establish the axiomatic nature of light by stating that light is the most apparent of all phenomena since everything else is recognized and defined in terms of it. Suhrawardi argues that light is the necessary condition for things to be observed and therefore it is light and not being that should be the constitute element of an ontology.

Suhrawardi tells us that the principality of light and its ontological significance came to him first through *ishraqi* means. In the *Ḥikmat al-ishrāq* he says:

> The issues and truths therein (*Ḥikmat al-ishrāq*) first came to me not through rational inquiry, but their attainment was through a different means. Finally, after understanding

> them, I sought their rational basis in a way such that if I ignore them, nothing can make me doubt their validity.[2]

It is therefore imperative that in any discussion concerning Suhrawardi's ontology one has to realize the visionary nature of this ontology and that ultimately his philosophical analysis is based on his mystical experience.

2. EXISTENCE AND ESSENCE

For Suhrawardi, to know something is to know its essence and not its existence. Let us now see how Suhrawardi argues for this position and what its *ishraqi* implications are.

Contrary to the Peripatetics, Suhrawardi maintains that existence is a mere concept and has no external reality or manifestation.[3] His argument for the principality of essence *(aṣālat al-māhiyyah)*, which distinguishes him from most of the Muslim philosophers, undermines the role of existence as that upon which the reality of a thing depends. In *The Philosophy of Illumination*[4] he argues that all beings exist equally and it is not the case that some existent beings exist more than others, an indication that existence is a universal concept. The problem which follows from this is that such things as "whiteness" are also of a universal nature which nevertheless are regarded to be universal essence as well. If "existence" were not pure "whiteness" or "sweetness", then it would not be a universal concept, but would be a particular. But, if they were the same, then, it would be the same as essence. This means every existing being would have its own particular existence. Suhrawardi seems to argue that if this be the case then this "particular existence" would be equivalent to the essence of the thing. From this, Suhrawardi concludes that existence is a purely mental concept, whereas the particular essence has an actual existence which makes a white or black object be white or black. On this he states:

> Attribution of existence to blackness, essence, man and horses are regarded to be the same, and therefore the concept of existence is a concept that is more universal than each of them. The same is true of the concept of essence in its absolute sense and the concept of truth and the nature of beings in their absolute sense. Therefore, we claim that such categories (existence and universal essence) are pure mental concepts since if we (assume) that existence consists only of pure blackness,

> necessarily the same will not hold true with whiteness and (together) cannot include whiteness and essence.[5]

Suhrawardi goes on to further argue for the principality of essence by concluding the following:

1. Existent objects and existence are two separate things.
2. Existence can be conceived only in respect to an existent being.
3. Existent beings precede existence in their order of coming into existence.

Since existence as a universal concept requires an existent being in order for it to manifest itself, and since existent beings require an essence in order to be, then essence must precede existence in the order of actualization. In other words, since essence is needed for an existent being to exist and existence is contingent upon an existent being, then existence is contingent upon the essence.

Suhrawardi offers two types of arguments, the support for both of which is based on the impossibility of the existence of an infinite succession of contingent dependent beings. He argues that existence can exist if and only if existent beings exist. He states this in a very complicated argument which is as follows:

> If we say that whenever something is non-existent, its existence is necessarily not-actualized, then its existence is non-existent. This is because with the assumption that its existence is non-existent, whenever we conceive of existence and say that it does exist, it becomes necessary that the concept of existence be different from the existent object.[6]

Suhrawardi in the above argument seeks to demonstrate that existence has no actual reality and as a concept it is contingent upon the existence of the existent beings and therefore its presence is derived from the existence of the existent objects which themselves owe their existence to essence. This is the first argument for the principality of the essence (*aṣālat al-māhiyyah*) which became the basis of the *ishraqi* doctrine.

Suhrawardi's second argument for the principality of the essence is based on the fallacy of a teleological argument. On this Suhrawardi states:

> Therefore, if we say that what we assumed not to exist came into existence and the existence of that which was not and then was created, we realize that coming into being is

> different from existence. It becomes necessary that existence should have existence and we have to define existence by existence, and this continues *ad infinitum*. [It was stated that] an infinite succession of beings is impossible.[7]

In the above, Suhrawardi argues that if existence had actually existed, i.e. a table, and yet was different from essence, then it must have an existence and so on. This process could go on ad infinitum, which is absurd.

Suhrawardi's view on the principiality of the essence is absolutely crucial in the understanding of his philosophical views. To know something, for Suhrawardi, is to know its essence and that cannot be done through the senses, since senses can only perceive the appearance. Therefore, either we cannot know anything, which is absurd, or there is an alternative explanation. Suhrawardi's explanation of what this alternative is will be elaborated upon in the section on "Knowledge and Presence."

3. ON NECESSARY AND CONTINGENT BEINGS

Having argued for the principality of essence over existence by maintaining that essence is a necessary being and existence is contingent upon it, Suhrawardi goes on to equate essence with light.

Having argued against an infinite regress of contingent dependent beings, which is crucial for the validity of Suhrawardi's ontological frame work, Suhrawardi offers a complex argument that all existent beings except Light are of a contingent nature.[8]

To argue for this, Suhrawardi offers an argument in two parts. In the first part he argues that while no being exists by necessity (except the light of lights), all beings exist necessarily. His argument goes as follows: Things either exist by necessity or they are contingent. Contingent entities exist because of the presence of their cause and, should their cause be absent, the effect, which is the entity in question, would not exist either. Therefore, the existence of existent objects is due to the existence of their cause, and from this Suhrawardi concludes that objects, whether they exist or not, are contingent since they are caused. On the other hand, since every event has to have a cause and this process can not go on for ever, one can conclude that there has to be an ultimate cause whose existence is necessary.

The second part of Suhrawardi's argument is more complex. He states:

> If, as some have assumed, it is true that existence excludes the contingent from its contingency and makes it necessary, then it is necessary that non-existing should exclude the non-existent from non-existence and make it not-possible which means there cannot be such a thing as contingent being.[9]

Suhrawardi's argument maintains that if that which comes into existence loses its contingent nature and becomes necessary, then by a logical inference its opposite, which is non-existent by virtue of its non-existence, should make all non-existent entities not-possible. From this it follows that it is not logically possible for anything to be contingent.

1 $P \supset \sim\sim P$
2 $P \supset \Box P$

The converse would also have to be true.

1 $\sim P \supset \sim P$
2 $\sim P \supset \Box \sim P$

However, Suhrawardi has already maintained in the first part of his argument that all existing objects are contingent, which is contrary to the conclusion of the above argument. In the above arguments, Suhrawardi not only criticizes the ontological views of the Peripatetics which he elaborates upon in numerous places in *The Philosophy of Illumination, Intimations, Opposites,* and *Conversations,* but also strengthens his own *ishraqi* views through the implications of the arguments.[10]

4. LIMIT AND INFINITY

The discussion concerning limit and infinity for Suhrawardi has bearing upon his epistemology. While Suhrawardi argues against the existence of an infinite series of contingent dependent beings, he maintains that an infinite divisibility within a limited set with a beginning and an end can exist. The process of divisibility, however, will never come to an end and thereby the existence of such a set remains within the domain of logical possibility. Suhrawardi states:

> Know that in each succession (of beings) within which there is order, however they may be arranged. If they are within the domain of existence, they necessitate a limit or an end. Between each integer of this succession and another integer

> there exist infinite integers. Then it is necessary (for infinity) to be limited to these two integers and this is impossible. If in that succession two integers cannot be found in such a way that the numbers between them are not unlimited, then it is necessary that there be no unit unless (integers) between that and every other integer that is conceived in that succession be finite and therefore it will be necessary that all that succession be finite.[11]

This is a rather unusual approach to the problem of infinity. Suhrawardi's argument goes as follows: Either it is the case that the principle of infinite divisibility between two beings, i.e. two integers, is true or not. If it is true, then there must be an infinite set of numbers between two different integers. For example, between the numbers 2 and 3 there exists an infinite number of integers i.e. 2.1, 2.2, 2.3, etc. From this it can be concluded that infinity exists, but its existence is contingent upon the existence of a beginning and an end. Suhrawardi uses this argument both in a philosophical and mystical context and applies this conclusion in a number of Sufi doctrines as will be discussed later.

5. GOD'S EXISTENCE

In the *ishraqi* school God is equated with the light of lights from Whom emanate the lower levels of light, the angelic order and the archetypes. Therefore, the existence of God is fundamental for the validity of the philosophy of illumination and in particular the emanationistic scheme.

Suhrawardi argues that every event has at least one cause whose existence is necessitated if or when that cause is present. However, an effect is often a compound entity, and, therefore, when *A* causes B, it should be regarded as the cause of all its individual components. Since *B*, by virtue of being an effect, is a contingent being, all its components are contingent. The reverse is also true; that is, if individual members of a set are caused, then the set itself must be caused. From the above argument Suhrawardi concludes that:

> The cause of contingent beings cannot be contingent, because that will then be one in this set. Therefore, (the cause) must be something that is not contingent or non-existing and thus, the cause and the source of the existence of all the contingent beings must be a Necessary Being.[12]

Suhrawardi's argument again rests on the principle that an infinite chain of cause and effect is not possible and therefore the cause of an effect must be a Necessary Being. Having argued that the cause of all things is a Necessary Being, Suhrawardi then tries to respond to the possibility of having several necessary beings by offering the following:

If there be more than one Necessary Being, (i.e. A & B) then one of the following cases will occur:

1. A and B have nothing in common.
2. A and B have everything in common.
3. A and B have something in common i.e. C.

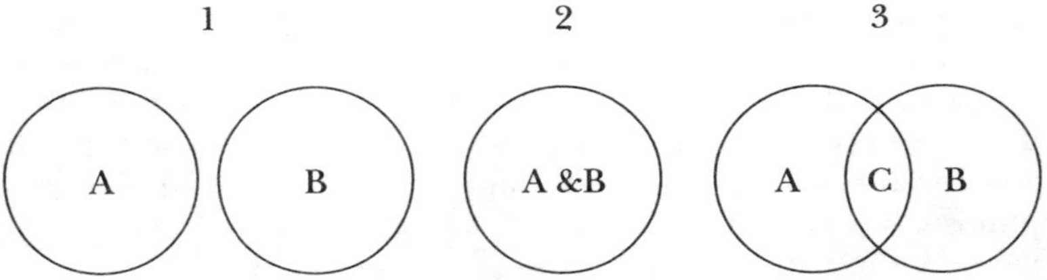

The first one can not be true since A & B at least have one thing in common, their property of being a Necessary Being. Therefore, it is not possible for several Necessary Beings to exist without sharing at least one common property.

The second alternative can not be the case either because if A & B had everything in common, then they would be the same. What makes A & B to be two different things is that they must have at least one difference between them. Therefore A & B can not have everything in common; otherwise they would be the same, which they are not.

The third option implies that A & B have something in common, and yet there are differences between them. This possibility is not a viable one either. As Suhrawardi states:

> If that which is their difference were not, then none of them would have existed. And if that which they have in common were not, then each one would not exist.[13]

Suhrawardi's argument requires further elaboration: If *A+C* is a Necessary Being, then *C* cannot be a contingent part of this Necessary Being. A Necessary Being by definition cannot have a contingent element in it. The same holds true with regard to *B+C*. If *C* is a Necessary being and a part of *A* and *B*, then we will arrive at the second alternative which we have already excluded.

Suhrawardi offers similar arguments in various places throughout his works.[14] For example, in the *Alwāh 'imādi*, he summarizes his views on the existence of a Necessary Being and its attributes as follows:

> Since there is no other Necessary Being, He has no match and because there is no force equal to Him in power and might, there is nothing to oppose Him. Since He has no location, He has no negation like the negation of whiteness that is black. All the power is emanated from Him and therefore nothing is His enemy. He is the Truth, meaning He exists because of His own essence and everything other than His essence is not real (*bāṭil*) since in their own essence they are not worthy of existence by necessity. Therefore, their truth comes from the ultimate truth and not of their own essence.[15]

By demonstrating that the existence of all beings is contingent, Suhrawardi has also prepared the path which leads to his *ishraqi* views where he equates God with Light and Light with Being.

6. SELF-BODY PROBLEM[16]

One of the central problems of philosophy has been to argue for the existence of "self" or "soul" and its relationship with the body.

In *Partaw-nāmah*,[17] he begins by offering several arguments for the existence of an independent "self" from the body. His first argument goes as follows: We often refer to ourselves and say "I" did this or that. If I would separate a part of myself (i.e. my hand) and put it on the table, I would neither refer to it as "I" nor would I be any different as far as my personality is concerned. On this basis he concludes that "I" or "self" is different from the body and therefore it has to be immaterial.

There are basically two problems with Suhrawardi's arguments. First, he argues that "self", which he calls "*nafs*", is above and beyond the body. On the other hand, he implies that there exists a correlation between them. For example, in *Partaw-nāmah*, he states:

> Know that *nafs* (soul) was not present before the body. If it were present prior to it, it would not have been one and many

> since this is impossible. The reason why a variety of souls (selves) could not have existed before the body is because all things when they share in the same thing, i.e. soul, are one, and when they become numerous they become different.[18]

Suhrawardi then offers his own view which is the instantaneous creation of the body and the soul. On this point he states:

> Therefore it becomes apparent that the soul cannot exist before the body and that they come into existence simultaneously. Between them there is attraction, love and anxiety but not like the attraction of beings and their accidents.[19]

With regard to dualism, a theory that maintains mind and body are two different and distinct entities which interact with each other, Suhrawardi argues that this distinction is a superficial one.

Suhrawardi in a number of treatises such as *Partaw-nāmah*[20] and *Hayākil al-nūr*[21] alludes to the dichotomy between a changing body and an immaterial self and states:

> All the parts of the body change and if your "self" consisted of these parts of the body, they would also be in a continuous state of change. (Thus) your self yesterday is not the same "self" as today, but each day your self is other than itself and this obviously is not the case. And since your knowledge is continuous and permanent it is not all body nor part of the body, but it is beyond all this.[22]

The problem Suhrawardi alludes to, however, is that for him the body is nothing but the absence of light, the lowest level on the ontological hierarchy of light. Therefore, a relationship between the "I" and the body is a relationship between light and its absence, which is not possible. Whereas the "I" is the seat of wisdom, the body handles lower functions. Therefore, that self and body are essentially of the same ontological texture. The only difference between them is their "intensity" which signifies they belong to different ontological statuses.

From the above, Suhrawardi concludes that the self and body are different aspects of the same phenomenon whose interactions are in accordance with the principles of *maḥabbah* (love) and *qahr* (domination).[23] The body, belonging to a lower order, has an innate love and yearning for the higher order, light, knowing that the higher order dominates what is below it. In the ultimate analysis, however, various levels are of the same source and thus there exists a kinship between the mind and the body. This theory is neither dualistic nor epiphenomenalistic, in that the mind and body are viewed in a different context all together. It can be called "spiritual monism" since it is based on the interaction of different manifestations of the same thing, namely light.

Suhrawardi's theory can be viewed from two ontological perspectives. Looking at it from below, the self and body are two different entities, since the lower order, to which the body belongs does not include the higher order, to which the category of the self belongs. However, looking at the same ontological hierarchy from the above, the self-body problem fades away since body is contained within the self whose nature is only a more intense light than the body.[24]

7. LIFE AFTER DEATH

Suhrawardi offers two types of arguments for the existence of life after death and the status of the soul after it departs the body. His first argument is an *ishraqi* one and the second a philosophical one. We shall consider the *ishraqi* view first.

Suhrawardi offers a profound eschatological analysis of an *ishraqi* nature, which can be said to be a "Neoplatonization" of Ibn Sīnā's view on eschatology with some original contributions of his own.[25] In books 4 and 5 of *Ḥikmat al-ishrāq*,[26] he begins a discussion on eschatology, prophecy and transmigration of the soul based on his ontological views. Adhering to basic Ibn Sīnian doctrine of the gradations of beings, Suhrawardi goes on to argue for the transmigration of the human soul on the basis of the inner qualities that he attributes to various ontological statues. As he states:

> Objects are in need of the lordly light which has a relation- ship with the body. This interestedness [of lordly light] is due to the inherent poverty of it (body) and its yearning towards the higher is due to its illuminationist relation. It, meaning body, is the epitome of receptivity and contains lights.[27]

In the above argument Suhrawardi demonstrates the mechanism by which the lower beings ascend towards a higher ontological state, the gate through this ascendence ultimately being man himself.

> The gate of all gates is the human body since it consists of that which other gates precede it such that, entering through it is required first.[28]

The question that arises now is what happens to the soul when one dies. The entire section 4 of *Ḥikmat al-ishrāq* provides an *ishraqi* analysis in light of which the above is answered. In a section entitled "On the Status of the Human Soul After its Departure From the Body,"[29] Suhrawardi is explicit in putting forward his eschatological doctrine. There he argues that the status of the human soul after death depends on the degree to which one is able to ascend on the ontological hierarchy before death. In this regard, Suhrawardi considers pursuing a balanced life based on knowledge and action to be a key in determining one's status after death. On this he states:

> The good fated ones who are balanced in knowledge and action and the ascetics who are pure and virtuous once departed from their bodies, join with the archetypes which are the origin of their bodies.[30]

With regard to the fate of those whom Suhrawardi does not consider to be living a "balanced life" he says:

> The masters of cruelty and misery who have gathered around hell . . . transmigration be true or not, once they depart from their corporeal bodies, they will have deprivations and absences from the archetypes (*ṣuwar-i mu'allaqah*) in accordance with their character.[31]

Establishing a correspondence between one's deeds in this world and the status of one's soul in the hereafter is not a new concept. Suhrawardi's orginal contribution is the use of the concept of *ṣuwar-i mu'allaqah,* literally meaning the "suspended forms," in elaborating on his eschatological doctrine. Suhrawardi reminds us that these forms are different than Platonic archetypes and describes them as follows:

> The suspended forms are not the same as the Platonic forms (*muthul*), because Platonic forms are luminous and are in the world of intellectual enlightenment which is immutable. However, these are forms (*ṣuwar*) that are suspended in the world of transcendence, some of which are dark and some luminous.[32]

The above is perhaps the original contribution of Suhrawardi, since in his archetypal world there are inherently evil things which he identifies with "darkness." Perhaps this is where Zoroastrian dualism is best exemplified in Suhrawardi's thought since the "benevelant God" (Ahuramazda) and the "malevolent God" (Ahriman) have their own good and bad angels who are necessary beings. It is precisely introducing of this type of dualism into the archetypal world of traditional Platonic ideas and the relation of it to life after death which is a significant contribution of Suhrawardi to the ongoing eschatological debates in Islamic philosophy. It is a concept which is certainly not shared by many of his successors. In Suhrawardi's world of suspended forms (*ṣuwar al-mu'allaqah*), there are also perfect forms of evil which he identifies with darkness.

Finally, Suhrawardi concludes his eschatological doctrine by establishing a relationship between his ontology, angelology and his doctrine of the suspended forms. He argues that in fact the souls of those who have lived a balanced life give rise to an angelic order who in turn determine different gradations of the *ishraqi* ontology. Furthermore, he concludes that the ontological status of individuals is determined on the basis of this hierarchy and states:

> From the souls of the balanced people who possess the suspended forms and their manifestations which are the heavens, different levels of angels are created whose numbers are unlimited. They have different status in accordance with different levels of the heavens upto the state of the purified ones and theosophers. That status is higher and more noble than the world of angels.[33]

His arguments follow those that are typical of the Peripatetics, in particular Ibn Sīnā. One of his arguments has to do with the immortality of the cause of the self or soul. On this he states:

> Know that the self remains and death for it is not conceivable because its cause is the Active Intellect, which is immutable. Therefore, the effect will remain immortal because of the immortal nature of the Cause.[34]

However, Suhrawardi fails to adequately demonstrate that if a given cause is immortal, the effect too becomes immutable and immortal, a relationship which he seems to take for granted. It is true that there has to be an affinity between a cause and its effect, but to establish a necessary relationship between a cause and its effect and to ascribe the existential attributes of the cause to its effect is unfounded.

Suhrawardi offers a number of other arguments, especially in the *'Alwāh-i 'imādī*,[35] and *Partaw-nāmah*, for the existence of life after death which generally follow the same pattern, namely by establishing the existence of an immaterial and independent "self" from the body.

8. LOGIC

Suhrawardi classifies all knowledge on the basis of whether it is acquired through the sense perception or whether it is innate. He argues that the knowledge that is attained through innate ideas is beyond logical analysis. Therefore, logic as such can be applied only to the category of acquired knowledge.[36] So far, Suhrawardi has remained within the logical paradigm of the Peripatetics as exemplified by Ibn Sīnā's book of *Healing* (*Shifā*).[37] Logic for Suhrawardi is only a tool for analysis, and in that capacity it is subservient to philosophy. H. Ziā'ī summarizes Suhrawardi's views on logic as presented in the *al-Muṭāraḥāt* in the following three principles:

> (1) Logic deals with conception and assent insofar as they may be true; (2) logic is a speculative art (*sinā'a naẓariyya*) which deals with conception and assent, the form of syllogism and the secondary intelligibles; (3) logic is an axiomatic art of the rules (*sinā'a qānūniyya*) which guards the human mind against error in thinking.[38]

As far as formal differences between Suhrawardi and Peripatetics are concerned, Suhrawardi does not adhere to the nine books of Aristotle's *Organon*. First of all, the *Categories* are absent from Suhrawardi's analysis and there are only brief references to them in the *Topics*, *Rhetoric*, and *Poetics*. While there is no separate treatment of Aristotle's *Categories* as most of the Peripatetics (i.e. Ibn Sīnā) have done, Suhrawardi does consider the Aristotelian categories and in fact reduces them from ten to four, with motion being a new category.

H. Ziā'ī argues in his work, *Philosophy of Illumination*,[39] that while Suhrawardi does not deviate from the Peripatetic logic in a major way in the *Intimations* and *Conversations*, he does offer a "new structure" of logic in the *Ḥikmat al-ishraq*. This new structure according to Ziā'ī divides the field of logic into three general areas:

1. Semantics
2. Principles of proof
3. Errors of formal and material logic

On this Ziā'ī states:

> This new structure may be an attempt on the part of Suhrawardi to recognize the traditional *Organon* according to his general bipartite division of logic into expository propositions and proofs.[40]

In the forthcoming chapter, I will demonstrate how Suhrawardi applies logic to comment on such topics as knowledge by definition, sense perception, etc. Suhrawardi's use of logic can best be seen in his semantical analysis and his criticism of logic as applied by the Peripatetics, which he argues can only lead to a partial discovery of truth.[41]

9. ANGELOLOGY

Having used the symbolism of light and darkness, Suhrawardi then goes on to develop an elaborate angelology based on Zoroastrian angels. He achieves this by identifying different grades of lights with various angelic orders. Between the light of lights and total darkness, there are levels upon levels of light with different degrees of intensity such that each level corresponds to an angel.

The new schemata of angels changes the traditional view of angels as the force behind the movement of the heavenly bodies. According to Suhrawardi, angels serve a number of functions, the most important of which is their intermediary role between the light of lights and man. For instance, an angelic order identified as the "lordly light" (*al-nūr al-isfahbadi*) is defined by Suhrawardi as that which is "within the soul of man" such that "everywhere its signs are manifested and all things attest to its presence."[42]

Suhrawardi's ontology and its byproduct, angelology, are meant to map out the interior reality of man rather than to provide a logical explanation for such things as angels "out there." The Peripatetic view of the function of angels, especially that of Ibn Sīnā and Fārābī, who simply saw the angels as beings who perform certain functions out there in the universe such as rotation of the heavens, was criticized by Suhrawardi. While Suhrawardi accepts the view that angels have realities, he maintains that the number of angels are equivalent to the number of the fixed stars, meaning a virtually unlimited number of them, a departure from the traditional Peripatetic view.

From the hierarchy of angels arise two angelic orders: a longitudinal (*ṭūlī*), and a latitudinal (*'araḍī*) order with two separate functions. The longitudinal angelic order represents the vertical axis or hierarchy of light similar to a ladder. The latitudinal angelic order for Suhrawardi is where the "archetypes" or "forms" reside. Suhrawardi goes on to argue that at the top of the longitudinal order of light there stands the supreme light which he calls by its Quranic and Mazdean names, *al-nūr al-a'ẓam* (the Supreme Light) and *Vohuman (Bahman)*. From this light of lights, issues the lower order that is illuminated by the light above it and the process of one light issuing a lower one continues until it reaches darkness. The higher light, which is marked by intensity, dominates (*qahr*) the lower order and the lower order is marked by yearning and love for the higher one.[43] This process remains valid for the entire succession from the *nūr al-anwār* to darkness. As we will see later, Suhrawardi applies this scheme to offer his epistemological view which for him can replace the Aristotelian categories as a means of epistemic analysis.

For Suhrawardi there exists a veil between each level of light which acts as a "purgatory" or *Barzakh* and allows the passage of only a certain amount of light. The primordial, original and all-encompassing nature of this system, through which Suhrawardi expresses a number of esoteric doctrines, is such that he calls it *al-ummahat* (the mothers), since all that exists originates from this hierarchy and therefore it contains within itself the "ideas" (*a'yān al-thābitah*) whose unfolding is the world.

In his attempt to equate the angels of ancient Persia with the Platonic forms or archetypes, Suhrawardi considers the longitudinal order to have given rise to a latitudinal order and that to him is none other than the Platonic forms or ideas. Each being in the world has its own archetype (*arbāb al-anwā'*) within the latitudinal axis which Suhrawardi identifies with the Zoroastrian angelology. For example, he identifies water with the Mazdean angel *Khurdād*, fire with *Urdībihisht*, vegetables as *Murdād*, and minerals as *Shahrīwar*. These angels and many more are the archetypes whose actualization or manifestation from the archetypes (*al-a'yān thābitah*) appear in the material forms mentioned above.[44]

Suhrawardi considers the heavenly bodies and the more visible and materialized aspect of the angelic order to have come from the longitudinal order, while the latitudinal order gives rise to more esoteric phenomena such as the lordly light.

Since Suhrawardi knows that in the final analysis the ultimate truth to which he is alluding lies at the heart of all the divinely revealed traditions, the use of various symbols from different traditions becomes secondary. Therefore, symbols, be they Mazdean or Quranic, allude to truths which are profoundly Islamic as well as Zoroastrian.

Suhrawardi's angelology[45] relies on the symbolism of many traditions in order to provide a map of man's interior. It is a cosmological doctrine which alludes to the presence of a unifying element in all the traditional religions of man, namely a universal truth.

10. PHYSICS

In putting forth his views on physics,[46] Suhrawardi begins with a discussion regarding the nature of the universe, which from his point of view is pure light. The views of the *Ash'ari'te* Atomists, who were one of the predominant intellectual schools of the time, were based on the principality of form and matter and therefore the study of physics for them became the study of matter. Suhrawardi argued against them by saying that since material bodies are constituted of light, the study of physics is the study of light.

Having defined the nature of things as light, Suhrawardi goes on to classify things according to the degree of their transparency. For example, all those entities which allow light to pass through them, such as air, are in a higher ontological category than those which obstruct light, such as the earth.

In explaining meteorological phenomena, Suhrawardi follows Ibn Sīnā and Aristotle, but he rejects their views with regard to the occurrence of change within the nature of things. For example, Aristotle argues that boiling water is due to the coming in contact of the atoms of fire and water. Suhrawardi states that boiling is because there exists a quality in water such that when it comes close to fire this potentiality is actualized. He argues that fire does not come in contact with the water, nor does the volume of water change. Therefore, the only conclusion one can draw is to argue for the existence of a special quality or attribute within water. As he states:

> Qualitative change is due rather to the coming into being of a quality which is intermediate between the qualities of the original bodies and which is shared by all the particles of the new compound.[47]

It is obvious that such a theory has implications not only for the field of physics, but also as an esoteric doctrine that seeks to explain how the association of different things may bring about a qualitative change. This principle is one of the crucial elements in the development of spiritual alchemy which appears in Islamic esoteric writings.[48]

11. PSYCHOLOGY

Suhrawardi's views on psychology are closely related to his concept of epistemology, which in turn is directly related to the ontological hierarchy that serves as the foundation of his philosophy. The following diagram helps to demonstrate this connection:[49]

DOMINANCE→

Light of lights→ Angelic order→ Souls→ Heavens→ Bodies of lights
Universal Intellect→ Intelligence→ Souls→ Heavens

←LOVE

Such a hierarchy influences the human psyche in the following manner: The ontological status of a being necessitates a certain psychological apparatus, and how the psyche and the faculties of this being function depends on their place within the hierarchical structure of the universe.

Suhrawardi's view of psychology, though influenced by Aristotle's psychology as discussed in the *De Anima*, does not follow Aristotle's classification, and in fact is closer to Ibn Sīnā than to Aristotle. Suhrawardi classifies all beings into three categories: vegetable, animal and human. The only major difference between his view and the Peripatetics lies in his notion of body as the theurgy of *Ispahbad.*

According to Suhrawardi, the classification of different faculties can be illustrated by the following diagram[50]:

Vegetable Soul	Feeding (*ghādhiyyah*)	Attraction (*jādhibah*)
	Growth (*nāmiyyah*)	Retention (*māsikah*)
	Reproduction (*muwallidah*)	Digestion (*hāḍimah*)
		Repulsion (*dafi'ah*)

Animal Soul	Power of motion (*muḥarrikah*)	Power of lust (*shahwah*)
	Power of desire (*nuzū'iyyah*)	Power of anger (*ghadhab*)

Sensus Communis (ḥiss mushtarik)	The center where all the information and data of the external world is collected. The location is in the front of the brain.
Fantasy (*khiyāl*)	The place where *sensus communis* is stored. It is located in the back of the cavity.
Apprehension (*wahm*)	Governs sensible things which the senses are not capable of gathering and it is located in the middle cavity.
Imagination (*mutakhayyilah*)	Often identified with apprehension but its function goes further and it synthesizes and analyzes.
Memory (*ḥāfiẓah*)	The place where apprehension is stored. It is located in the back of the middle cavity.

12. ESCHATOLOGY

Suhrawardi's notion of eschatology is derived from his notion of psychology.[51] He concludes that the goal of man is to become illuminated and return to his origin in the other world. The other world is only a continuation of this one, and the status of the soul in the hereafter depends on the degree to which a person is purified here and now.

Suhrawardi identifies three groups of people with respect to the degree of their purity and illumination and establishes a causal connection between their purity and their ontological status in the other world. These three groups are:

1. Those who remained in the darkness of ignorance (*ashqiyā'*).
2. Those who purified themselves to some extent (*sudad*).
3. Those who purified themselves and reached illumination (*muta 'allihūn*).

In his book *Yazdān shinākht*,[52] he demonstrates the type of connection that he establishes between one's ontological status in this world and that of the other world. He argues that regardless of the degree of one's purity, the soul is in essence immortal. This argument is as follows:

> Know that the soul remains; it is inconceivable for it to perish since its cause (of coming to be) which is the active intellect, is eternal; therefore, it remains eternal because of its cause (which is eternal).[53]

13. *HIKMAT* VERSUS PHILOSOPHY

Like many other Islamic philosophers, Suhrawardi makes a distinction between philosophy and *ḥikmat* which is crucial for the understanding of not only *ishraqi* doctrine but also the post-Suhrawardian philosophy, especially in Persia and the sub-continent of India. The distinction between philosophy and *ḥikmat* which is held by a great number of Islamic philosophers is believed to have been advocated even by such peripatetics as Ibn Sīnā, who after reaching the zeinth of his philosophical maturity demonstrated *ishraqi* tendencies. In the introduction to *manṭiq al-mashraqiyyīn*[54] he tells us that "there are branches of wisdom that do not originate from the Greeks."[55] In his book *al-Mashāri' wa'l-muṭāraḥāt*,[56] Suhrawardi tells us that while most of Ibn Sīnā's writings are devoid of any theosophical significance, there are references to the existence of a type of wisdom other than the Greeks and their discursive method.

Suhrawardi may have believed that, due to the circumstance under which Ibn Sīnā lived, he had to remain silent in regard to his *ishraqi* ideas. Therefore Suhrawardi feels that he not only has to disclose the *ishraqi* tendencies of Ibn Sīnā but also to continue them. For example, in his work "*The Occidental Exile*" (*al-Ghurbat al-gharbiyyah*), Suhrawardi picks up the story where Ibn Sīnā had ended his short work, *Risālat Ḥayy ibn yaqẓān*.[57] Both of these stories are highly symbolic and demonstrate the spiritual stages of the inner being of a seeker of truth and his relationship with the active intellect, which Suhrawardi identifies as the "glorious old master" (*Pir-i Burnā*).

Ibn Sīnā was well aware of the dangers of popularizing the wisdom of illumination, and his silence in this regard may well be attributed to this very point. In the *al-Ishārāt wa'l-tanbīhāt*, he says,

If you corrupt this wisdom, God be the judge between you and me.[58]

If it was Spinoza who said, "God is not so mindless as to create a two legged creature and leave it to Aristotle to make him rational," Suhrawardi would add to this: "and to make Aristotle the only gate through which truth can be attained." This is because Suhrawardi neither considers Aristotle to be the founder of rationality nor can the type of wisdom he advocates be the only one that leads to truth. As S.H. Nasr states:

> He [Suhrawardi] believed that this wisdom is universal and Perennial, the *philosophia perennis* and *universalis*, which existed in various forms among the ancient Hindus, Persians, Babylonians and Egyptians and among the Greeks up to the time of Aristotle, who for Suhrawardi was not the beginning but rather the end of philosophy among the Greeks who terminated this tradition of wisdom by limiting it to its rationalistic aspect.[59]

The inherent distinction between philosophy and *ḥikmah* for Suhrawardi is a natural one and emanates from the fact that the faculty of intellectus and praxis are two separate faculties.

In his work *Yazdān shinākht,* Suhrawardi alludes to this distinction and argues that there lie two powers within the soul: one apprehends and the other one generates action. Suhrawardi then goes on to make the functioning of these two faculties be contingent upon each other and states:

> Theoretical (faculty), for example, is such as knowing that the world is created, and practical [faculty for example] is to know that oppression is evil . . . theoretical is subject to discursive science and from practical (faculty) a knowledge is required to know what should become known.[60]

This is not to say that Suhrawardi opposed a rational approach to philosophical issues, nor was he "anti-philosophy," as Ghazzālī and some other Sufis were. In fact, reasoning and independent judgment are an essential part of one's quest for the pursuit of truth. Suhrawardi's respect for a rational process of reasoning goes so far as to say: Do not follow me or anybody else and know that the only criterion is reason.[61]

Therefore, whereas philosophical speculation for Suhrawardi is important, it however originates from a faculty that is subservient to intellectual intuition (*dhawq*). Suhrawardi goes so far as to categorize different knowers in accordance with their mastery of rationalistic philosophy and *ḥikmat*. His classifications go as follows:

1. Those who have mastered *ishraqi* wisdom but are not well versed in discursive reasoning. (i.e. Bāyazīd, Kharraqānī)
2. Those who have mastered discursive reasoning but yet lack *ishraqi* inclination (i.e. Fārābī)
3. Those who have mastered both discursive reasoning and *ishraqi* wisdom. These are perfect philosophers and are entitled to be the "vicegerents of God" (*khalīfat Allāh*).

While it is clear that Suhrawardi recommends the study of the Peripatetic philosophy first, especially in the *al-Talwīḥāt* and *al-Mashari' wa'l-muṭāraḥāt*,[62] he puts the study of discursive philosophy in perspective.

Having defended the study of discursive philosophy as a prerequisite to the understanding of *ishraq*, Suhrawardi then tells us of the unique characteristics of the type of wisdom that he is propagating.

Suhrawardi considers himself to be the unifier of what he calls "*al-Ḥikmat al-laduniyah*" (Divine Wisdom), a tradition that begins with Prophet Hermes (*khiḍr*) and has persisted throughout time in various forms. As to the source of this wisdom he argues:

> The light of the path which stretches into the past is the substance of Pythagoras . . . and was sent down upon Tustarī and his followers. The substance of *Khusrawāniān* [wisdom] has been sent down to Kharrqānī and Sayyar Basṭāmī.[63]

Therefore, Suhrawardi is arguing that while philosophy and *ḥikmat* issue forth from the same source, they nevertheless are distinct in that philosophy is the necessary condition and theosophy the sufficient condition for the attainment of truth. Suhrawardi, as the unifier of different traditions of wisdom, considers philosophy and theosophy to be two types of wisdom, each of which is suitable for a purpose. Truth for Suhrawardi ultimately should rely on knowledge that is attained through illumination, while it has to sustain the scrutiny of logic and rational reasoning and be compatable with them.

On the relationship between philosophy and *ḥikmat*, Suhrawardi in the introduction to *The Philosophy of Illumination* states:

> . . . This book is of a different methodology, and a path (of truth) that is nearer than the other one(discursive) . . . . Its

> truth and other enigmas first did not come to me through thinking or discourse but its attainment was of a different nature. Finally, when I attained the truth, I questioned its rationale in such a way that if I ignore the reasoning process, no doubt can come upon me.[64]

Suhrawardi claims to have first discovered the truth which he calls *ḥikmat*, and then he embarked on a path to find the rational basis of his experiential wisdom. It is certain that philosophy in Suhrawardi's thought plays a different role from theosophy, and so does the means by which one comes to attain mastery of each type of wisdom. These two traditions of wisdom for the master of *ishraq* are not only different in their form and their content but also originate from two different sources. Discursive philosophy comes from the rational faculty, whereas *ishraqi* wisdom is issued forth from the faculty of intuition.

A major problem that is often alluded to is that whereas the results of logical analyses are verifiable, such is not the case in regard to various truth claims that are of an *ishraqi* nature. Suhrawardi argues that his views can be verified only by those who have been initiated into the science of *ishraq* through a spiritual master who has become the vicegerent of God on earth (*khalīfat Allāh*).[65] On this he states:

> Of course, it is not feasible for one who has not referred to a sage who is the vicegerent (of God) and possesses the knowledge of this book to gain access to the secrets of this book.[66]

Often Suhrawardi is very explicit in his instructions as to how the types of wisdom he advocates can be attained. For Suhrawardi *Ḥikmat al-ishrāq* is a blueprint for those who wish to have an experience of illumination. It is crucial to realize the importance of asceticism and practical wisdom to the *ishraqi* doctrine as a whole, even though this is contrary to some of the later interpreters of Suhrawardi who put more emphasis on his intellectual and philosophical aspects.

The prime concern of Suhrawardi's entire philosophy is to demonstrate the journey of the human soul towards its original abode. One begins by gaining an awareness of the path that he ought to follow. Having followed the teachings of a master who can direct the disciple through the maze of spiritual dangers, one reaches a state where spiritual knowledge can be obtained directly without mediation. In this state, Suhrawardi considers knowledge to come from the divine soul (*nafs al-qudsiyyah*), a mode of cognition distinct from that of the Peripatetics. To demonstrate the spiritual journey of man, Suhrawardi establishes a tightly woven web of ideas and concepts, the validity of which depends on the entire system, which itself rests upon the principality of light.

Notes

1 Nasr, *Three Muslim* Sages, 69.
2 Suhrawardi, *Opera* 2, 10.
3 Suhrawardi, *Opera* 3, 46.
4 Suhrawardi, *Opera* 2, 64.
5 Ibid., 64.
6 Ibid., 65.
7 Ibid., 65.
8 Suhrawardi's arguments can also be found in *Opera* 2, 106ff.
9 Suhrawardi, *Opera* 2, 62.
10 For more information on Suhrawardi's ontology see: H. Ziā'ī, *Knowledge and Illumination* (Atlanta: Scholars Press, 1990), 125–187.
11 Suhrawardi, *Opera* 2, 63.
12 Suhrawardi, *Opera* 3, 33.
13 Ibid., 34.
14 Suhrawardi's views on the existence of a Necessary Being, essence and existence as presented in his Persian works can be found in *Alwāḥ 'imādī,* 134–153; his arguments are basically the same as those presented in *Partaw-nāmah.* The arguments prestented in his Arabic works, especially in the *al-Talwiḥāt,* 33–39, are also similar to those of *Alwāḥ 'imādiyah* and *Partaw-nāmah.* Such arguments are based on the impossibility that the chain of causality could go on for infinity.
15 Suhrawardi, *Opera* 3, 141.
16 Suhrawardi's argument for the existence of the self and its relationship with the body can be found in the *al-Talwiḥāt,* 68, and 80–82; and *Būstān al-qulūb,* pp.342–387.
17 Suhrawardi, *Opera* 3, 23–24.
18 Suhrawardi, *Opera* 3, 25. Suhrawardi in this section uses the words "self" and "I" interchangably. However, in all these cases he is alluding to what constitutes the identity of a person.
19 Suhrawardi, *Opera* 3, 26.
20 For more information on Suhrawardi's theory of Personal Identity, see *Partaw-nāmah,* 26–31.
21 It is argued that Suhrawardi's choice of the word *Hāyakil* is influenced by the Ismā'īlīs, who use this term extensively. This also may have been one of the likely causes of his death since ṣalāḥ al-Dīn Ayyūbī was highly antagonistic towards Ismā'īlīs.
22 Suhrawardi, *Opera* 3, 85–86.
23 For more information see: H. Corbin, *En Islam iranien,* vol. 2 (Paris: Gallimard, 1971–1972), 107–110.
24 Suhrawardi's view on the existence of a self in his Persian works can be found in the following works: *Hayākil al-nūr,* 4–92; *Alwāh 'imādī,* 116–165; *Būstān al-qulūb,* 342–387; and *Yazdān shinākht,* 412–444. In his Arabic works he discusses the issue in the *al-Talwiḥāt,* 68, 81, 82. However, most of the arguments are derivations of the argument that I have discussed.
25 For more information on a "spiritualized" reading of Ibn Sīnā, see:

J. Michot, *Dieu el la destinée de l'homme ma'ād chez Avicenne,* (Peetrs: Louvain Pub., 1987).

26 Suhrawardi, *Opera* 2, ch.4, 5.

27 Ibid., 216.

28 Ibid., 217.

29 Ibid., 229.

30 Ibid., 229.

31 Ibid., 230.

32 Ibid., 231.

33 Ibid., 235.

34 Suhrawardi, *Opera* 3, 65.

35 For more information on Suhrawardi's view on the existence of life after death, see *Alwaḥ 'imādiyah,* 155ff.

36 Suhrawardi, *Opera* 1, 1–4.

37 *Shifā* 1, 2–4.

38 H. Ziā'ī, "Suhrawardi's Philosophy of Illumination" (Ph.D. Diss., Harvard University, 1976), 53–54.

39 Ibid., 57.

40 Ibid., 82.

41 For more information on Suhrawardi's logic see: H. Ziā'ī, *Knowledge and Illumination* (Atlanta: Scholars Press, 1992).

42 Ibid., 70.

43 It is not until Mullā Ṣadrā's time that the mechanism by which beings yearn for the higher order is thoroughly discussed. His notion of "Transsubstantial motion" (*ḥarakat al-jawhariyyah*) explains the inner yearning of beings towards a higher ontological status.

44 Hīdajī, in his commentary upon Sabziwārī's *sharḥ-i manẓumah,* offers a complete list of the words and phrases of the ancient Persian sages which Suhrawardi refers throughout his writings. For more information see *Ḥashiy-yi hidajī* (Tehran), 283.

45 For further discussion of Suhrwardi's angelology, see H. Corbin's introduction to Suhrawardi, *Opera 2,* and G. Webbs, *Suhrawardi's Angelology,* (Ph.D. Disst: Temple University, 1989).

46 For a discussion of Suhrawardi's physics, see H. Corbin's introduction to *Opera* 2.

47 *A History of Muslim Philosophy,* vol. 1, ed M.M. Sharif (Wiesbaden: Otto Harrassowitz, 1963), 391.

48 For more information on alchemy and its spiritual symbolim, see S.H. Nasr, *Science and Civilization in Islam* (Cambridge: Harvard University Press, 1968); and T. Burkhardt, *Alchemy: Science of the Cosmos, Science of the Soul,* trans. W. Stoddard (Olten: Walter, 1974).

49 For a more complete discussion, see H. Corbin's introduction to *Opera* 2.

50 I have followed the outline presented by S.H. Nasr in *A History of Muslim Philosophy,* ed. M.M. Sharif. p. 216.

51 In the later part of the *Ḥikmat al-ishraq,* Suhrawardi devotes a major section to the discussion of eschatology using the language of illumination. See *Opera* 2, 216.

52 Suhrawardi, *Opera* 3, 419–422.

53 Ibid., 65.
54 Ibn Sīnā, *Manṭiq al-mashraqiyyīn* (Tehran: Ja'farī Tabrīzī Pub., 1973), 63ff.
55 Ibid., 63.
56 Suhrawardi, *Opera* 1, 194–197.
57 Ibn Sīnā, *Risālat Ḥayy ibn Yaqẓān*, ed. Aḥmad Amin (Egypt: Dār al-Ma'ārif Publication, 1966).
58 *al-Ishārat wa'l-tanbīhāt*, 419.
59 S.H. Nasr, *Three Muslim Sages*, 61.
60 Suhrawardi, *Opera* 3, 422–423.
61 Suhrawardi, *Opera* 1, 140.
62 Ibid., 194.
63 Ibid., 502–503.
64 Suhrawardi, *Opera* 2, 10.
65 This notion, which may also have political connotations according to some scholars, has been instrumental in the latter developments of Shi'ite political thought. For more information see: H. Ziā'ī, "The Source and Nature of Political Authority in Suhawardi Philosopy of Illumination," in *Political Aspects of Islamic Philosophy*, ed. Butterworth (Cambridge: Harvard University Press, 1992).
66 Suhrawardi, *Opera* 2, 259.

3

PRACTICAL SUFISM

1. SUHRAWARDI'S VISION

The beginning of the mystical traditions is often traced back to the vision of their founders, and the mystical dimension of Suhrawardi's thought is no exception. Suhrawardi in *The Philosophy of Illumination*[1] tells us that in "a strange day", the truth and the secrets of the Divine were revealed to him. Having had a vision, he then sets forth to write down the principles of his transcendental theosophy for those philosophers who are well versed in esoteric sciences as well as discursive philosophy.

In his introduction to *The Philosophy of Illumination*, Suhrawardi tells us that the content and truth of this book were not attained through discursive reasoning. Having attained the truth "in another way,"[2] he goes on to say that he then sought the justification of his findings in a more discursive context. Suhrawardi further tells us that the certainty that is attained through this direct means of cognition is such that it stands independent of the process of logical reasoning that also leads to the same conclusion.[3]

Since for Suhrawardi it is this special mode of knowledge that differentiates between those who truly know and those who do not, he goes on to categorize the seekers of wisdom accordingly.[4]

1. Those who are immersed in theosophia and do not concern themselves with discursive and rationalistic philosophy.
2. Rationalisitc philosophers who do not concern themselves with theosophy.
3. Learned men who have benefited both from theosophy and discursive philosophy.
4. Theosophers who are neverthless mediocre or weak in discursive philosophy.

5. Rationalistic philosophers who are mediocre or weak in theosophy.
6. Students of theosophy and discursive philosophy.
7. Students of theosophy alone.
8. Students of discursive philosophy alone.

What is the nature of the knowledge of a theosopher which enables him to know the truth and to attain the certainty that is not part of discursive knowledge? Clarification of this crucial point in Suhrawardi's philosophy requires a lengthly disscusion concerning Suhrawardi's epistemology.

It should be first mentioned that there is a difference between this special mode of knowledge and what is commonly known as "mystical vision" or mystical experience. Suhrawardi tells us that he himself was puzzled as to how one comes to know a thing. He ponders upon this question and finally in a state of utter frustration he has a vision of Aristotle who tells him what the solution is:

Aristotle: If you turn to your own self (*dhāt*) and inquire, you will certainly find your answer.
Suhrawardi: How is that?
Aristotle: Is it not the case that you understand yourself? Is this understanding of the self, or is it the understanding of the self through something other than the self? If it is the case that the understanding of the self is through something other than the self, for your self there is another self who understands you and it is no longer you who understands yourself. Now that this is the case, necessarily one questions this new self that is the true element for the understanding of the self. Does this self understand itself, or does it need something else? If this be the case, then it goes on *ad infinitum*, which is impossible. The other assumption is that you come to know of your self through the effect or an idea that you attain the truth of your self and that the truth of your self can never be understood without any mediation.
Suhrawardi: I agree that I can never know myself directly and it is only through the picture or the idea of a self that I can know myself.
Aristotle: If what you say were the case, then if this idea or picture does not correspond with your self, it does not represent your self, and because this idea is not an indication of your self then you have not understood your self.
Suhrawardi: Suppose this idea corresponds to my self. If this idea comes to my mind through my "self", then it is precisely repre-

sentative of my self and no other thing. Do you still believe that one's self cannot be understood through such a thing?

Aristotle: This idea certainly corresponds to your self but does it correspond to the universal self or to your particular self that has specific characteristics and attributes?

Suhrawardi: I assume the latter by saying that the pictorial idea corresponds with my "self" that has certain characteristics and therefore represents my self.

Aristotle: Every picture that forms in the mind is of a universal character, and as much as you limit these concepts to having attributes, etc. yet, since they are of multiple nature, they are still universal. If in case due to an obstacle in the outside world, the validity of a universal concept is violated because of the particular characteristics of an individual, it nevertheless remains universal at a conceptual level. The inevitable fact is that you understand your unique self, a self that is truly free from any sharing or commonness. The result is that this particular understanding that you have of your unique and uncommon self cannot be understood through a picture or idea. Therefore, understanding of the self is never through the "idea" (or picture).[5]

Suhrawardi in his state of dream-vision asks Aristotle if the Peripatetic philosophers are the true masters of wisdom. Aristotle tells him that such figures as Bāyazīd and Ḥallāj, the masters of the Sufi tradition, are the true philosophers and not the Peripatetics, presumably because they came to know their "self" first.[6]

Aristotle's advice to Suhrawardi is that to know anything one must first "know himself." This knowing, which for Suhrawardi takes place both on a practical and a philosophical level, is a central theme of *ishraqi* philosophy. On a practical level, the "I" is the source of all sublime desires veiled by the temptations of the corporeal dimension of man. On a philosophical level, Suhrawardi considers the "I" to be the foundation of the illuminationist epistemology.

It is precisely this illuminationist epistemology that can lead to the visionary experience of fifteen types of lights by those who are on the spiritual path. Suhrawardi tells us those who disengage themselves from the world of matter are able to arrive at the "eighth heaven" (*aqlīm al-thāmin*), which he identifies with the archetypeal world (*'ālam mithāl*).[7] Suhrawardi mentions such figures as Hermes, Plato and the prophet Muhammad to be among those who have had a vision of these lights, each of which

Suhrawardi identifies with a particular attribute. According to Suhrawardi, these fifteen lights, some of which have peculiar descriptions are "the purpose of the path of knowledge."[8] These visionary lights which emanate from the world of intellect are the essence of power and knowledge and he who experiences these lights also attains the power to rule over the material world. The necessary condition for this experience is, however, separation (*tajrīd*) from one's corporeal body. These lights are:[9]

1. A light which shines upon the novice and is pleasant but not permanent.
2. A light that shines upon others and is more like a lightningbolt.
3. A light that is soothing and enters the hearts of the gnostics. It is as if warm water is poured on you, a pleasant sensation is then experienced.
4. A light that descends upon the hearts of the men of vision and lasts a long time. This is a dominant light which induces a form of intoxication.
5. A light of extreme grace and pleasure which is induced through the power of love.
6. A light that burns and is induced through knowledge that is attained through intellection.
7. A light which at first is luminous and is more intense than the light of the sun.
8. A luminous and pleasant light appearing as if it comes from the hair and lasts a long time.
9. An emanating light which is painful but pleasurable.
10. A light coming from some figures and lies in the brain.
11. A light that emanates from the self *(nafs)* and shines upon the entire spiritual components.
12. A light whose attainment is marked by intensity.
13. A light that gives birth to the "self" and appears to be suspended. The incorporeality of the self can be observed through this light.
14. A light which induces a special heaviness such that it exerts a pressure beyond one's ability.
15. A light that is the cause of the movements of the body and the material self.[10]

Suhrawardi tells us that he has "seen" and experienced these lights and that they are the reason sages are able to perform miracles.[11] As he states:

> He who worships God with sincerity and dies from the material darkness and frees himself from the corporeal body and abandons the consciousness of the material issues will witness that which others are incapable of seeing.[12]

Vision for Suhrawardi is a mode of being whose epistemological significance is to provide the knower with a mode of cognition that is attained through the pursuit of the spiritual life. The many components of the spiritual life, however, are discussed in a more secretive and esoteric manner in his various works but the ultimate purpose of them remains the same: the experience of illumination through seeing the separation of the self from the body and the material world.

2. ON THE NATURE OF MAN

Suhrawardi adheres to the traditional distinction between the body and the soul. Body for him represents darkness, an absence or a lack of light to which he refers as "body"(*haykal*).

> Know that the "I" (*nafs nāṭiqah*) is of a Divine substance which the powers and engagements of the body withdrew it from its abode. Whenever the soul is strengthened through spiritual virtues and the body is weakened through fasting and not sleeping, the soul is released and unites with the spiritual world.[13]

Suhrawardi, who repeatedly offers arguments for the existence of an independent self from the body, follows a Neoplatonic scheme by considering the body to be a veil that prevents man from seeing the intelligibles:

> Know that it is matter that prevents intellection since until you have abstracted something from matter and what is in matter, you can not be the subject of intellection.[14]

Corporeality by nature is the antipode of intellection or thinking, which he regards as belonging to the incorporeal world. The self, constitutes the true identity of a person, "a living substance which exists by necessity of its own essence."[15] On the contrary, the body has a tendency towards the lower world, and, relying on sense perception, denies the more transcendental pleasures and seeks the highest of the attainable pleasure of each senses.

Suhrawardi, who follows the hierarchical structure of Islamic ontology, explains the place of self and body in this context. Identifying the self with light, Suhrawardi tells us that the self has a higher ontological reality for which the body, being lower, has a natural yearning. Suhrawardi's analysis of the place, nature and types of light is an elaborate one which will be discussed at a later point, but this hierarchical structure puts in place a mechanism whereby the need, yearning and desire for man to follow the spiritual path becomes a necessary and natural process. No wonder Suhrawardi argues that all beings involuntary yearn for light rather than the inferior status of darkness.

All beings by nature seek perfection, which explains why even animals are drawn to light.[16] The ontological necessity of the spiritual ascendance is illustrated in the mystical narratives of Suhrawardi, in particular through the language of the birds. The nature of man is such that in encountering the worldly pleasures, he is overcome by forgetfulness. In the *Risālat al-ṭayr* he tells us:

> With God's grace, he who can remain steadfast in his determination at the time when lustful desires attack, is superior to angels and if one is overcome by them, is inferior to animals.[17]

Suhrawardi begins his *Risalāt al-ṭayr* describing the journey of a group of birds who in their flight to their original abode fall in the trap of the external beauty of the world and become prey to hunters. Identifying the self with one's body as a mistake that the ego makes is a central theme in many mystical traditions, in particular Islam and Hinduism. Suhrawardi tells us due to the forgetfulness of human nature, we become accustomed to the corporeal world to the point of considering it to be our natural abode.

Speaking as one of the birds, Suhrawardi tells us that he was reminded of his original condition when he saw that some of the birds had partialy freed themselves. Through the guidance of his peers he too is partially freed and begins his flight while his legs are still in chains. The birds' entrapment represents the human condition, trapped in the world of forms, chained by our lustful desires, hunted by our own ego and afraid of the hardships of the spiritual path. A few, however, are able to remember man's origin and destination.

The birds continue their journey until the eighth city which symbolizes the archetypal world. The man in charge of the city tells them that they must proceed to the top of the mountain where His Majesty resides. The Birds finally arrive at the Divine throne, only to hear Him say that only he who has chained you can free you from bondage. Suhrawardi symbolically alludes to the fact that it is man who has condemed himself to his condition, suffering and bondage, and only he can free himself. The question now is how man can overcome his condition.

Suhrawardi's answer to this question is two-fold. On the one hand, man's condition is due to his weakness and giving in to his lustful desires. On the other hand, this is not the fault of man since our condition is derived from an ontological reality in which matter is the lowest part which constitutes the body. However, man does possess the potential consciousness to understand the exalted status of our "self", which can then break the chains and free us.

In *The Red Intellect*,[18] Suhrawardi discusses the forgetful nature of man through another narrative. A bird who has also forgotten his origin meets a red-faced man who tells the bird he is the first man of creation. But he too is a prisoner of the material world which Suhrawardi identifies with darkness. The red-faced man explains how man in his original Adamic state is white and luminous, but when mixed with the darkness of the created domain he has turned red. The first son of creation describes man's condition of fallenness by alluding to the wonders he has seen around the world.

> I asked, from the wonders of the world, what have you seen? He said: "The Qāf mountain, the Ṭūbā tree, twelve workshops, David's shield, the sword of Blark, the fountain of life."[19]

The immensely rich symbolism Suhrawardi employs here provides us with a spiritual map which aids the *sālik* to find his path. The Qāf mountain is our original abode from which everything comes and to which all things return, a place that Suhrawardi refers to as "*nākujā ābād*" (the nowhere but prosperous land). The luminous pearl is the first object of creation, the intellect which is the cause of illumination but whose misuse can lead to disasterous results. The Tūbā tree symbolizes life and its fruits are the archetypes. It is upon this tree that the *Sīmurgh* (griffin), symbol of divine unity, has its nest. The twelve workshops are the levels of reality or being, each of which is the existential cause of the one below it. The lower level of this hierarchical scheme is where the Davidian shield is woven. David, the Prophet of the old testament and the Quran alike, is known to have had a legendary shield known for its impenetrability. This shield symbolizes the attachments of our world which have made a prisoner of us all.

The shield of attachments is cut loose only by the sword of Blark, the power of will (*himmah*). Suhrawardi tells us that through determination, one should seek the fountain of life which he identifies as *Sophia perennis.* Having overcome oneself and the temptations of the body, the fountain of life is then attained.[20] Suhrawardi expresses this concept in a beautiful ode:

> I am the falcon who hunters are in search of at all times.
> My prey are the black eyed Gazelle
> Who emanate from themselves *ḥikmah*
> I am far from word play, to me it is the meaning that matters.[21]

3. ON THE SPIRITUAL JOURNEY AND ASCETICISM

Much has been written on the spiritual journey of man and the Sufi encounter with the path of love and knowledge. Suhrawardi follows the traditional views of the spiritual path and man's quest for gnosis *(ma'rifah).* What is different in Suhrawardi's approach is the symbolism he employs to allude to the centrality of various components of the Sufi path in particular asceticism.

In his *A Day Among Sufis*[22] Suhrawardi describes the conversation of a Sufi master and a novice in a Sufi house (*khāniqāh*). Following a series of questions and answers between master and disciple that offers a concise and profound understanding of the medieval cosmology, the master indicates that he regards all such conversations as vain. Using astronomy as an example, the master indicates three different modes of knowing, two of which are not relevent to one's spiritual path.

Those who reflect upon the heavens, the master says, are of three types: a group of them see the cosmos through the external eyes and see a dark sheet with several white dots on it. These are the commoners and this much the animals see too. Another group see the cosmos through the eyes of the cosmos and these are astronomers . . . but there are those who do not see the secret of the heavens and stars through intellection [reasoning] *(istidlāl)*, these are seekers.[23]

The *sālik* asks the master how "the eye" opens with which one can see reality. In one of the most unique examples of Sufi symbolism and an exquisite literary style, Suhrawardi offers a prescription for asceticism. Because the significance of this passage further establishes the role and place of asceticism in the overall school of *ishraq*, we present the translation of the entire section.

> I asked the Shaykh, "I do not have that insight. What is the solution?" The Shaykh said, "You have indigestion. Fast for forty days and then drink laxative so you may vomit and your eyes may open." I asked, "What is the prescription for that laxative?" He said "The ingredients of that are attained by you." I said "What are the ingredients?" He said," Whatever is dear to you from wealth, property, possessions and the pleasures of the body and such things are ingredients of this laxative. For forty days eat pure but little food . . . . If you must use the bathroom soon, then the medicine has been effective, your sight will be illuminated, and if the need arises, for another forty days fast and use the same laxative so it may work this time too. If it does not work, apply it time and time again, it will work . . . ."
>
> I asked the Shaykh, "Once the inner eye is opened, what does the seer see?" The Shaykh said, "Once the inner eye is opened, the external eyes and lips should be shut and the five external senses should be silenced. The inner sense should begin to function so that if the patient grasps, he may do so through the inner hand and if he sees, he sees with the inner eye and if he hears, he hears with the inner ear and if he smells, he smells with the inner sense . . . [then] he sees what he sees and when he sees.[24]

In this most interesting analogy, Suhrawardi clearly shows the integral relationship between the spiritual yearning, the role of the master and his supervision to cure the disease of the soul and the place of asceticism in this. In the above narrative the seeker's inability to open his inner eye is analogized as indigestion. In the forty days of fasting, known among the Sufis as *chillah*, an attempt is made to contain the desires of the ego (*nafs*). This attempt is regarded by most Sufis to be the cure of spiritual illnesses and so is analogized as a laxative, that which flushes out impurities. To allude to the worldly attachments which prevent openning of the intellect, Suhrawardi uses the image of indigestion.

Perhaps the most important part of the passage is the allusion to the existence of a relationship between the external and internal senses. For Suhrawardi the attainment of knowledge begins by sense perception and as the process of inner purity continues, one begins to understand through the inner senses. Suhrawardi identifies the external senses with the "women's quarter" and the limitations of the sense perception as bondages of the children's world. He who frees himself and penetrates the women's quarter, Suhrawardi tells us, may arrive at the "man's quarter," a condition that is necessary for the understanding of the incorporeal world (*'ālam-i tajarrud*).[25]

In his work, *On the State of Childhood,*[26] Suhrawardi continues this theme and equates his past – when he attained knowledge only through sense perception – with childhood. Alluding to the necessity of initiation, a child meets a master who teaches him the esoteric sciences. However, the child reveals the secrets to the uninitiated, thereby casting the pearl of esoteric sciences before the swine of unpreparedness which results in the loss of what he had learned. Self-guarding remains an essential part of the spiritual path, necessary to the transition from the childhood and the acquisition of knowledge through the senses.

Again in the treatise, Suhrawardi calls for the abandonment of all attachments and he considers worldly desires to be a veil and a hindrance to the awakening of the inner senses. Acknowledging the difficulty of detaching oneself from wealth, position, etc., Suhrawardi states:

> I asked the Shaykh if there is any one who can give up all that he has Shaykh answered, "A true human is he who can." I asked "if he has nothing how does he live?" Shaykh replied "He who thinks like this does not give up anything, but he who gives up everything does not think like this."[27]

Knowing the truth therefore requires the functioning of the inner senses which does not happen unless one detaches himself from his worldly possessions. To explain the nature of the knowledge that is attained by the inner senses, Suhrawardi gives the example of the inability of a child to understand the pleasure that is derived from sexual intercourse.[28] Just as physical maturity is needed for sexual intercourse, spiritual maturity is required for the attainment of knowledge through the inner senses. On the Sufi path, spiritual maturity comes through initiation, ascetic practices and observance of the moral codes of Islam. The pleasures of experiencing the incorporeal world through the inner senses (*'ālam al-dhawq*) are so great that the inner self of the Sufi yearns to burst open. It is this inner joy which is the basis of Sufi music, dancing (*samāʿ*), poetry and art.

To explain Sufi dancing through the inner senses, Suhrawardi says:

> The soul took away that ability from the ears, it [the soul] says, you [ears] are not worthy to hear this music. The soul deprives the ear from hearing and hears itself since in the other world, hearing is not a function of the ear.[29]

It is man's inner yearning for the transcendent that makes him wish to dance like a bird who wants to fly while taking its cage with it. The Sufi, too, in his attempt for spiritual flight, carries his body with him.

In the latter part of *On the State of Childhood*,[30] Suhrawardi goes through various Sufi practices such as shaking of the sleeves, throwing away of the Sufi garment, fainting during *samāʿ* and drinking water following the *samāʿ*. In each case, Suhrawardi offers his interpretation by means of neo-Platonic scheme.

According to Suhrawardi, the spiritual journey and the states and stations of its path arise from three phenomena: virtue (*ḥusn*), love (*mihr*) and reflective sadness (*ḥuzn*). In his *On the Reality of Love*,[31] Suhrawardi attributes virtue to the knowledge of God and love to the knowledge of the self and finally to a sadness which comes from "the knowledge of what was not and then was."[32] The knowledge of God is a virtue, a good, indeed the *summum bonum*, whereas the knowledge of the self leads to the discovery that the self is divine, resulting in the love and yearning that Sufis experience. Finally, there is the sadness that is experienced by reflecting on the created order, for it signifies separation of man and his departure from his original abode.

In the treatise *On the Reality of Love*, where the language of esoteric symbolism reaches its climax, Suhrawardi describes the story of creation by first refering to the first object of creation,[33] the intellect. Having stated that the *summum bonum*, knowledge, love and sadness, or the pain of separation, are three aspects of creation, Suhrawardi goes on to describe how each one came from the other one. Using such Sufi symbolism as "city of the soul" (*shahrastān-i jān*), "young-old master" (*pīr-i jawān*), "the nowhere but prosperous land" (*nākujā ābād*), and perennial wisdom (*jāwidān khirad*), Suhrawardi goes through the sacred journey in great detail, offering the spiritual topography[34] of this journey. Various realms, domains and dangers of the journey of the soul towards the "eternal city" (*shahristān-i azal*) are discussed and once again at the end of this treatise, Suhrawardi concludes that until "the cow of ego is slaughtered, one does not set foot in that [eternal] city."[35]

The centrality of eradicating the ego and the lustful desires of the flesh through ascetic practices is a common theme in the Sufi doctrine which is echoed time and time again in various treatises of Suhrawardi. The consistancy with which Suhrawardi argues for this is a clear indication that classical Sufi beliefs and practices are an inherent part of the *ishraqi* school of thought and are not marginal in Suhrawardi's philosophy as some have suggested.

Suhrawardi brings this treatise to an end with an emphasis on the dual nature of truth, the practical and theoretical, and their relationship with the *nafs* of he who chooses not to engage in an inner effort, *jihād*, against his *nafs* . . . .

> Neither through the iron of asceticism does he plow the ground of the body so it may become worthy to plant the seeds of action, nor [does he] use the vehicle of thought to extract knowledge from the well of thought so [he] may arrive from the known to the unknown. He wanders in the desert of self-infatuation . . . not every cow(ego) is worthy to be slaughtered and not in every city is there such a cow and not everyone has the heart to sacrifice this cow and the chance to do so is not bestowed upon one at all times.[36]

Time and time again the theme of the spiritual journey and its essential components are discussed in various treatises, and interestingly, in each narrative a new set of symbolism is employed to allude to the traditional Sufi concepts. In his *The Language of Termites*,[37] as in many other writings, Suhrawardi identifies the *nafs* as the enemy that stands between the divine self and the experience of illumination. He states:

> Whatever hinders good is evil and whatever blocks the [spiritual] path is infidelity (*kufr*). To be content with whatever one's sensual self (*nafs*) presents and to adapt oneself to it is impotence on the path of mystical progression (*dar ṭarīq-i sulūk*). To look with delight upon oneself, even if one has God in mind, is renunciation. Liberation (*khalāṣ*) is to turn one's face utterly towards God.[38]

Suhrawardi's writings are not only rich with symbolism but also with his many references to the Quran and *ḥadith* as well as poems by himself and others. All of these provide us with an insight into the sacred universe in which Suhrwardi himself had his mystical flight like *Sīmurgh*, the bird whose spiritual biography is elaborated upon in *The Chant of Sīmurgh*.[39] In this treatise Suhrawardi is most explicit about the significance of ascetic practices and their relationship to having an experience of various lights, each of which represents a type of mystical experience. Suhrawardi tells us that "all knowledge comes from the chant of *Sīmurgh*"[40] and on that basis he divides the chant of *Simurgh* which he equates with *scientia sacra*, into three parts: on the virtues of this unique knowledge, on what is relevant to "brethren of purity" (*ahl-i tajarrud*) and finally on inner peace (*sakīnah*).

On the virtues of this knowledge and its superiority over other types Suhrawardi tells us that the desired end of this knowledge is truth and furthermore it is based on vision and observation. It is self-evident that "witnessing is stronger than reasoning,"[41] for one can always question the process of reasoning but not a direct and unmediated relation to the object of one's knowledge. Suhrawardi offers a philosophical analysis of how this is possible, which will be discussed in the forthcoming chapter.

As to what is manifested to the knower of the particular mode of knowing, Suhrawardi tells us that from this incorporeal world lights descend upon the soul (*rawān*) of the brethren of purity. These lights come like lightning and last only a few moments, Suhrawardi says, and they are heart warming and pleasant. Often they stop and "when ascetic practices are intensified, lights come in abundance until they reach a level where whatever people look at, reminds them of the stature of that [incorporeal] world."[42] Those who are not engaged in austere and serious ascetic practices do not see the lights even when they might come to them. Ascetic practices refine the character and make a person receptive to having a vision of these lights. Suhrawardi offers the analogy of beating on a drum at the time of war or riding on a horse, which induce emotions in a person even if one is not ready for the experience.

When the intensity and duration of the vision of these lights reach their climax it is called *sakīnah*, which is a feeling of inner peace unlike any other experience. Referring to Quranic verses where the notion of *sakīnah* is discussed, Suhrawardi considers it to be a station where the Sufi "from the heaven hears sublime and soft voices and receives spiritual correspondence and attains certainty."[43]

We conclude our discussion of Suhrawardi's view on the spiritual journey of man and its integral part, asceticism, with a brief reflection on the concluding section of Suhrawardi's *Būstān al-qulūb.*[44] Having discussed a number of traditional philosophical issues in the *Būstān al-qulūb,* Suhrawardi then changes the theme and the language to one that borders poetry and prose and concludes this treatise with a summary of the essential components of the practical aspects of the Sufi path, which are as follows:

1 Fasting: Suhrawardi first discusses the centrality of fasting and hunger, which he identifies as the foundation of the ascetic path. He states:

> Know that the foundation of asceticism lies on hunger . . . if he who wants to pursue spirituality does not experience hunger, nothing will be achieved. All [spiritual] illnesses are due to being full and overeating.[45]

2 Staying awake: The second instruction of Suhrawardi is to reduce sleeping to its minimum. Arguing that God is always awake and that the Quran tells us to become "God-like,"[46] he concludes that lack of food reduces sleeping time and causes other human passions to be reduced as well.

> So, the less they [Sufis] eat, the more they will become subjects to divine attributes and also, the less they eat, the less they sleep.[47]

Suhrawardi maintains that where and when possible, one should remain awake during the night and if that is too burdensome, one should remain awake in the latter part of the night and even if one finds this to exceed one's ability, then one should observe the sunrise, for there is much benefit in remaining awake.

3 Invocation: The invocation of divine names (*dhikr*) brings an inner change which prepares the human psyche to become receptive to illumination. He goes so far as to say that even the Prophet Muhammad before receiving revelation was engaged in ceaseless invocation. Suhrawardi tells us that invocation begins on a verbal level and then the Sufi reaches a point at which his entire being invokes the divine name. The Sufi at this stage remains silent.

> First it is the invocation by tongue, then by heart. When the soul (*jān*) begins invocation, the tongue remains silent.[48]

4 Spiritual Master: Although invocation is important, Suhrawardi is quick to remind us that a spiritual master is needed to give the mantra (*wird*). The spiritual master is necessary if one is to be guided properly on the Sufi path and the initiate should give himself to the master. As Suhrawardi states:

> When master (*pīr*) meets the seeker and knows that he has the potential the [master] encourages him to perform the invocation that he deems necessary. . . . Every day [the master] comes to the initiate [*murīd*] so he may interpret events or dreams that have occured to the initiate.[49]

Suhrawardi explicitly states that "without a master one does not get anywhere," and considers one of the most important responsibilities of the spiritual master to be the overseeing of the spiritual retreat of the *sālik* for forty days.

> Not less than forty days the initiate has to observe a retreat (*khalwah*) and if one *khalwah* does not open [the *salik*], then a second, third . . . should be done.[50]

5 Moral Virtues: Observing such moral virtues as truthfulness, humility, compassion, honesty, and not being jealous of others are also essential parts of the Sufi path. Even such details as using good perfume and reciting poetry as one goes through daily life are recommended by Suhrawardi.

4. UNITY AND THE FINAL DESTINATION

The spiritual journey and its essential components, initiation, spiritual master, asceticism, etc., are only means through which one becomes the *Sīmurgh*, the symbol of unity. Any ordinary man who like *hudhud* (hoepoe) would throw away his comfortable life and pluck his own feathers, and aim at the *Qāf* mountain, he too becomes a *Simurgh* whose chanting reawakens those who are sleeping, thereby giving them spiritual birth. The *sālik* whose endeavors have born fruit and who has endured much suffering on his quest for illumination now has become the possessor of the esoteric truth whose spiritual flight in the sacred cosmos transcends the world of form and therefore looks upon it with domination.

> This *Simurgh* flies without moving and without wings . . . He is colorless and in the east lies his nest and the west is not devoid of him . . . his food is fire . . . and the lovers of the secrets of the heart tell him their inner secrets.[51]

Sīmurgh represents the perfect man (*al-insān al-kāmil*) whose intellect has been elevated to the worlds above and has become receptive to illumination. In *The Chant of Sīmurgh* Suhrawardi devotes the latter part of the treatise to thorough discussion of the end of the spiritual path, when one is no longer on the path but is "the truth, the way and the light." Sufis are rarely as explicit as Suhrawardi in revealing the esoteric truth.

Suhrawardi divides the final state of the Sufi path into three modes, first on annihilation (*fanā*), second on knowledge and perfection, and third on love. *Fanā* for Suhrawardi is a state of being in which one transcends even spiritual ecstasy and is marked by total loss of consciousness, to which Suhrawardi refers as "the greater *fanā*" (*fanā'-i akbar*). Once one is annihilated and also annihilates the consciousness of his annihilation, the highest possible station in the Sufi path, "annihilation of annihilation" (*fanā dar fanā*), is attained. As long as man is happy with [his] knowledge, he is imperfect . . . he attains perfection when knowledge is lost in its object.[52]

Unity and annihilation, Suhrawardi argues, have many connotations ranging from the common understanding of annihilation to what the spiritual elites understand by that concept. Suhrawardi tells us that there are five interpretations of *fana* beginning with "there is no deity except God," which Suhrawardi considers to be the common understanding of unity. The second group, and a more profound understanding, is "there is no 'he' except 'He.'" This group sees God as the Beloved and experiences the immanent aspect of the transcendental. The third group are those for whom God is not a "He" but a "You," a more personal reference which also indicates presence and vision. The fourth group of Sufis are those who say "there is no 'i' except I" and those are few who are superior to others for they have transcended duality, be it "He" or "You" as pronouns indicating the nature of their relationship with God. This group knows that the only reality is that of God and that their "I-ness" is due to the only true "I" which is God. Finally, there is a fifth type of unity which only a few Sufis have attained. This manifests itself in the very being of those whose souls testify that "all things perish except His face." In this non-dual state of being, one sees God not as a "He" or a "You" or even an "I" but sees nothing for there is no one thing to see. This for Suhrawardi represents the highest possible station for a Sufi.

The second mode of the final stage of the path is that of knowledge. In a section entitled "He who is more knowledgable is more perfect," Suhrawardi discusses the second characteristic of one who has achieved unity.

This knowledge, Suhrawardi tells us, is attained through presence.[53] He who attains it gains access to the secrets of the heavens and then the earth. Suhrawardi is extremely cautious regarding the secretive nature of this knowledge and considers revealing it to be forbidden. Since it is through love that one comes to unite with God and God is omniscient, then he who unites with God in a sense also becomes omniscient. We will elaborate on this in more depth in the forthcoming chapter.

The third aspect of the final mode of being is love. Suhrawardi's exposition of love is most interesting in that loving something requires a lover and a beloved and this implies duality. Love in its ultimate sense is an absorption, a perfection, a state of not desiring for where there is desire, there is imperfection. He who knows he has his beloved desires nothing more. This state of transcending desires and living with the beloved is the perfection of the consciousness "for when the consciousness attains that [knowledge of God], the highest of its perfection is from the illumination of the light of truth."[54] "He who seeks the fountain of life will wonder much in darkness if he belongs to those who are meant to find the fountain,"[55] but Suhrawardi tells us that the Sufi has to set foot on the spiritual path like Seth. Refering to the concept in the *Būstān al-qulūb*, he states:

> He who comes to know of himself, inasmuch as his ability allows, attains knowledge of God, and the more he endures ascetic practices the more he becomes perfect and his knowledge increases.[56]

In one of his lengthiest treatises, *Yazdān shinākht*,[57] Suhrawardi elaborates on eschatology with regard to two types of death, namely physical and "spiritual death." His treatment of physical death is brief but his exposition of spiritual death and rebirth, which is the natural consequence of practical wisdom, is in-depth.

Practical wisdom, Suhrawardi argues, brings detachment of the "self" from the bodily desires so that the presence or absence of the body does not make any difference. This state of being which is to be achieved in this world is similar to the natural death in that the body is left behind except that in spiritual death one can have a vision of the incorporeal world.

> The self (*nafs*), which is not simple and is complete and pure, when departed from the body unites with the world of intellect and spiritual substances which it resembles in perfection.[58]

Suhrawardi maintains that language is incapable of expressing what is observed, for the vision of these spiritual substances is ineffable and analogy is not helpful either since there is nothing to analogize it to. The power of the purified self at its peak is such that it can learn a great deal in a short time. A person of this stature does not learn through sense perception and other intermediaries, but learns directly from the sources of knowledge. The power of initiation of a *sālik*, now a learned master who learns without a teacher or text, does not think or conceptualize, but it is as if truth is revealed to him. Such people are rare, Suhrawardi says, but he who attains this stature becomes vice-gerent of God (*khalīfat allāh*). Referring to pure and practical wisdom, Suhrawardi says that although some are stronger in pure and some in practical wisdom, if they achieve perfection they become one in their being perfect. Having alluded to the distinction between pure and practical wisdom on numerous occasions, he goes on to elaborate on the necessity of having a prophet (*nabī*). Suhrawardi considers men of vision to be prophets of a sort:

> There is a need for a person who is an avatar (*nabī*) and a spiritual guardian (*walī*) . . . the need for such a person is more than the [need for] having eye lashes or eyebrows . . .[59]

Suhrawardi's description of the *valī* is similar to Plato's philosopher and the guardians which in Shi'ite Islam are refered to as the "spiritual jurist guardian" (*walī-yi faqīh*). He is the culmination for which man was created and through Gabriel he comes to know of divine secrets by virtue of his unmediated and direct knowledge. Suhrawardi then warns that although "from the time of Greeks until now, no one from the great and righteous sages has revealed these secrets,"[60] but he has briefly alluded to them in the *Yazdān shinākht* so it may encourage the restless soul. The safeguarding of the esoteric doctrines is so central that Suhrawardi sees the solution in transmitting them in the form of oral tradition. Suhrawardi tells us that Aristotle said, "Divine wisdom should never be revealed or written except that it be transmitted orally from person to person."[61]

Notes

1 Suhrawardi, Opera 2, 258–259.
2 Ibid., 10.
3 Ibid.
4 Ibid., 12.
5 Suhrawardi, *Opera* 1, 70–71.
6 Suhrawardi's choice of such Sufi masters as Bāyazīd and Ḥallāj as true philosophers is also a further argument against those whose reading of Suhrawardi's philosophy is a Peripatetic one.
7 Suhrawardi, *Opera* 2, 252.
8 Ibid.
9 Ibid., 253.
10 Suhrawardi regards these as "the principles of the eighth heaven" within which are mysterious beings. See ibid., 254.
11 Suhrawardi, *Opera* 2, 254.
12 Ibid., 255.
13 Suhrawardi, *Opera* 3, 107.
14 Ibid., 139.
15 Ibid., 140.
16 Ibid., 182.
17 Ibid., 199.
18 Ibid., 226.
19 Ibid., 229.
20 Ibid., 237–238.
21 Ibid., 238.
22 Ibid., 242.
23 Ibid., 247.
24 Ibid., 248.
25 Ibid., 263.
26 Ibid., 252.
27 Ibid., 259.
28 Ibid., 263.
29 Ibid., 264.
30 Ibid., 263–266.
31 Ibid., 268.
32 Ibid.
33 Suhrawardi is referring to the Ḥadith: "In the beginning God created a precious pearl and called it the intellect." For more information on this see Paul Ballanfat, *L' itineraire des esprits*, note 233 and note 528.
34 This is a term first used by Henry Corbin. For more information see: Henry Corbin, *La Topographie spirituelle de l'Islam iranien*, ed. Darius Shayegan (Paris: Editions de la Difference, 1990).
35 Suhrawardi, *Opera* 3, 290.
36 Ibid., 291.
37 Ibid., 294.
38 Ibid., 310.
39 Ibid., 314.
40 Ibid., 315.

41 Ibid., 317.
42 Ibid., 320.
43 Ibid., 323.
44 Ibid., 396–401.
45 Ibid., 396.
46 Suhrawardi is referring to the famous Quranic verse "takhallaqū bi-akhlāq allah." For more information see the new edition of the Lāhījī's *Sharḥ-i gulshan-i rāz,* ed. by M.R. Barzegar Khāliqī and 'A. Garbāsī. Also see *Kashf al-asrār,* Vol.2, p.186.
47 Suhrawardi, *Opera* 3, 397.
48 Ibid., 399.
49 Ibid.
50 Ibid., 400.
51 Ibid., 315.
52 Ibid., 324.
53 For more information on this see: Mehdī Ḥā'irī, *The Principles of Epistemology in Islamic Philosophy: Knowledge by Presence* (New York: SUNY Press, 1992).
54 Suhrawardi, *Opera* 3, 330.
55 Ibid., 330.
56 Ibid., 377.
57 Ibid., 404.
58 Ibid., 439.
59 Ibid., 454.
60 Ibid., 457
61 Ibid.

4

PHILOSOPHICAL SUFISM

Suhrawardi's philosophical Sufism is the application of the Neoplatonic scheme to traditional Sufi concepts in an attempt to provide rationally justifiable answers to such questions as the inherent yearning of man towards transcendence, the role of asceticism in intensifying this yearning and the nature of mystical experience. Suhrawardi, who has consistently argued that *ḥikmat* has two dimensions, practical and theoretical, also tells us that what the intellect can understand, the heart can see. "Know that the human self has two powers: one is that which finds out, the other is the one that which does things."[1]

In the previous section, the practical aspect of Sufism has been discussed. We will now turn to a discussion of the more philosophically oriented aspects of his mystical thought.

1. ON LIGHT AND ITS VARIETIES

The centrality of light as an axiomatic phenomenon in Suhrawardi's philosophy has been alluded to before. In the *Ḥikmat al-ishrāq*[2] Suhrawardi devotes a major part of the book to an exposition of the nature, place and varieties of light that exist as a hierarchy at the top of which exists the light of lights, from which all lights emanate. At the bottom, there is darkness or absence of light (*'adam*) represented by corporeality or inanimate objects (*barzakh*).

Suhrawardi's classification is based upon intensity of light or darkness which is different from the traditional Ibn Sīnian concept of hierarchies of realities, each of which are different in the degree to which they possess "being." The ordinary light that the eye can see is only one manifestation of the light of lights with a specific intensity. All things in existence are therefore various degrees and intensities of light and darkness. The most important of these created beings is the rational self (*nafs nāṭiqah*), which Suhrawardi refers to as *nūr Isfahbadī*, arguing that due to its purity it is independent of matter. Since all the beings in the hierarchy influence that which is below them and are influenced by what is above them, the influence of a soft light is soft and a hard one even harder. Suhrawardi tells us that there are several types of lights with different attributes; they are as follows:

Incorporeal light (*nūr mujarrad*) =	The light that subsists by itself.
Accidental light (*nūr 'araḍī*) =	The light that depends on something other than itself.
Corporeal darkness (*ghasaq*) =	It is that whose true nature is darkness.
Accidental darkness (*hay'at-i ẓulamānī*) =	The type of darkness that depends on something other than itself and requires space and has the accident of darkness.
Purgatory (*barzakh*) =	An object or an object-like entity that hides and reveals the lights.

There is intrinsic yearning (*maḥabbah*) on the part of the lower members of this hierarchy towards the higher ones that is marked by love and adoration whereas the relationship between the higher members to the lower ones is one of dominance (*qahr*). The lower want to go higher and all of them ultimately aim at uniting with the light of lights.

If all beings are made up of light then what accounts for their difference? Certainly their essence being light is not the differentia but what is in common among them all (*mā bih'il–ishtirāk*). In other words, light is that which at the same time unites and differentiates (*mā bih'il-imtiyāz*) among all existing beings through its intensity and weakness. As Suhrawardi states:

> All lights inherently and from the point of their "light-ness" have no difference; their only difference lies in their perfection or shortcoming or matters outside their essence.[3]

Suhrawardi, who considers the attributes of an object to be shortcomings and absences of light, then goes on to equate God with light, which explains why his mystical experiences have all come to him in the form of "divine flashes" (*bāriqa-yi ilāhī*). Light here is equated with God because it is the phenomenon by which and through which things are known. Suhrawardi offers the following as a justification of his argument:

> If you seek the reason for a criterion for the incorporeal light, it is this: light is a thing which in its nature is obvious and reveals all other things. It is inherently more obvious than anything else whose appearance is added (*iḍāfah*) to its truth.[4]

The light of lights which exists by necessity (*wājib al-wujūd*) is the source of all existence to which Suhrawardi refers to with a variety of names, i.e. all-encompassing (*al-muhiṭ*), the supreme (*al-a'ẓam*), the sacred light (*al-muqaddas*) and the all-victorious (*al-qahhār*).[5]

Following the Ibn Sīnian classification of beings into necessary, contingent, and impossible, Suhrawardi goes on to say that lights are either self-subsistent, in which case they are "substantial light" (*nūr jawharī*), or incorporeal light (*nūr mujarrad*), both of which Suhrawardi says are rich (*ghanī*). There is the contingent light that is referred to as accidental light (*nūr 'araḍī*), which is revealed to be indigent (*faqīr*) or poor. Finally, there is darkness which is nothing other than the absence of light[6] which he refers to as darkness (*ẓulamāt*), obscurity (*ghāsiq*),[7] form (*hay'ah*)[8] or *barzakh* which he defines as body.

Suhrawardi's exegesis of the corporeal world as an inherently indigent phenomenon and his analysis of corporeality in terms of light is fundamentally related to the spiritual journey of man. In a sense, Suhrawardi lays the philosophical foundation for the explanation of the journey of the soul from the darkness of the corporeal world to the luminous world of the incorporeal light and the light of lights. A thorough reading of the dense philosophical arguments of the second part of the *Ḥikmat al-ishrāq* reveals a firm mystical doctrine. In a section entitled "Principles On How Unity Emanates Multiplicity," Suhrawardi states:

> Since between the lower light and higher light there is no veil, necessarily the lower light sees the higher light and the higher illuminates the lower [one]. Therefore, from the light of lights a beam of light shines upon the lower.[9]

Each of these incorporeal lights receives a direct emanation from the light of lights as well as the light that is directly above it. So, every light receives two levels of light simultaneously, but this process does not continue *ad infinitum.* In the process of emanation light solidifies until it reaches corporeality which Suhrawardi divides into many different parts.[10] Suhrawardi, in the *Ḥikmat al-ishrāq,* using a peculiar and dense philosophical language, offers a detailed account of the various types of light, their interaction with one another and their final destination, which is full integration, or to use a Sufi term, annihilation into the light of lights. In a section entitled "On the Freeing of the Pure Lights and their Transfer to the Luminous World,"[11] Suhrawardi tells us:

> Whenever the regent light (*nūr mudabbir*) is not overcome by its engagement in corporeality, its yearning for the heavenly world of lights is more than his yearning for obscurity (*ghāsiq*) and as its luminous status is increased, so is its love for the dominary lights . . . and thus it is freed from the human body and returns to the world of pure-light and resides amongst the heavenly lights and due to the purity of the light of lights, it becomes pure too.[12]

2. ANGELOLOGY

Suhrawardi's ontological views based on light and its varieties and the emanationistic scheme are interwoven into his angelology with each angelic order performing an ontological task, which gradually helps the *sālik* to find his original abode by providing him with spiritual topography of the sacred world and its many paths and pitfalls.

Suhrawardi's angelology represents an intricate web of lights, elements and symbols, a great number of which are drawn from the Zoroastrian tradition. His view of the function and the role of angels is radically different from Ibn Sīnās which attributed rotations and many other functions to the heavenly bodies and astronomical issues. For Suhrawardi, angels are means through which his metaphysical doctrine as well as esoteric views can be expressed and therefore the language with which he puts forward his angelology, sometime philosophical and sometime symbolic, is one that borrows heavily from other traditions.

Suhrawardi says that from the light of lights arise two angelic orders, the latitudinal and longitudinal. The latitudinal order for him is the same as Plato's archetypes to which Suhrawardi refers as "masters of the species" (*arbāb al-anwāʿ*) and whose definition of them is somewhat similar to Plato's. "The form of material species has to be in the illuminative world and be necessary, permanent and unchangeable."[13]

The various angelic orders which themselves give rise to other angelic orders are as follows:

1. The longitudinal (*ṭūlī*) order represents the archangels and is the first emanation which Suhrawardi identifies with Bahman from the Zoroastrian tradition. This order, which is referred to as the nearest light (*nūr al-aqrab*), is a direct emanation of the supreme archetype (*hurmuzd*).
2. The latitudinal (*'araḍī*) order which arises from the masculine aspect of the supreme hierarchy represents Plato's archetypes. Suhrawardi uses Zoroastrian names for these forms such as *Urdibihisht* for fire, *Khurdād* for water, *Murdād* for plants *Shahrīwar* for minerals and *Aspandārmaz* for love. The elements of this order do not bring one another into existence as the longitudinal order does. Since all things in the world are manifestations of these latitudinal archetypes, Suhrawardi refers to them as "theurgy" (*ṭilismāt*) or icons (*ṣanam*). He calls these archetypes the "masters of species" since each one has its celestial domain over which it rules and exercises its particular influence in the created order.
3. From the feminine aspect of the longitudinal order, which is characterized by love and receptivity, comes the solidification of the angelic order which manifests itself as fixed stars and heavenly bodies. These observable bodies, which in a sense are absences of light, are ontologically distant from the light of lights.
4. Finally, Suhrawardi tells us of another angelic order which is effused from the latitudinal order. This intermediary angelic order, which is called lordly light (*al-anwār al-isfahbadīyyah*) or regent light (*al-anwār al-mudabbirah*), consists of the angels of mercy and the guardians of the earth and all its inhabitants.

The lordly light which exists within the soul of every man is represented by Gabriel, the archetype of humanity (*rabb al-naw' al-insān*), which Suharwardi identifies as the "holy spirit" (*ruḥ al-qudus*), equating it with the spirit of the Prophet Muhammad. In addition to this angelic entity, Suhrawardi tells us that every man has his own guardian angel who resides in the angelic world and who divides in half before entering the human body. Half of it remains in the angelic world and the other half enters the prison of body from which it always seeks its release in order to become united with the other half.

Suhrawardi's angelic scheme is significant not only because it unites his ontology and metaphysics but also because it demonstrates that Islam, the Zoroastrian religion and for that matter all the divinely revealed religions, allude to the same truth when they are viewed from an esoteric point of view. Suhrawardi enters into a hermeneutic discussion of the sacred meaning of the Zoroastrian angels to explain how they fit within the metaphysical doctrine of Islam. The Zoroastrian fire, Suhrawardi argues, is the divine light and *farwahar* as archetype of the human souls which descends upon the human body after it is conceived.[14]

Another application of Suhrawardi's angelology lies in his epistemological doctrine and the problem of knowledge. Having argued that angels are independent realities in the world, he then follows an Ibn Sīnian scheme to say that angels are also representations of man's inner forces that have been externalized. The externalization serves as a spiritual map of the inner guides. He who learns how to follow them properly will be led to the heart of the *ishraqi* doctrine, that is, "To know everything, one has to first know himself."[15] Knowledge of the self and self-knowledge therefore are necessary conditions for anyone in his spiritual quest who seeks certainty. In the words of Henry Corbin, self-knowledge is necessary "for all those who are called to a direct and unmediated relationship with the divine world."[16]

The power of guidance helps us to overcome our fundamental alienation from ourselves which in the *ishraqi* school is denoted as ignorance of oneself. In its epistemological context, Suhrawardi's angelology provides us with means through which God guides us to self-knowledge and, eventually, knowledge of the Divine itself.

> Zoroastrian angels, however, are not simply 'aspects' of the supreme divinity, but Seven Powers (*Amshāspands*), the Seven *Avestan Amerta Spenta,* the holy immortals. Their holiness is an active and activating energy that communicates and grants being to all things.[17]

Suhrawardi introduces the Zoroastrian angels amidst the exposition of his metaphysical arguments in order to show the fundamental harmony between the *Weltanschauung* of the Islamic and Zoroastrian religious universes. The following shows Suhrawardi's use of the

Zoroastrian angelology of "Persian theosophers" (*ḥukamā-yi Fārs*) and their compatability with Islamic metaphysical principles.

Mīnū=	Incorporeal world
Gītī=	Corporeal world
Hūrqalyā=	Archetypal world
Surūsh=	Gabriel
Farvadīn=	The lower world
Gawhar=	Pure essence
Bahrām=	Victory, which often appears in the form of a mad ox, white horse or sometimes a hen.
Hūrakhsh=	Sun
Shahriyār=	Archetype of species
Isfahbad=	Light in the body
Kiyān kharrah=	The incorporeal light which descends upon those who have attained the divine wisdom. The priest-kings of the ancient Persia were considered by Suhrawardi to have attained Kiyān kharreh, the wisdom that is necessary for being a wise king.

Suhrawardi describes the above as follows:

> Once the soul becomes illuminated and strong through the rays of divine light, it reaches the throne of kiyānī and becomes fully grounded in power and prosperity.[18]

As we have discussed, Suhrawardi's angelology unites his ontology, metaphysics and cosmology. This is nowhere more evident than in his mystical narratives. Once again we see that Suhrawardi's analysis is elaborated upon in the language of mysticism and practical reasoning. Because philosophical discourse alone does not fulfill the spiritual thirst of the seeker, Suhrawardi translates his philosophical and *ishraqi* analysis of angelology into the language of practical wisdom, as we see in such treatises as *The Chant of Gabriel's Wing* and *The Red Intellect.*

In *The Chant of Gabriel's Wing,* we see a discussion of Suhrawardi's cosmology and ontology within the context of a seeker's quest for truth. When the *sālik* leaves the pleasures of the body and enters the desert, he sees ten old men (*pīrs*) whose beauty and glory are mesmerizing. Having been asked where they come from, the old man who represents an angelic order says, "We are a group of incorporeals and come from the 'nowhere but prosperous land' (*nākujā ābād*)."[19]

The ten old men, whose hairs are white and have substance but do not occupy space are the ten levels of light which correspond to the Ibn Sīnian levels of intellect. The seeker then asks, "What is your occupation?" to which the old man responds, "We are tailors." The angelic function is to "sew" the world below them, that is, the world of generation and corruption, the corporeal domain. They are the intermediaries between the pure and the corruptable world of ours. In highly symbolic language Suhrawardi writes:

> I asked, "Why are the old men that are above you observing silence?" He replied, "Because they do not mingle with your types. I know their language and they do not speak to you.[20]

The old man is the archangel Gabriel who explains to the *sālik* that due to his limited spiritual accomplishment he can not understand the language of the beings residing in the spiritual world.

Suhrawardi uses analogies from nature to explain how creation takes place and what the function of each of the levels is. Whereas the creation of the other nine old domains is not easily observable due to their softness, Gabriel's creation is more solid and thus more visible.

The relationship between the ten angelic orders is one of the spiritual unity and oneness. Gabriel tells the *sālik* that the old man whose mantle is on the top is the spiritual master of the second one and so on until the ninth master who trained him and gave him his Sufi cloak. Here, the emanationistic ontology of Suhrawardi is explained in terms of a chain of initiation emanating from Ibn Sīnā's first intellect *(al-'aql al-awwal)* or Suhrawardi's Bahman (*al-nūr al-'aqrab*), the closest light to the light of lights.

Suhrawardi's visionary narrative continues with the *sālik* questioning the relationship between the old man and the world. "Do you have children, property and the like?" the *sālik* asks.[21] Gabriel responds by saying that he does not have mates but each of them has a child who works at a mill while they are staring at him with one eye and at the mill with the other eye. Suhrawardi uses the imagery of children to allude to each angelic order giving birth to or emanating a lower level of reality down to the tenth level which is pregnant with the created order. Gabriel then tells the *sālik*, "When the time is proper, they come to me and do not leave again and new children go there."[22] Those who have purified themselves and have become what Suhrawardi calls "brothers of purity" can return to the angelic order where they belong. As to the problem of the unchangeable and immutable nature of the angels and the very act of emanating, which implies the occurrence of motion in angels, the *sālik* asks how they came to have children. The *sālik* poses a rather old philosophical issue, namely the relationship between change and sameness in the created domain. The old master offers an explanation whereby he impregnates "a black slave," who symbolizes the corporeal world, without a change occurring in him. Having questioned the tenth angelic order's relation with the corporeal world, the *sālik* then questions its relation with God and whether the old master praises God. The old master replies:

> Absorption in divine presence does not allow for praising [Him], and if there be praise, it is not by virtue of tongue; no motion or movement is associated with it.[23]

The old man Gabriel, the archangel of revelation and the intermediary between the corporeal and incorporeal world, then teaches the *sālik* the esoteric secrets necessary to understand the true meaning of the Quran which is none other than the secret of creation.

In a esoteric phrase, the old master tells the *sālik* that "everything in the four corners of the world is due to the wing of Gabriel."[24] Referring once again to the emanationistic scheme of lights, the old master indicates that God's words are so luminous and profound that from them comes a lower word and so on until the "last words which are the words of Gabriel and the spirits of man (*arwāḥ*) are from this last word."[25] The relationship between words and spirits as realities in the archetypal world will be elaborated on in the forthcoming section, but it suffices to say that Suhrawardi uses various Quranic references as well as other sacred scriptures to allude to the two-fold function of angels as entities between the world of light and the world of darkness. It is noteworthy that Suhrawardi considers the luminous nature of angels to be an added relation (*iḍāfah*) not inherent to angels. The angelic order are contingent beings, from the closest to the light of light, Bahman, to the last one, Gabriel.

> Gabriel has two wings: the right wing is pure light and the entirety of that incorporeal wing is a relation (*iḍāfah*) of his existence to God. And there is a left [wing] with a mark of

> darkness on it . . . that is a sign of its existence which has one-side to non-existence. If you view its existence from a relational point with God, it exists [because of] His existence. If you view its essence, it is worthy of non-existence.[26]

3. THE ARCHETYPAL WORLD: *MUNDUS IMAGINALIS*

In his numerous treatises and in particular *The Chant of Gabriel's Wing,* Suhrawardi alludes to the archetypal realities which illuminated human faculty can witness. The nature of the archetypal world is such that human consciousness can have a vision of these abstract and incorporeal beings. Imaginal beings are realities that transcend place and time but are as real, if not more real, than the corporeal world.

Suhrawardi, speaking as a *sālik,* asks Gabriel to discuss his original abode. Their conversation goes as follows:

> I asked from which direction have you, the exalted ones, come. The old man who was at the corner replied that they are a group of incorporeals who have come from "the nowhere but prosperous land" (*nākujā ābād*). I did not understand that, so I asked to which region that city belongs? He said "It belongs to the domain where the index finger can not point to." So I came to know that the old master knows [the secrets].[27]

Describing the archetypal worlds, Suhrawardi uses several terms that are uniquely his own such as "nowhere but prosperous land" (*nākujā ābād*), "ruinous but prosperous land" (*kharāb ābād*) and "the city of the soul" (*shahristān-i jān*), all of which he identifies as the eighth domain (*iqlim-i hashtum*). Henry Corbin refers to this domain as *mundus imaginalis* and considers it to be a level of reality that has no external existence and yet is real, in fact, more real than the external world, the seemingly real. This real world therefore is the "imaginal" as opposed to "imaginary" which implies both non-real and non-existence.

First, let us see what the nature of this imaginal domain is which Suhrawardi considers to be the ontological origin of the corporeal world. Suhrawardi considers the existential cause of the archetypal world to be the "accidental intellects" which have come to be in a variety of forms. Although these intellectual entities are subject, quality, quantity and many other accidental attributes, they are independent of matter. It is imperative to know that for Suhrawardi these "suspending archetypes" (*muthul mu'allaqah*) are different than Plato's forms or archetypes which he regards to be in the fixed world of archetypes. The suspending archetypes which are between the corporeal world (*'ālam-i barzakh*) and the angelic world (*'ālam-i qahriah*) are not only numerous but also independent of place and time which explains why the external senses are unable to see them except in rare and small glimpses.[29]

The imaginal world is the spiritual topography of a domain that can only be seen by those who have turned away from the *sensus communis* and rely on spiritual hermeneutics (*ta'wīl*), a profound issue which he discusses both in the *al-Talwīḥāt*[30] and *Alwāḥ-i 'imādī*.[31] Seeing the archetypes requires transcending all obstacles in order to go beyond what Suhrawardi symbolically refers to as the *Qāf* mountain. Then one reaches the mysterious cities of the world of suspending archetypes where such spiritual entities reside.

In the *Ḥikmat al-ishrāq*,[32] Suhrawardi mentions several cities of the imaginal world, all of which belong to the eighth domain. They are *Jābilqā*, *Jābirsā* and *Hūrqalyā*, the cities which are "nowhere". According to Suhrawardi, in the last one, wonders exist. As he states: "And there are eight domains therein, *Jābilqā*, *Jābirsā* and *Hūrqalyā*, the substance of wonder."[33]

For Suhrawardi, *Hūrqalyā* represents the archetypes of the heavenly bodies whose harmonious functioning produces a sublime music that only those who are discoverers and seekers of the truth can hear.[34] In fact, the beauty of the wonders of *Hūrqalyā* which those who have purified themselves can only experience through the inner senses, represents the sacred world of the Sufis whose journey has reached its climax. Suhrawardi analogizes the status of this perfect man with God since both the Sufi master and God can create archetypes, a state of being Suhrawardi calls "Be" (*kun*), referring to the Quranic verse in which God creates the world by saying, "Be", and it was.

> And the brothers in purity have a special status in that they are able to create archetypes that are self dependent, and that state is named "Be."[35]

Suhrawardi concludes by saying that the outward beauties, shapes and forms of this world have their ontological roots in the *mundus imaginalis*, a world which is real but accessible only to a few. Nowhereland, therefore, is the place which transcends the world of forms, time and space. It is a land only reached by the seeker of truth who has suffered on the path and whose psyche has been opened to the unseen worlds.[36]

4. VISION

Suhrawardi formulates a theory of vision based on his illuminationist ideas. According to him, knowledge by presence, the epistemological basis of the *ishraqi* school, provides a framework which explains vision, in both its physical and its intellectual sense. Suhrawardi argues that "vision" (*mushāhadah*) can only take place in accordance with the principles of illumination. He first refutes the existing theories of how vision occurs and then offers his own view.[37] According to the first theory, a ray of light comes from the object of perception and in meeting the eye leaves an impression which we call the act of seeing. The second theory takes the opposite angle by saying that a ray of light emanates from the eye and meets the object and that constitutes the very act of seeing. Suhrawardi rejects both views and offers his own theory which is as follows:

> Once you see that sight is not the correspondence of the observed in the eyes and is not the exiting of a ray from the eye, then except for the encounter of the lit object with the healthy eye, it is not anything else . . . . And the result of this encounter in regard to sight is due to the absence of the veil between that which sees and that which is seen.[38]

Suhrawardi's argument can be better formulated as follows: The existence (*wujūd*) of an existent object has a presence that the "rational self" (*al-nafs al-nāṭiqah*) comes to realize once it is within the domain of its presence. Threfore, in seeing something, it is not the case that the subject sees the object but that it is the presence of the self that comprehends the presence of the object once it is in its domain. In order for this interaction to take place, there has to be the absence of a veil (*ḥijāb*) between the knower and the known. Since the subject, being the self (which for Suhrawardi is light), comes into contact with the object that is also illuminated, then the self "witnesses" (*shāhid*) the object. To clarify the issue, one can give the example of a room with several people in it; however, because the room is dark they cannot see each other. It is only after the light is turned on that they are able to see one another.

Since self for Suhrawardi is light and observation as such requires the presence of light, then in a statement such as "I know P," "I" as the knower and "P" as the object of knowledge both depend on light as the necessary condition for the "I" to know "P."

5. VISION AND INTELLECTION

In conjunction with the explanation concerning the very act of seeing, something has to be said about vision in its intellectual context. For Suhrawardi, intellection is a form of vision (*mushāhidah*) through which one sees the archetypes in the imaginal world. In fact, to think in the authentic sense is to think of the archetypes which do not lend themselves to speculation but whose reality can only be "seen" through intellection. This is an extremely profound point which Suhrawardi raises since the very act of intellection necessitates the existence of an intellectual world whose residences are the archetypes. It is noteworthy that Suhrawardi distinguishes between these archetypes and Plato's archetypes and states:

> These suspending forms are not like Plato's in that Plato's forms are fixed luminaries in the luminous intellectual world . . . but these archetypes are suspending and do not have a place so it is allowed for them to become the manifestations of this world.[39]

As we discussed, objects of the intellectual world had themselves been "seen" with the eyes of the universal intellect (*'aql-i kulli*), a vision that is only possible for the "brethren of purity." This is equivalent to "presence," a form of being before an object or seeing of an object. This presence or mode of knowledge which belongs to the intellectual elite is only attained after one has come to know one's self. This point will be further elaborated upon.

6. KNOWLEDGE AND PRESENCE: HE WHO KNOWS MORE "IS" MORE?

Since Suhrawardi takes the concepts of the self, light, and consciousness to be equivalent, it follows that when the self is more illuminated, the domain of its presence increases. As such, when the ontological distance of a being to the light of lights decreases, the power of one's presence increases and so does the domain of one's knowledge. He who knows more is therefore ontologically speaking closer to God and therefore "is-more." This "is-ness" or presence is not only a status which is to be gained through the pursuance of intellectual wisdom but also requires practicing the Sufi path.

The following formula demonstrates Suhrawardi's view of the relationship between knowledge and presence:

Existence (*wujūd*)= Presence (*ḥuḍūr*)= "revealedness" (*ẓuhūr*)
To argue for position, Suhrawardi first demonstrates that "I" is nothing but pure light in its onotological sense. He then uses this conclusion in order to formulate his theory of knowledge by presence. In a section entitled "He Who Perceives His Essence as Being Incorporeal Light", Suhrawardi states:

> Everyone who has an essence is not ignorant of it, nor is he in the dark as to the appearance of his essence to him. And it is not a dark corporeality (*ghāsiq*) in others since luminous corporeality also is not a light in its essence, let alone darkness. So, he is pure incorporeal light which has no spatial location.[40]

As I have discussed previously, by "light" Suhrawardi means that phenomenon of which nothing more apparent can be conceived. Defining the self in terms of light and light in terms of apparentness allows Suhrawardi to draw the following conclusion: The self is a simple, single and indivisible entity, since if this were not the case, it would have to be defined in terms of its components. That implies the components would have to be more axiomatic than the self, which is contrary to our definition of the self.

Suhrawardi's argument can be demonstrated as follows:

1. Knowledge of the self is the same as the very reality of the self.
2. The reality of the self is light.

∴3. Knowledge of the self is light.

4. Light can be understood only by being in its presence.
5. Knowledge of the self can only be understood by its very presence.

Although Suhrawardi does not present his arguments systematically and often does not make clear the relationship that exists between light, self, presence and knowledge, his arguments can be constructed in a number of ways. For example, on the basis of the following statement we can offer a different version of the argument.

> He who can understand his own nature will be incorporeal light.[41]

Based on our foregoing discussion, it follows that:

1 God is light.
2 "I-ness" is light.
3 "I-ness" is God.
4 He who knows himself, knows God.

God or the light of lights, omnipresent and omniscient, makes seeing possible by virtue of being "the light of heavens and earth," as the Quran says. In the external and physical sense, the light of lights provides the necessary condition for observation whereas in the case of inner senses omniscience and omnipresence stand in direct relationship with one another.

The knowledge crucial to the attainment of the particular mode of being which Suhrawardi refers to as presence is specifically self-knowledge. Knowledge of the self, as the divine substance bestowed upon us, is fundamentally knowledge of the Divine. God therefore becomes the focal point where the concepts of self, light, presence and knowledge come together into a unified whole. It is in lieu of such a view that Suhrawardi offers his epistemology both in its practical domain and its purely philosophical and intellectual sense. Knowledge of the self can be attained through the Sufi path which we have described in the previous chapter. Knowledge of the self and how it is that the self knows itself is the subject of Suhrawardi's philosophical epistemology to which we now turn.

A. EPISTEMOLOGY

Suhrawardi's theory of knowledge consists of two segments. First, there is the deconstructionist segment in which Suhrawardi criticizes various theories of knowledge, in particular knowledge by definition, sense perception and *a priori* concepts. He first offers a series of arguments to establish the fact that none of the existing theories of knowledge lead to certainty. Arguing that although each theory of knowledge leads to one aspect of reality, they all fail to explain how knowledge is actually possible. Peripatetics therefore offer at best a limited theory of knowledge.

Second, having offered his critique of the Peripatetics, Suhrawardi goes on to offer his own epistemological view known as "knowledge by presence" which explains how knowledge of the self is attained.

We will first discuss Suhrawardi's critique of the Peripatetics and then analyze his theory of knowledge by presence.

1. KNOWLEDGE BY DEFINITION

Traditionally, "definition" has been a means through which knowledge of the external world can be attained. This method, which was primarily developed by Plato and often referred to as the "Socratic Method",[42] is based on a dialogue in which a "thing" is defined and redefined until we can know what that "thing" truly is. Aristotle elaborates on this theory of knowledge by definition when he argues that definition should reveal the true identity of a thing by disclosing its essential nature. As he states "Definition is held to concern essential nature and is in every case universal."[43]

Suhrawardi's theory of knowledge by definition is a rapprochement between Plato's and Aristotle's position. It is an attempt to reconcile the Peripatetic philosophy of Aristotle and the intellectual intuition of Plato into a single and unified theory of knowledge. Suhrawardi's notion of knowledge by definition, despite his disagreement with the Peripatetics, remains rather similar to theirs. However, he attempts to offer the view that an adequate definition is one that not only tends to capture the essence of a thing and its relation to its attributes, but also brings about a harmony between Aristotle's views and those of Plato.

In his book *The Philosophy of Illumination*, Suhrawardi offers his criticism of the Peripatetics in a chapter entitled "Destruction of the Peripatetics' Rules of Definition"[44] by arguing that Peripatetics, in distinguishing between "general essence" *(jins)* and "specific difference" *(faṣl)*, have made a grave mistake.

It is important to realize that despite Suhrawardi's criticism of the Peripatetics on the subject of definition, he does not discard definition as an entirely invalid means of attaining knowledge. What he is trying to do is allude to the limits and inadequacy of definition in arriving at certainty. As we will see in his other works, he elaborates on these problems and argues the conditions under which definition could act as a means of attaining knowledge. Let us now turn to examine Suhrawardi's view of definition in order to formulate his theory of definition.

Suhrawardi in *The Philosophy of Illumination*[45] as well as the *Conversations*[46] and *The Intimations*[47] devotes a chapter to the analysis of the theory of definition. In the second chapter of *The Intimations* he argues that it is not sufficient for a definition of an existent being to disclose only the essential nature of that thing, since other attributes of a thing should also be considered as part of the identity of a thing even though they may be of an accidental nature. Therefore, a definition should include not only the essence but other elements as well.

> A formula (*qawl*) is indicative of the essence of a thing and combines (*yajma'*) all of its constituent elements. Regarding the principle realities, it [the formula] is a synthesis (*tarkib*) of their genera and differentia.[48]

This is a radical departure from the Aristotelian approach since its underlying assumption is that the identity of a thing not only consists of its essence but includes its other attributes which are also important. The other significance of this approach is that if the differentia or "the particular essence" (*faṣl*), is not known, then the definition of that thing remains incomplete. On the basis of Suhrawardi's argument we can arrive at the following two conclusions:

1 Since we can never know all the "constituent elements" of a thing, it can never be defined properly and adequately and therefore it cannot be known by definition.
2 If a definition should include not only genus but also all the differentia and other constituents of a thing, that necessitates an *a priori* knowledge of the differentia since the differentia are an exclusive property of an existent being.

Suhrawardi's treatment of the topic of definition in *The Intimations*, which is done in three sections, "Essential Nature," "Description," and the "Fallacies in the Construction and Use of Definition,"[49] is followed by an even more extensive treatment of the topic in the *al-Muṭārahat*. What follows is a brief review of Suhrawardi's view as illustrated in twelve different sections of the *al-Muṭāraḥāt*.[50]

Having defined five different types of definition, Suhrawardi continues to analyze the very complicated issue of the relationship between mental concepts and their corresponding objects in the external world. He argues that while it is conceivable to define a thing so that its genus and differentia remain united, it is not possible to do so in regard to the class of those things whose genus and differentia are one and the same, such as colors.[51] A color, he says, is not like "Man is a rational animal" in that there would be a concept of man and a rationality so that the latter is a predicate of the former. Color is a genus without a differentia, therefore, no definition of it can be offered such that it would encompass its genus and differentia.

From the above argument Suhrawardi concludes the following:

1 Peripatetics are wrong in assuming that definition can be used unequivocally and without any qualification as a means to attain knowledge. In this case alone, (i.e., colors) we clearly realize the limits of definition in that it is only capable of defining certain things.
2 Color can never be known by definition since color can not be defined by something other than itself.

In *The Conversations*,[52] Suhrawardi once again stresses that a definition which is able to include the sum of all the differentia and other characteristics of the thing in question would be an accepted mode of cognition. In stating this, he implicitly is arguing that since it is not possible to define all the attributes of a thing, any attempt to define a thing would be in vain.

Suhrawardi, in some of his works in Persian such as *Partawnāmah*,[53] and *Hayākil al-nūr*,[54] makes reference to the problem of definition but does not discuss it in as much detail as he does in some of his Arabic works. In *The Philosophy of Illumination*, he summarizes his views regarding the Peripatetic view of definition by saying:

> He who mentions a number of essentials cannot be certain that there may not be another essential which he has ignored. Commentator and critic should inquire (of his certainty), and if he says that were there another essential, we would have known it, (we should say) there are many attributes that are unknown to us . . . . The truth of things is known only when all of the essentials are known, and if there be another essential that we are unaware of, then knowledge of that thing is not certain. Thus, it becomes clear that the limits and definitions (*ḥadd*) as the Peripatetics have accepted will never become possible for man. The master of the Peripatetics [Aristotle][55] has confessed to this existing difficulty. Therefore, the limit and definition cannot exist

> except in regard to those items whose collective body[56] is an indication of particularity.[57]

Suhrawardi in the above argument has demonstrated that the differentia of a thing is an exclusive property of that thing (i.e. the purring of a cat). Then, if we do not know what that property is, we will never know the identity of the thing through definition. The purring of a cat in this case has to be defined through another definition, and this definition in turn needs to be defined through another definition which for Suhrawardi is absurd. There ought to be an axiomatic principle so that everything else is defined in terms of it. In fact, Suhrawardi, in his *The Philosophy of Illumination*,[58] maintains that knowledge by definition is possible if and only if there be a first principle so that everything else is measured against it and yet itself is not subject to any definition because of its axiomatic nature. This axiomatic phenomenon for Suhrawardi is light and its derivative presence that underlies the very foundation of his epistemology.

2. KNOWLEDGE BY SENSE PERCEPTION

Suhrawardi's view of sense perception is difficult to formulate in that his views in this regard are scattered throughout his various writings. Quṭb al-Dīn Shīrāzī, the famous Avicennan commentator of Suhrawardi, in his work *Sharḥ-i ḥikmat al-ishrāq*,[59] argues that Suhrawardi believes in five internal senses and five external ones. Quṭb al-Dīn Shīrāzī[60] maintains that Suhrawardi not only believes that the five senses are for the attainment of knowledge of the outside world but also that there is a hierarchy of senses that begins with the sense of touch and ends with sight.

The internal senses for Suhrawardi are of five types, and their existence helps to synthesize the information that the external senses has attained. If these senses did not exist, then all the knowledge acquired through the senses could not have been interpreted in our mind.

In a section he entitles "On the Evidence that Peripatetic Principles Necessitate that Nothing be Known or Defined," in the *Ḥikmat al-ishrāq*,[61] Suhrawardi criticizes the Peripatetics in regard to their views on sense perception. His argument as presented in this chapter can be summarized in the following points:

1. "Substance has unknown differentia."[62]
2. "Essences are defined by negation."[63]
3. "The Soul and other mental concepts have unknown differentia."[64]
4. "Accident, e.g., blackness, has been defined as a 'color that is observable to the eye', and the totality of sight is an accidental concept, and now that you know color, it becomes necessary that accidents cannot even be conceived of."[65]
5. "Of course, the concept of being, that for them (Peripatetic) is the axiomatic principle, is now known."[66]
6. "If it is perceived that knowledge of things is through their non-essential attributes and that those attributes have attributes and the same continues, then this becomes problematic since according to this assumption it becomes necessary that in the world nothing can be known."[67]

The first three principles have been discussed in the previous section and they only demonstrate the inadequacy of the Peripatetics insofar as they rely on definition for the attainment of truth. In the fourth principle, Suhrawardi argues that there are objects in the external world which can only be perceived but not defined, i.e. colors. These types of phenomena he calls "simple truths" (*ḥaqā'iq basiṭah*) which neither can be known through knowledge by definition, nor be grasped by sense perception.[68]

As to the "compound truth" (*ḥaqā'iq murakkabah*), Suhrawardi argues that this category of things can be reduced to its essential components, which are the simple truths, and to know them one has to see them. For instance, a building or a tree can be reduced to a number of forms and colors that can only be the objects of perception.

The above view is part of the response that Suhrawardi provides in his sixth principle against the Peripatetics, who maintain that a thing can be known through its attributes and accidents. The problem is that an attribute has to be defined by another, which means the process can go on *ad infinitum*, and nothing can be known, which is absurd.

Suhrawardi's view of the function of sense perception can be better understood if we examine some of the consequences of his argument. Suhrawardi further argues that the data attained through sense perception is non-verifiable in that one can never know if others are experiencing the same data. Therefore, he concludes that the nature of the knowledge attained through sense perception is private and exclusive. As Suhrawardi states:

> It should be known that your ideas and others' are not the same as long as your ideas and those of others are not attained through the same means of cognition.[69]

So far, from the first two arguments of Suhrawardi, the following conclusions can be drawn:

1 Only the simple truth can be known through sense perception.
2 Knowledge of the simple truth is private, exclusive and non-verifiable by outsiders.

What Suhrawardi has not made clear yet are the sources of these concepts. In the *The Philosophy of Illumination,*[70] we find an argument which is the key to the understanding of this problem. There, Suhrawardi argues that there are those who maintain that in order to know something one has to have prior knowledge of it; otherwise, how would one know it even if he came across it? This problem was first raised by Plato himself and has since been repeated by many philosophers. The implication of Suhrawardi's response to this objection also provides the key to solving the problem regarding the sources of knowledge. Suhrawardi states that this problem can only be raised in a circumstance under which something is unknown. If something is completely unknown or completely known in all its aspects, it can not be known. Something can be known if it is partially known and partially unknown. It is only then that the unknown part can be known through an inference from known to the unknown.

> If the desired entity is completely unknown, then it cannot be known, and it is the same if something is completely known but that it has to be known in some aspect and not known in others so the unknown can become known through it.[71]

Now, since simple truths exist only in their pure form, i.e colors, and are not made up of several parts as forms and shapes are, they can be either completely unknown or entirely known. If the former is the case, then we can never come to know of colors, which is not the case. If it is the latter, the question then arises as to how it is that we know them in their entirety since neither definition nor sense perception can tell us what a color or simple form or shape is.

While Suhrawardi alludes to this in various places, he does not treat the subject in detail. What he does say is that we have a pre-knowledge of certain things, which are axiomatic in nature. These axiomatic phenomena, resembling Kant's *a priori* concepts, are what Suhrawardi refers to as *fiṭriyyah*. These are the concepts that allow us to recognize something when we see it. For example, recognizing that one line is shorter than another one without measuring it is due to the presence of these innate ideas although the act of cognition begins with our senses.

To recapitulate on Suhrawardi's view of knowledge by sense perception, the following can be said: Existent beings for Suhrawardi are either single or compound. If single, then they have no differentia and therefore we can not know them by their accidents (*lavāsim*). Sense perception can be helpful to decipher the simple from the compound and further to realize and reduce the compound to its essential elements which are simple. The knowledge of the simple can neither be defined nor be grasped through the senses without the aid of innate ideas.

3. KNOWLEDGE THROUGH INNATE IDEAS

Suhrawardi, both in his critique of the Peripatetic view of definition and in the problems associated with sense perception, argued for the necessity of an innate knowledge that can serve as the foundation for various modes of cognition.

In *The Philosophy of Illumination*,[72] he discusses the notion of innate ideas by mentioning four modes of cognition and the place of innate ideas among them. His argument, briefly stated, is as follows: Some types of knowledge are either innate or not. In order for one to know a thing, one has to rely on that which is already known to him, and this process can go on *ad infinitum*, a process Suhrawardi maintains is impossible. Therefore, attainment of knowledge, at least partially, requires having pre-knowledge of that which one seeks to know, and this knowledge can only be innate. As Suhrawardi states:

> Human knowledge is either innate (*fiṭriyyah*) or it is not. Whenever in recognizing an unknown, if focusing one's attention [i.e. sense perception] and referring to one's heart is not sufficient, and if it is not an affair that can be known through the vision (*mushāhidah*) that is a characteristic of the

> great *ḥakims*, then necessarily in knowing we need pre-given knowledge . . . and the process, if carried out in certain order will lead to the innate ideas.[73]

Suhrawardi seems to be suggesting that innate ideas are a necessary condition if sense perception and even definition is to be possible. In other words, if knowledge by sense perception is not going to lead to an infinite succession of beings, each of which makes the other object known, then innate ideas have to exist. It is, therefore, reasonable to conclude that innate ideas for Suhrawardi are the necessary condition if some knowledge is to be attained through definition or perception.

4. SUHRAWARDI'S PHILOSOPHICAL EPISTEMOLOGY

As I have demonstrated, it is difficult to identify Suhrawardi's epistemology with any particular epistemological paradigm (i.e. empiricism, rationalism, etc.). While Suhrawardi argues that ultimately one can attain certainty only through the knowledge which is attained by illumination, he does not discard the possibility of attaining knowledge through other modes of cognition.

Suhrawardi's philosophical epistemology as has been discussed is made up of the following three elements.

1. Definition
2. Sense Perception
3. Innate Ideas

To summarize Suhrawardi's view on the shortcomings of the above means of cognition, the following can be said: Suhrawardi maintains that definition is problematic because it has to define not only the essentials of an existent being as Aristotle indicates, but all its attributes and accidents as well.

This is necessary since they are as much a part of a thing as the so-called essentials are and defining all of them is impossible. Suhrawardi attributes this problem to the following reason:

> All definitions inevitably lead to those *a priori* concepts which themselves are in no need of being defined; if this were not the case there would result an infinite succession.[74]

Contrary to the less significant place that definition has in Suhrawardi's philosophical epistemology, sense perception is much more significant. This is partly because most things that cannot be defined can be known through the senses. It is for this reason that he says: "Thus, knowing and recognizing of some items becomes a task of the senses."[75]

Sense perception, Suhrawardi tells us, is able to distinguish between the simple and compound entities. Despite this ability, our senses cannot escape the same problem that definition faced. That is, when faced with a compound entity, they can come to know it by its simple constituents, but how do we know the simple elements? It is at this point that either there has to be an axiomatic principle in terms of which a simple thing can be known or we again have the problem of knowing one thing through another *ad infinitum.* On this Suhrawardi states:

> There is nothing more apparent than what can be sensed . . . since all our knowledge comes from the senses; therefore, all that is sensed is innate and can not be defined.[76]

Finally, there are the innate ideas that Suhrawardi considers to be necessary in order to connect the other two elements of his philosophical epistemology. The existence of innate ideas provides the necessary link between Suhrawardi's view of knowledge by definition and sense perception which enables him to offer a coherent and consistent theory of knowledge. The nature of these ideas and their structure, be it Kantian or Platonic, remains somewhat unclear in Suhrawardi's philosophical writings; what is clear is that for Suhrawardi they have a limited role and function.

Suhrawardi's concept of philosophical epistemology, therefore, is based on the idea that while different modes of cognition and schools of epistemology are useful in some domains, ultimately certainty comes through illumination, which is the type of knowledge that is attained without mediation. In the beginning of the *Ḥikmat al-ishrāq* Suhrawardi summarizes his view towards his theory of "knowledge by presence." He states:

> As we observe the sensible world, through which we gain certainty of their states of affairs, we then base a thorough and precise science on this basis (math, astronomy). By analogy, we observe certain things in the spiritual domain and then use them as a foundation upon which other things can be based. He whose path and method is other than this will not benefit from this and soon will be plunged into doubt.[77]

What Suhrawardi has clearly been trying to argue for is that philosophy in general and epistemology in particular have to have an *ishraqi* foundation. In Suhrawardi's epistemology, light becomes the substance of knowledge and knowledge the substance of light.

> If there be anything that needs no definition or explanation, it has to be obvious by nature, and there is nothing more obvious and clear than light. Thus, there is nothing that needs no definition except light.[78]

Having argued for the limited role of conventional modes of cognition, what has not been answered yet is how knowledge as such is possible. What is it that makes knowing and cognition feasible?

We can now proceed to consider Suhrawardi's answer to these questions, known as the theory of knowledge by presence.

B. KNOWLEDGE BY PRESENCE

The fundamental principle upon which Suhrawardi's *ishraqi* epistemology is based is that the "self" is capable of knowing certain things directly and without mediation by virtue of its very presence. Man, Suhrawardi says, can know himself only through himself, and that which is other than himself cannot be used to arrive at the knowledge of the self. He offers several arguments to prove that the self has the ability to know directly and without any mediation, beginning with the knowledge of the self.

The question Suhrawardi poses is, how does the self know itself? It is precisely the answer to this question which constitutes the core of his *ishraqi* epistemology, and it can be formulated as follows: There is a special mode of cognition which attains knowledge directly and without mediation, thereby transcending the subject/object distinction. This mode of cognition, which has come to be called "knowledge by presence" (*al-'ilm al-ḥuḍūrī*), is, as I will demonstrate, the only plausible explanation as to how the self can know itself.

The arguments that Suhrawardi offers in support of his claim that the self can only know itself by virtue of the very presence of itself are expressed by Suhrawardi through his writings in two different styles. In his Persian writings, which I have discussed in the previous chapter, this view is expressed symbolically, whereas in his other works, especially in his tetralogical works, he is more philosophical.

The significance of the present discussion for Suhrawardi's mysticism lies in the concept that true knowledge, and for that matter the foundation of kowledge, is an ontological issue (i.e. presence) as opposed to an epistemological one. Knowledge is a question that is directly related to the question of being and existence and not an abstract epistemological issue. Furthermore, Suhrawardi's argument implies that certainty depends on the direct nature of the epistemic relationship between the subject and the object.

Mysticsm in general as reflected in the perennial tradition, *Sophia perennis*, and in particular in the Sufi tradition, for Suhrawardi is distinguished from other traditions of wisdom by the directness of the experience of the knower of the known. The higher the status of the knower, ontologically speaking, the more intense and direct is the experience. This point will be elaborated on further in the forthcoming section.

Suhrawardi offers three arguments to prove that the self can only know itself through the reality of its presence. We will proceed to consider these arguments.

1. ARGUMENT FROM "I/IT" DICHOTOMY

Suhrawardi presents his first argument by asking, "When I know *P*, do I also know myself?" If I do, then how did I come to know myself? Either I knew myself directly or through some other means. If I know myself through an intermediary, then the following problem arises:

> A thing that exists in itself (*al-qā'im bi'l-dhāt*) and is conscious of itself does not know itself through a representation (*al-mithāl*) of itself appearing in itself. This is because if, in knowing one's self, one were to make a representation of oneself, since this representation of his "I-ness" (*anā'iyyah*) could never be the reality of that "I-ness," it would be then such that that representation is "it" in relation to the "I-ness," and not "I". Therefore, the thing apprehended is the representation. It thus follows that the representation apprehension of "I-ness" would be exactly what is the apprehension of "it-ness" (*huwa*), and that the apprehension of the reality of "I-ness" would be exactly the apprehension of what is not "I-ness." This is an absurdity. On the other hand, this absurdity does not follow in the case of apprehension of

> external objects, for the representation and that to which that representation belongs are both "its."[79]

According to this argument, one either knows himself through himself or something else i.e. a representation. If the latter be the case, then "self" *A* is known through a representation (*mithāl*) *B*. Suhrawardi then argues that knowledge of *A* which is attained through *B* is really not knowledge of *A*, but is seeing *A* through *B*. Suhrawardi's argument allows for knowledge of the outside world to be attained through a representation (*mithāl*), which is rather similar to Hume's notion of "ideas" and "impressions." However, knowledge of the self which is to be attained through anything other than the self is not knowledge of the self, but knowledge of that which is other than the self. Suhrawardi goes on to argue that if I am to know *A* through *B*, then in a sense I am equating my understanding of *B* with *A*, which is an absurdity. How can my self be the same as my understanding of *B*, through which *A* is supposed to be known? In other words, if I am to understand the self through something other than itself, then the problem arises that the understanding of something is the same as the thing itself.

Let us examine Suhrawardi's argument further. When one says "I know P," he is saying that there exists an "I", such that I knows "itself" and also this "I" knows "P". This implies that, when one claims to have any type of knowledge, one is implicitly saying that I know myself before knowing anything else. Therefore, in claiming that one knows something not only is knowledge of the self assumed, but that "I" seems to be the object of its own knowledge. It seems to be the case that in the statement "I know myself" the knower, which is the "I," and the known, which is the "self," and the relationship between them is one and the same. If this were not the case, then there would be an "I" versus "it" which is the self. Now, either this "it" is made up of the same substance as the "I" (i.e. unchangeable), or it is not. This "it" is either identical to the "I" or "it" is something totally different. M. Ḥā'irī[80] argues that "If we accept this argument of Suhrawardi, then the "I" and its representation "it" would then be both identical and different in one and the same respect,"[81] which is a logical contradiction and therefore an absurdity.

An analysis of how Suhrawardi arrives at this conclusion is as follows: If "I" did not know "it" directly and without mediation, then "it" has to know itself through objectifying itself which would be called "it." On one hand, "I" and "it" are the same, since "it" is a representation of the "I"; on the other hand, they are not the same since if they were the same, there would not have been an "I" and an "it". Therefore, "I" and "it" are different since they stand in a subject/object relation, but they are the same since "it" is a substitute for the "self" in the statement "I know myself." According to Suhrawardi, the following propositions would then have to be the same if the "I" were not the same as the "self."

1. I know myself.
2. I know it.
3. It knows myself.
4. "It" knows it.

Therefore, if it is the case that the "I" comes to know itself through its representation, then the above contradictions arise which maintain "I" and "it" are the same and different at the same time. That is the absurdity which Suhrawardi demonstrates in his first argument.

To summarize the views of Suhrawardi on the basis of his first argument we can classify his first argument into the following three categories:

A. Epistemological
B. Logical
C. Semantical

A. Epistemological

If "I" can only know myself through a representation of myself, then I know myself through what is not myself which is an absurdity. This is to say that my understanding and apprehension of something are the same as the thing in itself. Therefore, either the self cannot be known or it has to be known by itself. We all know ourselves; therefore, it is reasonable to conclude that we can know our "self" only through our "self."

B. Logical

If the "I" is to know itself through its representation, then either the "I" and its representation, the "it," are the same or not. If they are the same, then there cannot be two of them and therefore, "I" and "it" have to be one and the same. On the other hand, if they are different, then how can "it" be a perfect representation of the "I"? This is a logical contradiction which arises if we are to accept the "I/it" distinction.

M. Ḥā'irī in his work *The Principles of Epistemology in Islamic Philosophy*, maintains that there is a realm of "I-ness" and "It-ness."[81] I-ness naturally can only be known by itself and if it is represented by something other than itself, then "it" becomes "not I", whereas it should be nothing but "I". According to Ḥā'irī, the "I" and the "it" are not the same, but "it" exists because of the "I". If the self comes to know of itself through the idea or representation of the self (*mithāl*) then it clearly can never know itself since according to Suhrawardi and Ḥā'irī *mithāl* does not represent the "I" but demonstrates the "it." In fact, if two things are identically the same, then they can not be separated. Therefore, by virtue of the distinctness of the "I" and its representation, the "it", we can conclude that knowledge of "it" is not the same as the "I." If this were not the case, then the "I" and the "it" should have been the same and yet different at the same time, which is an absurdity.

C. Semantical

When I say "I know myself," if by "myself" I am referring to the representation of the I, then I am actually saying that "I know it." However, since "it" is "not I," then I am also saying that "I know not I," which is another way of saying "I do not know I." This too is an absurdity. According to Suhrawardi, then, if "I" is known through its representation, then the statement "I know myself" means "I do not know myself", which is contradictory and therefore absurd since I know myself.

Several conclusions can be drawn from the above arguments, which are among Suhrawardi's original contributions to Islamic philosophy. First, is that he seems to have succeeded in establishing the existence of a being that can only be understood by itself, but also that this understanding takes place by virtue of the reality of its presence. The second conclusion is that since "self" can only know itself by the reality of itself, any other thing is foreign to it and thereby will never know it as it really is. M. Ḥā'irī states this as follows:

> In this prime example of presence – knowledge, the meaning of knowledge becomes absolutely equivalent with the mean-

> ing of the very being of the self, such that within the territory of "I-ness" to know is to exist and to exist is to know.[82]

The third remarkable characteristic of Suhrawardi's argument, which can be regarded as an original contribution in the Islamic epistemological tradition, is that he has offered a theory of knowledge without relying on such notions as essence, appearance and reality. Instead, he argues that if the "I" understands itself by virtue of its presence, then its existence is its primary mode or its essential character. The very fact that the self can know itself by its mere presence leads to the conclusion that self is pure existence or pure presence.

2. ARGUMENT FROM PRE-COGNITIVE MODE OF KNOWLEDGE

Suhrawardi offers two arguments in support of the view that our knowledge of ourselves requires the existence of a pre-cognitive mode of knowing and that can only be possible through knowledge by presence. In his first argument, Suhrawardi attempts to demonstrate the absurdity of not accepting the argument. Through the use of *reductio ad absurdum*, in a very difficult passage he states:

> Indeed, if that which is unknown to you becomes known, then how do you know that it is what you sought? For inevitably either [your] ignorance remains, or [your] prior knowledge of it existed so that it could be known as such [. . .] For that which is sought, if it is unknown form in all aspects, it could have never been known.[83]

In the above argument Suhrawardi maintains that if I am to know *A* through *B*, then I must have come to know that *B*, in some sense, represents *A*. However, if we say this, then it is necessary for a person to first know *A*, and then the fact that *B* represents *A*. How can I begin to know myself through something other than myself, if I do not already know myself? This argument originally goes back to Plato, who argued that in searching for truth, we in essence must know the truth or else, even if we do find it, how will we recognize it? Suhrawardi is applying the same concept with a great deal of emphasis on the precognitive mode of knowledge. Therefore, prior knowledge of *A* is necessary if *A* is to know itself through *B*, otherwise any object of one's reflection may be a representation of *A*.

Suhrawardi's second argument for having precognitive knowledge is as follows: If *A* knows itself through its representation *B*, then the question arises as to how it knows that *B* represents *A*? If *A* does not know itself directly, then it must have come to know *B* through *C*, and this process goes on *ad infinitum*. In other words, either *A* knows itself directly or else there will be an infinite chain of representations, each of which is known through the other one. This, according to Suhrawardi, is impossible. From this he concludes that *A* knows itself directly and without mediation or representation. Suhrawardi is careful to point out that this process is true only in regard to the knowledge of the self of itself and not of the objects of the external world.

3. ARGUMENT FROM ATTRIBUTES

Finally, Suhrawardi offers an argument that is based on the primacy of the essence over the accident. The primacy of the essence over the accident is the underlying philosophical principle upon which the argument is based, despite the fact that Suhrawardi does not use the concepts of essence and existence explicitly to argue for his position. This view, which has come to be known as the "principality of essence" (*aṣālat al-māhiyyah*), as opposed to the "principality of existence" (*aṣālat al-wujūd*) held by the Peripatetics, is an integral part of the *ishraqi* school. To know something is to know its essence, and if one is to know the essence of a necessary being through its accident or in this case its predicate, then it is as if one were to know a major premise through a minor one. To argue for his position, Suhrawardi relies on the method of *reductio ad absurdum* by assuming that we know ourselves through the representation of the "I." On this he says:

> Indeed the thing which necessarily exists and which is self-perceived does not know itself from a representation of itself in itself. If it knows [itself] through its representation, and the representation of I-ness is not itself, then in regards to it [I-ness], it is the one perceived and it is the representation at that time. The perception of I-ness must be, by itself, the perception of that which it, itself, is, and must be the perception of itself, by itself, just like the perception of other than itself – and that is impossible – in contrast to the externals, representation and that which it has of it are both it. Moreover, if it is through a representation, it, itself, did not know it was a representation, and thus it knew itself through

> representation. And how was it not? It imagines that it knows the very thing by that which is attributed to itself from outside. It is an attribute of it. If it is judged according to every super-added attribute to itself, then it is a knowledge of other than itself. It already knew itself before all attributes and the like. It did not know itself through attributes which are super-added.[84]

The above argument seeks to establish the reality of the knowledge of the self by itself through an examination of the attributes of the self. The argument is based on a key concept, which is that if one is to know himself, then he must have had prior knowledge of himself. If this were not the case, then how could one realize that the thing which is supposed to be the representation of the self does actually represent the self? The representations of one's self, which in this case are the attributes of the self, are useful in recognizing the self if and only if those attributes truly represent the self. This too, however; requires having a pre-knowledge of the self. Thus, it can be said that if one is to know oneself through his attributes, then he has to know that these attributes are actually the attributes of the self. To know this, one has to have pre-knowledge of his own "self", which implies the "self" knows itself through itself as has been argued for in the first two arguments.

In the second part of this argument Suhrawardi maintains that one knows himself either directly or indirectly. In the first case, the problem is solved. However, if *A* is to know itself through its representation *B*, then it is reasonable to conclude that it cannot know *B* except through its representation *C* and this process can go on *ad infinitum*. . . . Therefore, it can be concluded that *A* can never know itself through its representation. Suhrawardi considers this to be an absurdity on two grounds. First, it leads to an infinite series of contingent dependent beings, which, he argues, is impossible for there is an end to everything. Secondly, we know ourselves, while the above argument indicates that we cannot know ourselves, an absurdity Suhrawardi rejects.

Suhrawardi has made an assumption here which is that the self knows itself. What if this is not the case and that the self is ignorant of itself? Suhrawardi does not reply to this point since our knowledge of ourselves is so certain and appears to be so "clear and distinct," as Descartes would say, that one may not mistake his notion of self with the actual self as it really is.

The above objection, in my opinion, is a shortcoming in Suhrawardi's philosophy. There is no question that the self knows itself. However, there is every reason to doubt that this knowledge of the self is the self as it really is. For example, it is true that my relationship to my headache is marked by certainty and directness. However, my concept of my headache and its characteristics, though certain to me, should not be mistaken for the true nature of that headache which may never be known to me. I have an idea of my "self", but how do I know this is my actual self or that my knowledge of it corresponds to the actual self? Suhrawardi would reply to the above by saying that the mode of cognition with which the self knows itself is such that it does not lend itself to any logico-semantical analysis. Therefore, it is not a proper analogy to compare one's relationship to one's headache and the knowledge of the self of itself. The problem with this argument is that Suhrawardi leaves no room for any verification of his claim by an outsider.

The above problem is one that Ḥā'irī also notices, but he does not elaborate on it and in fact considers it to be an issue open for further study. However, having offered a discussion of the concept of "awareness" and "presence", Ḥā'irī concludes that our knowledge of ourselves is one that goes beyond the "*noumena*" and "*phenomena*" distinction. As he states:

> The most outstanding feature of knowledge by presence, however, is that the immediate objective reality of the thing as it is, is its being known.[85]

4. CONCLUSION

Having demonstrated in the last three arguments that the self cannot be known by anything else except itself and that it is only through the sheer presence of the reality of the self that the knowledge of the self becomes possible, Suhrawardi goes on to conclude the following:

> You cannot be absent from yourself (*dhātika*), and from your realization of it, and since awareness is not possible through representation or super-addition, in your awareness of yourself you only need yourself which is visible to itself and not absent from itself, and nothing else. The awareness of the self itself must be by itself and cannot be absent from it such as the organs of the heart, the liver, and the brain, and all

> matter and material darkness and light is not implied in your awareness of yourself. Your self-awareness is not an organ nor is it materiality and unless you are absent from it, you have awareness of yourself, continuously and permanently.[86]

Two conclusions can be drawn from Suhrawardi's theory of knowledge by presence. First and foremost is that the self can only be known by itself, and therefore to know a thing is equivalent to gaining knowledge of an object so that the relationship between the object and the self is the same as the relationship between the self and itself.

The second conclusion is that whatever is not known through the presence of the self is therefore beyond the epistemic domain of the self. Consequently, gaining certainty with regard to those objects that are beyond the epistemic domain of the self is not possible.

5. PRACTICAL CONSEQUENCES OF A PHILOSOPHICAL ANALYSIS

With regard to the foregoing discussion, it can be said that the first step in Suhrawardi's epistemology is to argue for the existence of a self which is an immaterial and immutable substance. The proof for the existence of the "I" is the task of discursive philosophy. Suhrawardi, as a skillful philosopher, carries out the task of establishing the very existence of an independent self which, however, has many attributes that are attached to it. These attachments are the basic constituents of the human ego (*nafs*) whose existence is too obvious to argue for and include desires of the flesh.[87]

Suhrawardi holds the view that the self often appears to be nothing but a sum of desires towards wordly attractions and not two separate entities, a metaphysical "I" to which desires of the flesh are supper-added. In order to make this crucial distinction, Suharawrdi calls for further philosphical analysis to firmly establish that the "I" and its attributes are not the same. It is only then that we can see that whereas the nature of the "I" is divine and belongs to the luminous world, its attachments are ontologically rooted in the corporeal world. Rationalistic and discursive philosophy in this context is called for in order to establish the distinction between the self and its attributes.

Suhrawardi's third step in dealing with the self would be to go beyond the separation of the self from its attributes. At this stage

Suhrawardi argues that in order for the self to be able to reveal itself, the "veiling" attributes of the self should be destroyed. To do so, Suhrawardi prescribes practicing asceticism and he goes on to illustrate in great detail the type and nature of these practices as was discussed previously. Such practices eliminate the *nafs* and the attributes of the self begin to vanish one by one. As this process goes on, the self, whose relation to its attributes is like the relationship between accidents to essence, begins to reveal its "I-ness." This process will have to continue until the annihilation of the attributes of the self is completed, and once this process has been finished, the self will remain in its entirety without any veil from itself.

> When you have made a careful inquiry into yourself, you will find out that you are made of "yourself", that is, nothing but that which knows its own reality. This is your own "I-ness" (*anā'iyyatuka*). This is the manner in which everyone is to know himself and in that, everyone's "I-ness" is common with you.[88]

The methodology of bringing the self to its fullness and thus enabling it to reveal itself can be summarized as the following:

1. Realization of the distinctness of the self from its attributes.
2. Separation of the "I" from its attributes, both philosophically and practically.
3. Employment of asceticism as a means for destroying attributes and leaving the self in its pure form.
4. The self in its pure form is a single and self-evident phenomenon from which nothing more apparent can exist.
5. That from which nothing more apparent can exist is light.
6. Self is light. (F 4,5)
7. Things are known by coming into the mere presence of light.
8. Things are known by the presence of the self. (F 6,7)

It is in regard to the above epistemological scheme that philosophy and asceticism have their own place and in fact are able to become integrated into a tradition of wisdom that brings about a rapprochement between discursive philosophy, intellectual intuition and practical wisdom.

For Suhrawardi, the concept of knowledge by presence is therefore defined as an awareness or presence of the object before its essence. He reminds us that this essence, which he considers to be the same as the self, light, and knowledge, is such that by virtue of its presence bridges the subject-object distinction.

Since all things are ultimately made up of light, and because it is absurd to say that one needs light to find another light, in order for an epistemic relation to occur the veil that is separating the subject and the object has to be removed. In this case, self or light, which are equivalent in Suhrawardi's philosophy, is knowledge as well. 'To know is to exist and to exist is to know' therefore constitutes a major epistemological theme and one of the important contributions of Suhrawardi to Islamic philosophy.[89]

6. A CRITICAL ANALYSIS OF KNOWLEDGE BY PRESENCE

Despite Suhrawardi's genius, there are a number of objections that can be raised against some of his specific arguments. Here I wish to discuss several problematic points implied by the theory of knowledge by presence. Suhrawardi argues that after he thoroughly mastered the Peripatetic philosophy, he realized the inadequacies of such a philosophical methodology. He then improved certain aspects of the Peripatetic philosophy by adding and omitting certain arguments. At that point he had done what any brilliant philosopher would do. He then tells us that through asceticism and initiation he had a vision of the truth. He reminds us on numerous occasions that the path of spiritual realization requires ascetic practices.

What is problematic in Suhrawardi's claim is that through spiritual vision he has realized the validity of the philosophical principles which he advocates. This is exactly what distinguishes gnosis (*'irfān*) from philosophy. The problem is as follows: What if there exists an argument or a set of arguments in the works of Suhrawardi that are clearly false? In order to falsify Suhrawardi's philosophical paradigm it is only necessary to find one instance in which Suhrawardi advocates a false argument. There are indeed such instances.

Basing the validity of a philosophical argument contingent upon spiritual realization creates the following problems:

1. All the philosophical arguments must be sound, or else the spiritual vision of Suhrawardi is not authentic.
2. All the philosophical arguments *are* sound regardless of their apparent fallacies and therefore the vision is authentic.

As I indicated above, in the first case, it is not very difficult to find an argument of Suhrawardi with apparent flaws. How Suhrawardi can defend this position is puzzling. If I present a philosophical argument of Suhrawardi which is by any account fallacious to him, then he either has to admit that his spiritual vision was not real or that the validity of philosophical arguments is not necessarily related to one's mystical vision. Since Suhrawardi has based his views on the premise that the truth of philosophical arguments can be realized through one's illumination, then separating the validity of the arguments and spiritual vision would be a violation of the fundamental principle upon which the *ishraqi* school is established. Suhrawardi obviously will not grant that his mystical experience has been a false one since that would place the *ishraqi* school in a dilemma.

It follows that Suhrawardi will have to adopt the position that all the arguments which he has presented have been checked by his spiritual realization and are correct, regardless of their apparent fallacy. The falsification of his arguments is therefore of no consequence since he knows that ultimately these principles are sound. This argument does not go very far and, in fact, brings about even a more fundamental problem. There have been many eminent philosophers of the *ishraqi* tradition who have refuted each other's arguments. Let us take only two of the greatest masters of this tradition, Suhrawardi and Mullā Ṣadrā.

Mullā Ṣadrā is by all accounts a man of superior intellect and profound vision whose spiritual and philosophical acumen is comparable to Suhrawardi's. Mullā Ṣadrā takes issue not only with Suhrawardi's ontology, but in his commentary upon *The Philosophy of Illumination* he criticized specific arguments of Suhrawardi.

One can say that the apparent inconsistency between Mullā Ṣadrā and Suhrawardi exists only within the philosophical domain and that on an esoteric level they remain in agreement. This would have been acceptable if Suhrawardi and other *ishraqi* sages had not derived the validity of their philosophical propositions from the authenticity of their spiritual vision. Mullā Ṣadrā and Suhrawardi both claim to know the truth and both claim that the validity of their philosophical views is derived from the knowledge they have acquired directly in the form of revelation. Since they disagree with one another, one of the following alternatives must be the case:

1. The existing inconsistancies indicate they both are false.
2. The existing inconsistancies indicate one of them must be false.
3. They both are right.

One way of determining whose claim is correct is to apply the standard means of analysis and evaluation that philosophers have relied upon to determine the validity of their arguments. Those who do engage in such an analysis will soon find out that there are fallacies in the works of Mullā Ṣadrā and Suhrawardi as well as their commentators.[90] The problem to which I am alluding is a serious one, since if the validity of philosophical arguments is subject to the truth of one's vision, then philosophy becomes subjective and relative and one has to accept that Suhrawardi and Mullā Ṣadrā and their opponents are all correct, which is not possible because they contradict one another.

One may reply to my objection by arguing that truth is relative to the spiritual state of an individual, and while only the absolute truth can be known absolutely, knowledge of all other beings of the absolute truth is relative. Therefore, the existing differences between Mullā Ṣadrā and Suhrawardi are superficial and ultimately they are in agreement even though they do not know it.

The above reply is not convincing in that philosophical principles, especially those of a rationalistic nature, do not lend themselves to exegesis and interpretation in the same way that mystical assertions do. To further clarify the above, let us consider the following example. Suppose Suhrawardi argues that the following argument is correct and Mullā Ṣadrā argues it is false.

1. All men are mortal.
2. Socrates is a man. (A)

∴3. Socrates is mortal.

Assuming Suhrawardi and Mullā Ṣadrā both had a genuine experience of truth, then they must necessarily agree with *A*, since the conclusion of the above argument is true and their philosophical view is derived from the authenticity of their spiritual vision. Then how are we to account for their disagreement in this regard? In such instances as the description of truth, God, or even the nature of a mystical experience, inconsistencies can be explained by the fact that one's understanding of truth is relative to his spiritual state. In cases such as *A*, however, we have a clear and simple argument that is clearly either true or false. This creates a problem which is typical of those who have offered a philosophical analysis based on their mystical vision.

'Abd al-Razzāq Lāhījī, one of the most celebrated commentators of Suhrawardi, in his book *Gawhar murād*,[91] argues that the conclusion one arrives at through discursive reasoning is the same as that which is attained through illumination, with the only difference being the degree of clarity. Lāhījī raises an important issue which Suhrawardi has left unanswered, and that is, what if the knowledge attained through illumination is contradictory to the well established principles of knowledge? This is a question that Suhrawardi seems to take for granted by assuming that illumination and philosophical analysis, if carried out "properly",[92] will lead to the same conclusion. Lāhījī realizes that neglecting the validity of a logical principle at the expense of an esoteric judgment may lead to anarchy, since the authority of the judgment itself is not verifiable.

Lāhījī's response is a clever one. He maintains that if the result of one's discovery through illumination were contrary to the principles of logic, then the person should not claim to be illuminated. Although this principle guards the rational principles from subjective judgments, it gives priority to the discursive domain. As Lāhījī states:

> Therefore, a Sufi[93] would either be a theosopher or a theologian. Without a firm grasp in theosophy or theology, and without benefiting from the men of vision, in accordance with the words of the *'ulamā* or its contrary, any claim to Sufism is pure forgery.[94]

To further clarify the distinction between the principles of rationalistic philosophy and *ḥikmat,* Lāhījī makes a distinction between knowledge of the scientific principles versus metaphysical beings.[95] Whereas the scientific principles lend themselves to philosophical inquiries, *ishraqi* wisdom does not.

To summarize, there exists a fundamental problem at the heart of the school of illumination, which arises when Suhrawardi makes the validity of the philosophical principles contingent upon one's mystical vision. My proposed solution is that instead of arguing for a correlation between the spiritual realization and philosophical truth, Suhrawardi should separate them. It is perfectly justifiable for a mystic to remain ignorant of the science of biology and chemistry while claiming to know the truth. Accordingly, Suhrawardi has to differentiate between scientific and philosophical truth. He must then place them within a different category from truth that is attained through a mystical experience. Suhrawardi should say that knowledge of one category should not have any bearing upon the other one if he is to resolve the problem which I have discussed above. Suhrawardi should continue to consider philosophical training and especially mastery of Peripatetic philosophy to be a prerequisite for the pursuance of the *ishraqi* tradition. This is justifiable if Suhrawardi considers it to be a necessary training and nothing else. However, it would be a fatal mistake for him to say that the validity of all the philosophical principles, especially those contained in *The Philosophy of Illumination*, have been derived from his mystical experience, since some of those principles and arguments are clearly regarded as fallacious even by such giant commentators of Suhrawardi as Mullā Ṣadrā, Lāhījī and Sabziwārī. Regardless of this objection, Suhrawardi's philosophical arguments and mystical narratives are important and have their own merit. Within the philosophical domain, his works should be regarded as a brilliant commentaries on Ibn Sīnā's philosophy, with major differences in the fields of epistemology and ontology.

Notes

1 Suhrawardi, *Opera* 3, 422.
2 Suhrawardi, *Opera* 2, 117.
3 Ibid., 119.
4 Ibid., 113.
5 Ibid., 121.
6 Ibid., 108.
7 For Suhrawardi, *qhāsiq* is that which yearns to return to the real light.
8 For Suhrawardi, *Hay'ah ẓulamāniyyah* belong to the categories of the accident.
9 Suhrawardi, *Opera* 2, 133.
10 For more information on these divisons see, Ibid., 187.
11 Ibid., 223.
12 Ibid.
13 Ibid., 144.
14 For more information on the Zoroastrian and Mazdean angelology and Islam see H. Corbin, "Rawābiṭ-i ḥikmat-i ishrāq wa falsafa-yi Iran-i bāstān," *Majillay-i anjuman-i Iran shināsī*, no.3, (1946): 34ff.
15 Suhrawardi, *Opera* 1, 70.
16 H. Corbin, *Creative Imagination in the Sufism of Ibn 'Arabī* (Princeton: Princeton Press, 1969), 55.
17 R. Evans, "Henry Corbin and Suhrawardi's Angelology," *Hamdard Islamicus* 11, no.1 (n.d.): 12–20.
18 Suhrawardi, *Opera* 3, 186.
19 Suhrawardi, *Opera* 3, 211.
20 Ibid., 211.
21 Ibid., 213.
22 Ibid., 214.
23 Ibid., 216.
24 Ibid., 217.
25 Ibid., 218.
26 Ibid., 220.
27 Ibid., 211.
28 For more information see Henry Corbin's work on imagination: *Mundus Imaginalis or the Imaginary and the Imaginal*, trans. Ruth Horine (Ipswich: Golgonooza Press 1976).
29 Suhrawardi, *Opera* 2, 183–184.
30 Suhrawardi, *Opera* 1, 3–4.
31 Suhrawardi, *Opera* 3, 191.
32 Suhrawardi, *Opera* 2, 254–255.
33 Ibid., 254.
34 Ibid.
35 Ibid., 242.
36 Some of the advocates of the perennial view are of the opinion that the imaginal world is also the source from which the forms and patterns of Islamic art emanate. Among these can be named: S.H. Nasr, F. Schuon and T. Burckhart. Also, for more information on *Mundus imaginalis* see: Q.A. Dīnānī, *Shu'ā-i andisha wa shuhūd dar falsafa-yi*

Suhrawardi (Tehran: Ḥikmat Press, 1985 A.H.s.); and D. Shayagan, "Henry Corbin: The Spiritual Topography of Iranian Islam," *Iran Nameh* X, no.2 (Spring 1992): 280–296.

37 Suhrawardi, *Opera* 2, 133–134.

38 Ibid., 133.

39 Ibid., 230, 231.

40 Ibid., 110.

41 Ibid., 110.

42 Socratic method as exemplified throughout Plato's writings, in paticular in the *Meno* and the *Symposium*, intends to define and redefine a "thing" until one reaches an axiomatic definition which is also a means of understanding the forms. The Socratic method is related to the Platonic epistemology and the theory of "recollection" which lies at the heart of it.

43 Aristotle, *Posterior Analytics* (New York: Random House, 1941), 160.

44 Suhrawardi, *Opera* 2, 20.

45 Ibid., 29–36.

46 *Opera* 1, 17.

47 Ibid., 199. Throughout this work, especially towards the end of this book, Suhrawardi criticizes the Peripatetics on their concept of definition and categories.

48 Suhrawradi, *Opera* 1, 14.

49 Ibid., 14.

50 For more information see Ibid., 116ff.

51 Suhrawardi, *Opera* 3, 5.

52 Suhrawardi, *Opera* 1, 199.

53 Suhrawardi, *Opera* 3, 2.

54 Ibid., 85.

55 Aristotle, *Posterior Analytics*, 15.

56 What Suhrawardi has in mind is the category of things whose genus and differentia are the same, such as colors.

57 Suhrawardi, *Opera* 2, 21.

58 Ibid., sec. 9–14.

59 Quṭb al-Dīn Shirāzī, *Sharḥ-i ḥikmat al-ishrāq* (Tehran: Tehran University Press, 1951), 454–457.

60 Ibid., 455.

61 Suhrawardi, *Opera* 2, 73.

62 Ibid.

63 Ibid.

64 Ibid.

65 Ibid.

66 Ibid.

67 Ibid.

68 Ibid., 74.

69 Ibid., 54.

70 Ibid., 54.

71 Ibid., 54.

72 Ibid., 18.

73 Ibid.

74 Ibid., 104.
75 Ibid., 21.
76 Ibid., 104.
77 Ibid., 13
78 Ibid., 107.
79 Ibid., 111.
80 In *The Principles of Epistemology in Islaimc Philosophy: Knowledge by Presence,* M. Ḥā'irī argues that this is a case of logical contradiction when the law of subject-object relation is violated. For a complete discussion see pp. 69–92.
81 Ibid., 77.
82 Ḥā'irī, *The Principles of Epistemology in Islamic Philosophy,* (first edition), 142.
83 Suhrawardi, *Opera* 2, 110.
84 Ibid., 111.
85 Ḥā'irī, *The Principles of Epistemology in Islamic Philosophy,* 155.
86 Suhrawardi, *Opera* 2, 112.
87 This aspect of the "I" is better discussed in the Persian works of Suhrawardi where he is very explicit about such attributes. For more information see Suhrawardi, *Opera* 3, 170–191.
88 Suhrawardi, *Opera* 2, 112.
89 This concept has become one of the central themes of *ḥikmah* and was treated extensively by the masters of the School of Isfahan, Mullā Ṣadrā in particular. For more information see S.H. Nasr, "The School of Isfahan," in *A History of Muslim Philosophy,* ed. M.M. Sharif (Karachi: Royal Book Co., 1983), 904–932.
90 Proof for this would be the existing commentaries and critiques on Mullā Ṣadrā and Suhrawardi by so many eminent philosophers, e.g. Lāhījī, Sabziwārī, et al.
91 What distinguishes Lāhījī from other *ishraqi* philosophers is the fact that he argues that if one's vision does not correspond with the conclusions of logical analysis, then one should not preach any of them. The best course of action then, according to Lāhījī, is pursuing truth until the spiritual vision and the result of philosophical analysis correspond.
92 This argument of Suhrawardi's gives rise to a tautology since if one's vision does not correspond to philosophical principles, he has not carried out his analysis properly. This argument makes the verification of an argument impossible by an independent observer.
93 By "Sufi," Lāhījī is, here, referring to those who opposed any intellectual activity towards the attainment of truth. Sufis emphasize pure piety and asceticism at the expense of intellectual knowledge.
94 Qummī Lāhījī, *Gawhar Murād,* (Bombay: 1923), 16–17.
95 Ibid., 16.

5

INFLUENCE OF SUHRAWARDI ON ISLAMIC PHILOSOPHY

Suhrawardi's *ishraqi* school marked a turning point in the history of Islamic philosophy since it changed the direction and nature of philosophical thinking from a purely rationalistic approach to one that considered ascetic practices to be part of its epistemological paradigm. Most of the schools of philosophy that came after Suhrawardi were influenced by his teachings in one way or another. Some of them, such as the *Shaykhiyyah* movement, which agreed with certain strands of *ishraqi* thought, opposed others.

The school of illumination was not only instrumental in reconciling the two traditions of wisdom that had been in contrast with one another, Sufism and the Peripatetic philosophy, but also brought about a harmony between them. The result was that purification and asceticism became a necessary condition for the philosophical speculation, which ultimately leads to the attainment of truth.

The following discussion will demonstrate how Suhrawardi's ideas spread to different parts of the Islamic world and the different ways in which the *ishraqi* school played a role in the development of subsequent philosophical schools. The purpose is not to show specific links that exist between Suhrawardi and his successors by way of textual analysis, but rather to show the influence of Suhrawardi on various schools of thought.

By virtue of their historical, cultural and intellectual backgrounds, it was greater Persia and the sub-continent of India that became the cradle of the school of illumination, from which the influence of Suhrawardi's ideas spread in the following geographical areas:

A. Greater Persia
B. Sub-Continent of India

C. Syria, Anatolia, Spain and North Africa
D. The West

A. THE GREATER PERSIA

Suhrawardi's school of illumination left a profound and permanent influence on the tradition of wisdom in Persia. Suhrawardi's teachings and the bulk of *ishraqi* texts became a powerful philosophical movement whose climax was the "School of Isfahan." The masterly *ishraqi* expositions and commentaries of the teachings of Suhrawardi are still avidly studied today. Why was Suhrawardi so well received by Persian philosophers of this period? Was it only because he was a native of Persia? The answer lies in the rich and esoterically inclined religious ambience of Persians themselves which made them receptive to Suhrawardi's ideas.

Another reason was that the illuminationist school of Suhrawardi provided the basis upon which an esoteric interpretation of Shi'ite Islam could be formulated.[1] Shi'ite Islam puts a great deal of emphasis on intellect (*'aql*) as an instrument for the attainment of truth as well as acceptance of and adherence to the presence of an esoteric knowledge that lies at the heart of the Islamic message. Suhrawardi's school of illumination considers both intellectual discourse and the practice of asceticism to be the necessary components for the attainment of truth.

It is not accidental that Suhrawardi's philosophy, which emphasizes the elements of knowledge as well as practical wisdom, came to show itself during the Safavid period when Shi'ite Islam was adopted as the official state religion. Shi'ite Islam, which emphasized the twelve Imāms as a chain of initiators through which the Muḥammadan light (*nūr Muḥammadi*) manifested itself, was naturally receptive to *ishraqi* doctrine.

In addition to the religious and intellectual elements that enabled Suhrawardi's ideas to take root in Persia, there are other important commentaries and expositions which helped to consolidate his ideas. The most important work was the commentary of Shahrazūrī (680/1281) on *Ḥikmat al-ishrāq* and *al-Talwiḥāt*. Also, the commentaries of such masters as Ibn Kammūnah (667/1269), 'Allāmah Ḥillī (693/1293), Quṭb al-Dīn Shīrāzī, Athīr al-Dīn Abharī,[2] Naṣīr al-Dīn Ṭūsī and, finally, Mullā Ṣadrā were influential in spreading the ideas of Suhrawardi.

Abharī and Ṭūsī are known for their Peripatetic writings but were nevertheless highly influenced by Suhrawardi. For example, in his work *Kashf al-ḥaqā'iq fī taḥrīr al-daqā'iq*, a perfect representation of Suhrawardi's teachings, Abharī discusses a number of philosophical issues from an *ishraqi* point of view. Before the Safavid period, such figures as Sayyaid Ḥaydar Amulī and Ibn abī Jumhūr and his major work *Kitāb al-mujlī* played a major role in allowing the *ishraqi* school to reach its climax during the Safavid period. The religious ambience of Persia, its historical and cultural characteristics, and the existence of an essentially gnostic element in the Persian *Weltanschauung*, helped to establish Suhrawardi as a figure with whom Persians felt at home. As S.H. Nasr states:

> By the beginning of the eighth/fourteenth century the *ishraqi* school had become definitely established in Persia and henceforth it remained an important element of the intellectual life not only of Persians but also the eastern lands of Islam where the Persian Islamic culture has been dominant.[3]

The powerful political movement of the Safavids and the keen interest of the Safavid kings in nourishing the intellectual and mystical life of Persia brought about the culmination of the tradition of *ishraqi* wisdom in what has come to be known as the "School of Isfahan." Before embarking on a discussion of the School of Isfahan, I will briefly consider those *ishraqi* philosophers who paved the path for the emergence of this powerful paradigm.

1. ISHRAQI PHILOSOPHERS BEFORE THE SCHOOL OF ISFAHAN

Among the significant figures who emerged just prior to the Safavid period, who for all practical purposes are considered to belong to the school of Isfahan, are Ṣadr al-Dīn Dashtakī and his son, Ghiyāth al-Dīn Manṣūr Dashtakī. Manṣūr wrote extensively on the Peripatetics, such as his commentary on the *Ishārāt* and a treatise on ethics. However, it is his commentary on Suhrawardi's *Hayākil al-nūr* that shows the extent of Suhrawardi's influence even on certain peripatetics. His works offer a perfect representation of *ishraqi* philosophy and particularly influenced Mullā Ṣadrā, for whom he was often mistaken. In a sense, Manṣūr represents a successful attempt to bring about a rapprochement between the Peripatetic philosophy as represented by Ibn Sīnā and the *ishraqi* tradition.

A number of other intellectuals of this period not only carried out an *ishraqi* reading of Ibn Sīnā, but also paid attention to the gnosis (*'irfān*) of Ibn 'Arabī who was introduced to the Persians through the works of his student, Ṣadr al-Dīn Qūnawī. Among these figures we can name Ibn Turkah Iṣfahānī (8th/14th) whose attempt to bring together philosophy and gnosis, as represented in his major work, *Tamhīd al-qawā'id*, influenced many of his successors, in particular Sayyid Ḥaydar Āmulī. Āmulī interpreted Shi'ite Islam in the light of the writings of Suhrawardi, Ibn 'Arabī, Ibn Sīnā and created a philosophical synthesis. Āmulī's important work, *Jāmi' al-asrār*, exemplifies the type of spiritual hermeneutics (*ta'wīl*) that is practiced by the *ishraqi* masters.

Besides the previously mentioned Ibn A'bī Jumhūr, Rajab Bursī, who wrote *Mashāriq al-anwār* stands out among other figures of this tradition. He also attempted a synthesis of Ibn 'Arabī's gnostic doctrine, the works of the Peripatetics, and Shi'ite thought.

Concerning the attempt for a unified and well-integrated philosophical paradigm by the important figures of this period, S.H. Nasr states:

> The integration of *ishraqi* teaching into Shi'ism was . . . rapid and profound, with the result that during later centuries most of the *ishraqis* have been Shi'ite. During the period pre-dating the Safavids, such Shi'ite theologians as Sayyid Ḥaydar Āmulī and especially Ibn Abī Jumhūr prepared the ground for the integration of *ishraqi* wisdom into the perspective of Shi'ism.[4]

Philosophical activity in general and Suhrawardi teachings in particular which had gone through a period of decline, were once again revived during the Safavid dynasty when the intellectual, religious, mystical and artistic life of Persia reached its climax.

2. SCHOOL OF ISFAHAN

The founder of the School of Isfahan, Mīr Muḥammad Bāqir Dāmād Ḥusaynī Astarābādī, known as "Mīr Dāmād", and often referred to as the "third teacher", (*mu'allim al-thālith*), was one of the most outstanding figures of this period. Mīr Dāmād made an attempt to revive and reconcile Ibn Sīnā and Suhrawardi. He was in a unique position to revive philosophical activities since he was highly esteemed by the jurists as well as the court, which protected him from the orthodox jurists' accusation of heresy.

> He may be considered an *ishraqi* interpreter of Ibn Sīnā's metaphysics in the spiritual universe of Shi'ism.[5]

While Mīr Dāmād defended the rationalistic philosophy of the Peripatetics, he made a distinction between rationalism and illumination. Whereas Suhrawardi distinguished between Oriental and Occidental philosophy, Mīr Dāmād distinguished between *Yamānī*, the illuminative philosophy, and *Yūnānī* the discursive philosophy of Greeks.[6] *Yamanī* being the Orient represents the illuminative, while *Yūnānī* stands for discursive philosophy.

Mīr Dāmād commented on a number of philosophically significant topics, in particular the principality of the essence (*aṣālat al-māhiyyah*). The thrust of his philosophy is the relationship between the *ḥudūth* (creation) and the *qidam* (eternity) of the world. Mīr Dāmād accepted Suhrawardi's view of the principality of essence over existence but argued that, contrary to the *ishraqis* who consider the incorporeal world and the archetypes (*al-mujarradāt*) to have been created in the "divine essence" (*al-ḥudūth al-dhātī*), he considers them to have "corporeal creation" (*al-ḥuduth al-dahrī*). He argues that while the cause of the creation of these archetypes may be in the divine essence, the event or effect occurs in the created domain (*dahr*). In the *Qabāsat*,[7] Mīr Dāmād quotes Ibn Sīnā extensively and interprets him in a way that supports his own view of the corporeal createdness (*al-ḥudūth al-dhātī*). There are those contemporary interpreters[8] of Mīr Dāmād who argue that some of his interpretations of Ibn Sīnā were purely from an *ishraqi* point of view and therefore are not entirely accurate.

Mīr Dāmād devotes a major portion of his *Qabasāt* to a discussion of the principality of essence. His complex argument, which is essentially similar to Suhrawardi, is as follows: It is apparent that an existent being does not only exist by virtue of its own existence but because of its "essence" (*māhiyyah*). Now, either the essence precedes the existence in the order of creation or vice versa. In either case, the order can not be only a conceptual one in our mind or a random arrangement made for the sake of convenience, but this order must be intrinsic or innate to the ontological structure of the universe. From this, Mīr Dāmād concludes that the essence of an existent being must be the principal element, since it is inconceivable to have an existent being which is made up of pure existence (wujūd) and no essence. Mīr Dāmād's unique contribution to Islamic philosophy is his introduction of the notion of time concerning the priority and principality of essence over existence, which is perhaps the most important and complex part of Mīr Dāmād's philosophy.[9]

Among the fifty works of Mīr Dāmād which are committed to the revival of Ibn Sīnā's and Suhrawardi's philosophy from an *ishraqi* point of view, the following can be named: *Qabasāt, Taqwīm al-īmān, al-Ufuq al-mubīn,* and *Taqdīsāt.* Mīr Dāmād has also written a number of works in Persian, among which are *Jazawāt, al-Ṣirāṭ al-mustaqīm* and the collection of his works in Persian and Arabic entitled *Mashāriq al-anwār.*

Despite Mīr Dāmād's contribution to Islamic philosophy and Shi'ite gnosis as the founder of the School of Isfahan, his greatest achievement was training a number of students, some of whom came to dominate the intellectual scene and overshadowed the teacher. Among the students of Mīr Dāmād who played an important role in continuing the *ishraqi* wisdom of Suhrawardi by teaching and authorship, one can name Mīr Dāmād's son-in-law, Sayyid Aḥmad 'Alawī, the author of a commentary on Ibn Sīnā, Quṭb al-Dīn Ashkiwārī, who also wrote a book on the history of philosophy called *Maḥbūb al-qulūb,* and Mullā Khalīl Qazwīnī, who wrote a commentary on *Usūl al-kāfī* of Kulaynī and is regarded as an authority on Shi'ite jurisprudence. There were many other figures who are less known, such as Mullā Shamsā Gīllānī, who wrote extensively on Mīr Dāmād's view of creation and eternity and commented on Mullā Ṣadrā.

The second outstanding figure of the School of Isfahan and an *ishraqi ḥakīm* with legendary fame in Iran is Shaykh Bahā' al-Dīn Āmulī, whose influence goes beyond the sphere of philosophy and extends into architecture, jurisprudence, Arabic grammar and poetry. Āmulī, known as "Shaykh Bahā'ī", is not only respected for the ninety works he wrote in all areas of the Islamic sciences, but is also revered because he became the teacher of many scholars who went to Isfahan. While he is not particularly known for his works on *ḥikmat,* he nevertheless tried to reflect the spirit of *ḥikmat* in his architectural designs. His Sufi poetry written in the style of Rumi and reflected in his book *Ṭūṭī-nāmah,* is perhaps the best representation of his mystical views.

The greatest achievement of Shaykh Bahā'ī is the fact that he trained such scholars as Mullā Muḥsin Fyḍ Kāshānī, Sayyaid Aḥmad 'Alawī, and Mullā Muḥammad Taqī Majlisī, all of whom came to be prominent figures of the *ishraqi* tradition. It is for this reason, as well as for his unique achievements in architecture, that he has gained almost a mythical personality, so much so that performing miracles has been attributed to him.

The third figure of the School of Isfahan, Mīr Abu'l-Qāsim Findiriskī is less known despite his eminence and far-reaching influence. He traveled to India and had extensive contacts with Hindu Masters to whom he alludes in a major work, *Usūl al-fuṣūl*. Along with his commentaries on other traditional fields of Islamic intellectual thought, his *Risālat al-ḥarakah* and *Risālah ṣanā'iyyah* can be named. Mīr Findiriskī who offers a summary of *ḥikmat* in his book of poetry called *Qaṣidah*, tried to express his "experiential knowledge" through Ibn Sīnāian philosophical categories as did other members of the School of Isfahan. He also trained a number of fine scholars such as Mullā Rafī'ā Gīlānī and Āqā Ḥusayn Khunsārī. His most famous student is Mullā Rajab 'Alī Tabrīzī, the author of *Kilīd-i bihisht*.[10] Another figure of great importance in the School of Isfahan is Mullā Muḥsin Fayḍ Kāshānī, the best student of Mullā Ṣadrā, who wrote over 120 works. Beside writing on different religious sciences, he wrote extensively on such works as Ibn 'Arabī's *al-Futūḥāt al-makkiyyah* and Rūmī's *Mathnawī*. Kāshānī's work represents Shi'ite gnosis at its best. His major work, *al-Mahājjāt al-bayḍā' fī iḥyā' al-iḥyā'* was based upon Ghazzālī's *iḥyā' al 'ulūm al-Dīn*. "In fact, what Mullā Muḥsin did was to revive the work of Ghazzālī in the Shi'ite circle by 'Shi'ifying' it."[11]

Kāshānī brought the integration of the school of illumination to its completion. He used the rationalistic philosophy of Ibn Sīnā and the theosophical ideas of Suhrawardi to offer an analysis of the twelve-Imām Shi'ite Islam.

There are two other prominent figures of this school, Mullā 'Abd al-Razzāq Lāhījī and his student Qāḍī Sa'īd Qummī. Lāhījī is best known for his contribution to the field of *Kalām* (theology), which he carried out within the matrix of *ḥikmat*. Influenced by Mullā Ṣadrā, he wrote a number of works of a purely *ishraqi* nature such as *Ḥudūth al-'ālam*, and a commentary on Suhrawardi's *Hayākil al-nūr*. Qāḍī Sa'īd Qummī, who came to be known as the Ibn 'Arabī of the Shi'ite tradition, devoted his writing to the type of spiritual hermeneutics (*ta'wīl*) that was intended to elaborate on the esoteric meaning of the *Quran* and other Islamic doctrines and rites.

Towards the end of the Safavid period two events occurred. First, the Sufis, who had enjoyed relative freedom, began to be viewed as having deviated from the Islamic rites (*sharī'ah*) by the more esoteric jurists (*'ulamā'*) and therefore were persecuted. The second element was the weakening of the central government and the consequential dominance of the more austere and orthodox atmosphere. Despite this change, however, there were a number of *ḥakims* who emerged at the end of the Safavid period and provided a transition between the Safavid and the Qajar periods.

The first important *ishraqi* figure who belongs to this period is Ḥasan Lunbānī, (13/19 century), whose philosophical Sufism did not sit well with the esoteric *'ulamā'* and who was accused of being a Sufi. The second significant *ḥakim* of this period was Mīrzā Muḥammad Ṣādiq Ardistānī, who taught *ḥikmat* and carried on the tradition of Mullā Ṣadrā. During this period, such figures as Ardistānī and Mīr Sayyid Ḥasan Ṭāliqānī began to use *ishraqi* texts in the *madrasah*. Ṭāliqani, for example, taught Ibn 'Arabī's *Fūṣūs al-ḥikam* and Suhrawardi's *Ḥikmat al-ishraq* while being influenced by Mullā Ṣadrā.

Despite an environment hostile to Sufism and *ḥikmat*, both flourished until the Qajar period when another upsurge of intellectual activity occurred, although it never produced as many outstanding figures as the Safavid period did.

Before commenting on the status of the school of illumination during the Qajar period, it is necessary to say a few words about Mullā Ṣadrā both because of the extent to which he was influenced by Suhrawardi and because he came to dominate the philosophical scene during the Safavid and Qajar period. Mullā Ṣadrā 's monumental philosophical corpus, a synthesis of Ibn Sīnā and Suhrawardi, shaped and determined the course of philosophical activities in Persia even up until today. Therefore, the *ishraqi* tradition and its impact on the Shi'ite gnosis can be better understood if the intellectual relationship between these two giants, Suhrawardi and Mullā Ṣadrā, is made more clear.

3. SUHRAWARDI AND MULLĀ ṢADRĀ

It is generally believed that Suhrawardi's dominance of Islamic philosophy was substantially curtailed by Mullā Ṣadrā, whose criticisms and expositions of Suhrawardian doctrine established him as the foremost authority on transcendental theosophy (*al-ḥikmat al-muta'aliyyah*).

Suhrawardi and Mullā Ṣadrā represent two distinct approaches to *ḥikmat*. Mullā Ṣadrā's philosophical system includes that of Suhrawardi but he makes major changes so that it incorporates Ibn

Sīnā's Peripatetic interpretations as well as Suhrawardi's *ishraqi* ideas. The inclusive nature of his ideas established Mullā Ṣadrā 's dominance of Islamic philosophy in Iran until the present day.

The most important achievement of Mullā Ṣadrā is that he reversed the Suhrawardian ontology from one that was based on light to one based on the principality of Being. This important change took place in such a way that the overall philosophical structure of Suhrawardi remained intact with one exception: the predominance of the principality of existence over Suhrawardi's principality of essence.

Ṣadr al-Dīn Shirāzī wrote over fifty books which range from commentaries on the Islamic *ḥadīth*, such as the *Uṣūl al-kāfī*, to his Peripatetic writings, as in the case of *Kitāb sharḥ al-hidāyah*. There are also those works which defend the principles of illumination, such as *al-Shawāhid al-rubūbīyya, Ḥikmat al-'arshiyyah*, his famous commentry upon Suhrawardi's *The Philosophy of Illumination* called *Ta'liqāt 'alā sharḥ ḥikmat al-ishraq*, and finally his *magnum opus, al-Ḥikmat al-muta'āliyyah fī'l-asfār al-arba'at al-'aqliyyah.*

Mullā Ṣadrā's philosophy presents a unique synthesis of major intellectual currents in Islam. As S.H. Naṣr states, they are:

> *Kalām*, Peripatetic philosophy, *ishraqi* theosophy, and '*irfān*. In Mullā Ṣadrā we find elements of Ghazzālī, Ibn Sīnā, Suhrawardi and particularly Ibn 'Arabī. Moreover, there is Sufism especially in its gnostic aspect which serves as the background for this whole synthesis.[12]

The central difference between Mullā Ṣadrā and Suhrawardi lies in their ontological views. According to Mullā Ṣadrā, who advocated the principality of being and the gradations of Being (*tashkik*), each existent being has a different ontological status. Identifying pure Being as the absolute, Mullā Ṣadrā maintains that there is a unity amongst all the gradations of beings that emanate from Being. So far, Mullā Ṣadrā's system is similar to that of Suhrawardi, with the difference being that Mullā Ṣadrā has substituted Being for Light.

What constitutes the major difference between them is their account of the hierarchy they both advocate. Mullā Ṣadrā argues that gradation is applicable to the realm of existence (*wujūd*) and cannot include essence (*māhiyyah*).[13] Suhrawardi takes the opposite view by maintaining that gradation makes sense only if applied to essences. Sayyaid Jalāl Āshtiyānī, in his book *Hastī az naẓar-i falsafah wa 'irfān (Existence from a Philosophical and Gnostic View)*,[14] offers a lengthy discussion of the contention between Suhrawardi and Mullā Ṣadrā's view of Being and Existence. He summarizes Mullā Ṣadrā 's view as follows: "The existent being that has an essence must then be caused and existence that is pure existence . . . is therefore a Necessary Being."[15]

Therefore, for Mullā Ṣadrā, existence precedes the essence and is thus principle since something has to exist first and then have an essence. It is primarily this argument which lies at the heart of Mullā Ṣadrā's philosophy.

According to Āshtiyānī, there is another reading of Mullā Ṣadrā's argument that goes beyond the classical distinction between essence and existence. Āshtiyānī maintains that both in the *Asfār* and the *Mashā'ir*, Mullā Ṣadrā offers a middle road theory that is a rapprochement between those who argue for the principality of essence and those who advocate the principality of existence. Since all existent beings are essentially different in respect to their place on the hierarchy of existence, Āshtiyānī argues, essence and existence become one and the same in that every existent being has an ontological status which determines its degree of existence and this status bestows upon it its identity or essence.

It is in fact the above argument that demonstrates the extent of Suhrawardi's influence on Mullā Ṣadrā's ontological structure. The argument presented by Mullā Ṣadrā can be called a "middle road position" which goes beyond the traditional essence/existence distinction by arguing that they are two aspects of the same reality.[16]

A thorough discussion of the differences between the two giants of *ḥikmat* is beyond the scope of this work. It suffices to say that both figures left an indelible mark upon the intellectual fabric of Persia, the sub-continent of India and in particular on Shi'ism. Due to the hostility of the orthodox and esoteric jurists, Mullā Ṣadrā 's teachings were not taught in the intellectual centers for almost a century. However, once they were revived, during the early part of the Qajar period, their study came to the forefront of scholarship.

4. QAJAR PERIOD

The Qajar period in Iran also witnessed a prolific period of philosophical activity. These activities can be divided into two major trends, the majority who carried out the tradition of Suhrawardi and Ṣadrīan teachings and those who opposed them, such as *Shaykhiyyah.*

Perhaps for political reasons, the teachings of Mullā Ṣadrā and the Shi'a gnostic views did not receive the attention they deserved until Mullā 'Alī Nūrī, who devoted himself to the teaching and advocating of Mullā Ṣadrā's philosophy. Nūrī's commentary on the *Asfār* and *Mashā'ir* and his training of so many scholars made him one of the most prominent figures of the Qajar period.

Ḥājj Mullā Ḥādī Sabziwārī(13/19) is the main expositor of the *ishraqi* doctrine during the Qajar period, and the revival of Suhrawardi's teachings is mainly due to his efforts. Sabziwārī, who adhered to Mullā Ṣadrā 's teachings, studied with Mullā Ismā'īl Kushkī and Mullā 'Alī Nūrī in Isfahan. His ascetic practices are one of the reasons that have made a legendary figure of Sabziwārī. His emphasis on asceticism as a necessary element in philosophical training is most evident in his poems[17] and also important in the revival of the practical aspect of *ishraq.* Although belittled by some of the post-Ṣadrian philosophers, his emphasis on asceticism was important in the revival of the practical aspects of *ishraq.*

The works of Sabziwārī, in particular *Sharḥ al-manẓumah,*[18] have become standard texts for the students of Islamic philosophy in Iran. They present a complete discussion of philosophy and logic and raise objections against Mullā Ṣadrā's *Asfār,* especially his doctrine of the unity of the knower and the known (*ittiḥad al-'āqil wa'l-ma'qūl*) and the composition of form and matter. Although Sabziwārī primarily concentrated on Mullā Ṣadrā 's philosophy, his works are also regarded as expositions of *ishraqi* doctrine, especially his commentary upon Mullā Ṣadrā 's *al-Shawāhid al-rubūbiyyah* and his work in Persian, *Asrār al-ḥikam.* Sabziwārī's commentary upon the *Asfār* of Mullā Ṣadrā, one of the most comprehensive commentaries written on this work,[19] and his commentary upon Mullā Ṣadrā's *Mafātiḥ al-ghayb,* provide a valuable set of work for the students of Mullā Ṣadrā as well as the school of *ishraq.* Sabziwārī's interest in Sufism is most apparent in his Sufi poems and in his commentary on Rumī's *Mathnawī,* a classical work of Persian Sufi poetry. It is also said[20] that Sabziwārī wrote a commentary on the *Ilāhiyyāt* of Ibn Sīnā, which has been lost.

Many learned scholars consulted Sabziwārī on some of the more difficult philosophical questions to which he provided written answers. In one of the lesser known replies, Sabziwārī provided a brief answer to seven questions that were posed to him by a contemporary philosopher, Mīrzā Abū'l-Ḥasan Razavī.[21] Since the seventh question deals with the subject of knowledge by presence and clearly demonstrates the extent to which Sabziwārī was influenced by Suhrawardi, we have translated the entire section. This translation also indicates that the *ishraqi* theory of knowledge was of great interest among the intellectual community of the time.

QUESTION NUMBER 7:

M.A. Razavī: "Is the method of knowledge by presence,[22] which the sages of the Sufi tradition have promulgated, true or not? Is it accessible despite the differences among the followers of this method of discovery, and how can certainty of the truth of this theory be attained? As it (*Quran*) says: " If you do not know it, ask the learned", and also, "Remember that God gave birth to you through your mothers and you did not know anything." The prophetic *ḥadīth* says, "God did not make it necessary for people to answer but He made it incumbent upon the learned to answer."

I have dared to ask this while I am depressed, and my inner being is in a tumultuous state. I am thereby requesting that the answer be sent to me soon. May the prosperity of the two worlds be yours, your soul be enlightened, your intellect be well and your heart be free of every bondage."

Sabziwārī:

"Having a vision (*mushāhidah*) is an authentic principle and it is spiritual in nature. Spiritual discovery is a science through which knowledge of the self, knowledge of God and eschatological issues are known, and one becomes intellectually certain in a manner that is only attainable with regards to the domain of true knowledge. The mind proceeds from the knowledge of truth (*'ilm al-yaqīn*) to the beholding of the truth (*'ayn al-ya'qīn*) and finally becomes the truth (*ḥaqq al-yaqīn*).

God Most High has expressed the levels of certainty within the context of "fire" and has said: 'You will know soon, through *'ilm al-yaqīn*, you will see hell, and you will see it with the eyes of certainty.' Elsewhere He says, 'Hell can only be understood through knowledge by certitude.'

Therefore, the degrees of knowing the divine light are similar to the degrees of knowing fire. For example, if someone has never seen fire but has heard that whatever becomes united with it gains its attributes, he thereby knows that it loses its identity. Every candle and light are luminous from it and if it loses some of itself, it is not reduced. Whatever departs from it becomes its opposite in nature, such as smoke, which is dark. In darkness it is the master of all incorporeal lights.

It [fire] is like a luminous light that, if placed in a gathering, will illuminate everyone in colors, and forms manifest themselves in the presence of this light. Not every precious pearl that is placed in a gathering can do the same thing. Just as in illumination and warming, the sun is superior to fire in that 'there is not motion or power except through God,' and they call that being fire. There are those who believe in it on the basis of the following (those who know) and some who seek to believe because of its signs (smoke from fire), such as those who believe in God on the basis of clear signs. There are those who reach divine light and see existent beings through this light and see the essence of fire when the veil is removed for them. In their knowledge of God, these people are seeing the truth. People are like burning iron to whom the effects of fire appear when they understand it. They are those who have become the truth in their knowledge of God. Both of these types are men of true discovery and faith in what is obvious to them and are transcendental theosophers. There are different degrees amongst them and they know God but do not see God. Discovery of forms is the disclosure of forms as a particular to the senses and is divided in accordance to the five senses.

Therefore, discovery through vision, like the seeing of incorporeal entities by the ascetics [who see] a variety of lights, is an extensive discussion for another occasion. There are forms, phenomena and chants which are most sublime, and words that are pleasant and sounds that are fearsome and hopeful that are issued forth to the disciples. God said: 'The days of their life are like the divine breath,' and the prophet has said, 'He shelters us, feeds us and takes our thirst away' and also he said, 'God established balance between one's shoulders like the drink one has between meals.'

A formal discovery of the principles [of philosophy] is the manifestation of the divine name which hears all, sees all, and understands all things. A spiritual discovery of the principles, however, is the disclosure of the divine name. Hardship and ease are therefore apparent and following the Muḥammadean tradition is difficult and can only become easy through love and inner yearning.

The difference of opinion among the men of discovery and vision should not be regarded as an obstacle on the path of those who seek knowledge and practical wisdom, since differences exist everywhere. Are there not inconsistencies in the appearance of God's words and in the truth and in the appearance of the prophetic sayings as well as the sayings of the Imāms?

May he who wants the attainment of knowledge and sciences be successful."[23]

Another figure of great significance in propagating Suhrawardi's teaching is Muḥammad Riḍā Qumsha'ī. In the tradition of Sabziwārī and other great masters of this period, he taught Suhrawardi, Mullā Ṣadrā and Ibn 'Arabī. In fact, it was his attempt to integrate *ishraqi* tradition with Ibn 'Arabī's gnosis and Mullā Ṣadrā's metaphysics that made him one of the foremost authorities of Islamic philosophy in this period.

Towards the end of the Qajar period, Mullā 'Abdallāh Zunūzī and his son, Mullā 'Alī Zunūzī, wrote commentaries on Sabziwārī. They and Mīrzā Mahdī Āshtiyānī came to be known as the most important proponents of *ishraq* and Mullā Ṣadrā. 'Alī Zunūzī is particularly important, not only because of his important commentary upon Mullā Ṣadrā 's works, in particular the *Asfār*, but also because he represents the first encounter of traditional Islamic philosophy with European philosophy in Persia. Alī Zunūzī was asked by a Qajar prince to provide a reply to modern European philosophy, in particular Immanuel Kant. His response, the book *Badāyi' al-ḥikam*, earned him a special place within the Qajar period.

Mullā 'Abdallāh Zunūzī wrote an important book on *ishraqi* philosophy entitled *Lama'āt-i ilāhiyyah* which indicates how Suhrawardi's and Mullā Ṣadrā's teachings influenced the philosophers of the Qajar period.

There are many followers of Suhrawardi and Mullā Ṣadrā and their philosophical orientation who transmitted the wisdom of transcendental theosophy to the modern and contemporary *ḥakims* during the Qajar period. Among the outstanding figures of this period we can name Muḥammad Ismā'īl Iṣfahānī, Mullā Muḥammad Ja'far Langarūdī, Mullā Ismā'īl Khāju'ī, Mīrzā Mahdī Āshtiyānī and Mīrzā Ṭahir Tunkābunī. They constitute one intellectual trend among other movements which also reacted to Ṣadrian and *ishraqi* schools, among which the Shaykhiyyah movement is most conspicuous.

5. SHAYKHIYYAH SCHOOL

Initiated by Shaykh Aḥmad Aḥsāī (1153/1753), the Shaykhis are another continuation of the ideas of Suhrawardi and Mullā Ṣadrā during the Qajar period in Iran.[24] The Shaykhis, who seem more influenced by Mullā Ṣadrā's doctrine than they admit, reject many of Suhrawardi's ideas as presented by Mullā Ṣadrā.

While the Shaykkhīs adhere to Suhrawardi's view of the hierarchical structure of the universe, they reject his ontology based on light. Despite this, they accept the existence of an intermediary realm between the angels and human souls, which they describe as the domain of pure light. The Shaykhi's attempt to reconcile their *ishraqi* views with the more traditional theological themes is perhaps the root of their conflict with Suhrawardi's *ishraqi* school. Whereas Suhrawardi envisaged the grades of the existent entities as different intensities of light, the Shaykhīs argued that both the corporeal and the incorporeal world, the *hurqalyā*, are real.[25] Despite their disagreements, almost all the prominent figures in this movement, such as Shaykh Kāẓim Rashtī and Kirmānī, were influenced by the teachings of Suhrawardi and their reformulation by Mullā Ṣadrā.

6. CONTEMPORARY PERIOD

The golden age of philosophical activity during the Safavid period and its continuation during the Qajar period did not abruptly cease, as might be concluded from certain circles of Western scholars of Islamic thought. This tradition is still very much alive and active to this day. The philosophy of Suhrawardi and his chief expositor Mullā Ṣadrā become so fully integrated into the fabric of Persian intellectual thought that they remain to this day the cornerstone of traditional philosophical teachings in Iran.

In contemporary Iran, the teaching of *ḥikmat* has continued and flourished. Among the greatest masters of traditional teachings and *ishraqi* doctrine is 'Allāmah Sayyid Ḥusayn Ṭabāṭabā'ī, the author of *al-Mīzān,* and *'Alī wa'l-ḥikmat al-ilāhiyyah, Nihāyat al-ḥikmat* and *Bidāyat al-ḥikmah.* He has written numerous commentaries on Mullā Ṣadrā and the *ishraqi* doctrine, including a new edition of the*Asfar.* Other disciples of *ishraqi* tradition are Sayyid Muḥammad Kāẓim Aṣṣār, who has written a major work on transcendental theosophy entitled *Thalāth rasā'il fi'l-ḥikmat al-islāmiyyah,* and Abu'l Ḥasan Rafi'ī Qazwīnī, who has been the main defender of Mullā Ṣadrā 's school during the past half century. Qazwīnī has trained a number of fine scholars, such as Sayyid Jalāl al-Dīn Āshtiyānī, perhaps the most prolific writer in the field of traditional philosophy in Iran today. He has written extensively on a number of the commentators and authors of the *ishraqi* tradition.[26] The list of contemporary scholars who have kept the fire of *ḥikmat* alive is a long one.

Since the establishment of universities in Iran in recent years, Islamic philosophy and *ḥikmat* began to be taught outside of the traditional *madrasahs* for the first time. This was further facilitated by the appearance of scholars who have not only mastered the traditional teachings but also have become well acquainted with Western modes of thought. Among these scholars are Mīrzā Mehdī Ḥā'irī Yazdī and Seyyed Hossein Naṣr.

Ḥā'irī is a traditional master of Islamic philosophy whose extensive experience with the West marks one of the few examples of a serious encounter between traditional Islamic philosophy and Western philosophical paradigms. Such an encounter is best represented in his work entitled *The Principles of Epistemology in Islamic Philosophy: Knowledge by Presence.*[27]

Seyyed Hossein Naṣr is another exponent of Suhrawardi's philosophy who first edited the texts and introduced the Persian writings of Suhrawardi to both the Persian world and the West. His thorough familiarity with Western modes of thought as well as traditional Islamic philosophy has enabled him to present the *ishraqi* doctrine to the Western audience. Through his numerous writings and lectures, he has established himself as the chief proponent of the *ishraqi* doctrine in the West. Among his major works in the English language are *An Introduction To Islamic Cosmological Doctrines* and *Sufi Essays*. His most important philosophical works include *Knowledge and the Sacred, Three Muslim Sages, Ṣadr al-Dīn Shīrāzī and His Transcendental Theosophy,* and *Religion and the Order of Nature.*[28]

Besides Naṣr's major contributions in spreading the traditional teachings of Suhrawardi, Mullā Ṣadrā and other Shi'ite gnostics, he has trained a number of fine scholars, such as W. Chittick, the author and translator of many works on *ḥikmah.*

B. INDIA

In India, Suhrawardi's *The Philosophy of Illumination* was translated into Sanskrit and welcomed especially by the Zoroastrian community there. Besides the *ḥakims* and learned individuals who traveled to India, the keen interest of Sultan Muḥammad ibn Tughlug (725/1325) in philosophical and intellectual discussions helped to spread the school of *ishraq*. The Sultan, who had allocated large sums of money for the building of a library, was particularly interested in the works of Ibn Sīnā. Sayyid Athar Abbās Rizvī maintains in his book *A Socio-Intellectual History of the Isnā 'Asharī Shi'ism in India*[29] that most likely the works of Khwājah Naṣīr al-Dīn Ṭūsī and Quṭb al-Dīn Shīrāzī were amongst the *ishraqi* texts that had been taken to India by the followers of Suhrawardi. If *Durrat al-Tāj*, the central work of Shīrāzī, were available in India as Rizvī indicates,[30] then it is likely that other *ishraqi* works may have been available as well. Therefore, it appears that the ideas of Suhrawardi may have been discussed amongst the intellectual circles of India through the existing commentaries on the *ishraqi* doctrine.

Another example of the spread of Suhrawardi's ideas can be seen in the fact that several theological centers were established by Sand Niẓām al-Dīn in the early fifteenth century. His interest in these matters made the prominent *ishraqi* scholar, Jalāl al-Dīn Dawānī, consider moving to the area. However, Dawānī died while he was waiting for two of his students who had gone to the area for further investigation. Dawānī, a famous commentator of Suhrawardi, wrote *Lawāmi' al-ishrāq fī makārim al-ikhlāq*, and *Shawākil al-nūr fī sharḥ-i ḥayākil al-nūr*, the latter is a commentary upon Suhrawardi's *Hayākil al-nūr*. Although Dawānī did not go to India, many of his students did. Such figures as Mīr Mu'in, Mīr Shams al-Dīn, and in particular Abū'l-Fāḍl Kāzirūnī continued on the path of their teacher by propagating the transcendental theosophy of Suhrawardi. Suhrawardi's school continued to flourish in India, and with the rise of Akbar to power, the spread of *ishraqi* ideas reached its climax. Akbar's enthusiasm and tolerance for new ideas and religions provided the kind of ambience that the *ḥakīms* needed to freely teach the *ishraqi* doctrine, which had found a new home in the rich spiritual landscape of Indian culture. It was for this reason that a large number of *ḥakīms* moved from Iran to India, where they settled in numerous intellectual centers. Badā'ūnī, in his book, *Muntakhab al-tawārīkh,* offers an account of some of these masters. There he says:

> Some of the physicians in this region were so learned in the theory and skilled in the practice of medicine that they performed miracles like those of Moses and brought to mind the miraculous breath of the Lord Jesus.[31]

Among the most notable masters of the *ishraqi* school in this period were: Khatīb Abū'l-Fāḍl Kāzirūnī, who settled in Aḥmad Ābād, Shaykh Mubārak Nagorī and his son Shaykh Fāḍl, and finally Badā'unī himself. The tradition of *ḥikmat* has continued to flourish in India up to the contemporary period, even in the most orthodox centers.[32] In fact, it was the result of the influx of so many *ḥakīms* that many works were written on Suhrawardi, the best example of which is the commentary of Aḥmad ibn al-Harawī, *Anwāriyyah.*[33] This commentary, which is a classical work on Suhrawardi written in Persian, provides an overall account of Suhrawardi's *The Philosophy of Illumination.* Harawī, who lived in the 11/17 century in India,[34] made use of other commentaries such as those of Quṭb al-Dīn al Shīrāzī and Shahrazūrī, which indicates that these commentaries must have been available in India at the time through the followers of Suhrawardi.

Suhrawardi's influence in India went beyond the circle of *ishraqi* figures to become a profound influence on the Sufi tradition of the Chisti order. There are a number of other mystical schools that were influenced by Suhrawardi, such as the "Khayrābādī" school with its strong logico-philosophical tendency. Also, such grand masters as Shāh Walīallāh and Shaykh Aḥmad Sirhindī and their mystical schools came to be influenced by the illuminationist ideas of Suhrawardi, although the link with Suhrawardi requires further exploration.

The intellectual scene of Indian culture came to know of Suhrawardi in two separate periods. The first was in the first two centuries after Suhrawardi's death, as has been discussed. The second encounter of India with the illuminationist ideas of Suhrawardi was through the sages of the Safavid period, who belong to the school of Isfahan.

During this period many of the great masters of the *ishraqi* tradition traveled to India. Some of them who wrote important works on Suhrawardi and the doctrine of illumination include Qāḍī Nūrallāh Shūstarī, who authored two major books on the philosophy of illumination, *Majālis al-mu'minīn* and *Iḥqāq al-ḥaqq*, and Muḥammad Dihdār Shirāzī, the author of *Ishrāq al -nayyirayn*. In addition, there were such notable scholars as Mīr Findiriskī and Bahā' al-Dīn Iṣfahānī, also known as Fāḍil-i Hindī, who not only taught the Peripatetic philosophy, especially the *Shifā'*, but also knew the works of other commentators on the *ishraqi* tradition. Gradually, the teachings of Mullā Ṣadrā and his teacher, Mīr Dāmād, became extremely popular, even overshadowing the works of Suhrawardi. For instance, Mullā Ṣadrā's book, *Sharḥ al-hidāyah*, became an official text in the traditional school *(madrasahs)*.[35]

The school of *ishraq* and the texts that deal with the illuminationist doctrine are being taught even today in the traditional centers of learning in the Indo-Pakistani sub-continent. Outside of Iran, the sub-continent is the only region that is to this day receptive to the teachings of Suhrawardi.

C. SUHRAWARDI IN SYRIA AND ANATOLIA

The existence of large numbers of *ishraqi* manuscripts in Turkish libraries is an indication that Suhrawardi was studied by Turkish scholars. In fact, the Turkish libraries contain such an abundance of *ishraqi* texts of Ibn 'Arabī and others that such notable scholars as A.M. Schimmel and H. Corbin spent a number of years in Turkey to complete their research on Muslim gnostics and other *ishraqi* figures.

As far as the spread of Suhrawardi's ideas in Syria is concerned, his presence there and his numerous students and companions in Syria may have been instrumental in the spreading of his ideas. Suhrawardi does not mention the names of these associates but alludes to them as those who repeatedly requested of him to write various treatises, in particular *The Philosophy of Illumination.*[36] In fact, towards the end of this book he leaves a will asking his circle of friends to safeguard its content.[37] This indicates the existence of a circle of *ishraqis* who benefited from the esoteric teachings of Suhrawardi. It is reasonable to assume that they must have continued his work after Suhrawardi's death. One figure who may have been among his associates was Shahrazūrī. Although the date of his life makes it possible that he might have known Suhrawardi himself, it is likely that he was a disciple of one of Suhrawardi's students.[38] It is certain that Shahrazūrī's commentary on *The Philosophy of Illumination* and the *al-Talwīḥāt* (680/1281) were among the texts circulating within the group of *ishraqis* in Syria.

The discussions and debates of Suhrawardi with the learned men of his time in Syria, the bulk of his writing having been completed in Syria, and his circle of friends provide reasonable grounds to conclude that his ideas may have been studied by the intellectual community in Syria even though they were suppressed for political reasons.

D. SUHRAWARDI IN THE WEST

For uncertain reasons Suhrawardi's works were not translated into Latin and therefore his philosophy remained unknown to the West. One could postulate three reasons as to why his works were not translated. The first has to do with the existing philosophical paradigm of the period, which was more Ibn Sīnian in nature. Therefore, the rationalistic philosophy dominant in the Western world created an intellectual ambience that was not receptive to Suhrawardi's ideas. The second reason could have been that the great age of translation in Spain and the creative momentum that existed in southern Spain had come to an end. Since the translation houses (*Dār al-tarjumah*) were no longer productive, Suhrawardi did not receive the attention that he deserved. In my opinion, the third reason could have been Suhrawardi's affiliation with Ṣalādīn's son Malik Ẓāhir. Although Suhrawardi was not favored by the Ṣalādīn, he nevertheless may have been viewed by the Christian West as a court philosopher at a time when Muslims and Christians were involved in the Crusades. For this reason his works may have been set aside and gradually forgotten, except by a group of close friends or initiates.

S.H. Naṣr attributes the lack of interest by the West in teachings of Suhrawardi to a more fundamental problem, the philosophical and geographical departure of the East and the West.

> The West, which had been in many ways an 'orient' in the *ishrāqī* sense of the term and had passed a traditional civilization which . . . resembled the great oriental civilizations, was now becoming an occident, not only geographically but also in the *ishrāqī* sense of concerning itself with the domain of rationalization.[39]

Despite the existing intellectual currents which continued on their analytical and rationalistic path, Suhrawardi may have influenced certain intellectual strands in the West. S.H. Naṣr argues further that one of the intellectual circles that might have been influenced by Suhrawardi was the thirteenth century Oxford school of Roger Bacon and Robert Grossteste. While both of these figures were proponents of an empirical method of observation, their experiments were such that they were not necessarily inconsistent with a gnostic interpretation of nature. In fact, Nasr draws a parallel between the Oxford school of the thirteenth century and Quṭb al-Dīn Shīrāzī, the celebrated Muslim scientist and commentator of Suhrawardi, who had also continued an empirical method. Bacon and Grossteste used the kind of experimental method that considers the observation of nature to be a necessary part of illumination. "Bacon wore the dress of the *ishraqis* and lectured upon them."[40]

It is, however, even more likely that Suhrawardi had influenced certain intellectual circles in Spain where the intellectual milieu might have been more receptive to his ideas. For example, it is likely that Jewish Kabbalists who came to know of *The Philosophy of Illumination* may have taken this text to southern Spain where it was discussed among the Jewish mystics. It was this very text, some have argued,[41] that may have played an important role in the further development of Jewish illuminationists, thereby attracting attention to people who wrote extensively on illumination. Another indication that Suhrawardi's ideas did indeed travel into Spain is that Ibn Sab'in (7/13) of Spain, who lived in Morocco, alludes to the *al-Talwīḥāt* of Suhrawardi in his book *al-Risālat al-faqiriyyah.* Although it is difficult to establish whether he came to know of Suhrawardi while he was in Spain or in Morocco, it does demonstrate the large geographical span reached by Suhrawardi's ideas.

While illuminationist movements have emerged from time to time, it is difficult to establish a definite relationship between them and Suhrawardi's school. Such movements as the "Illuminated of

Bavaria," founded by Adam Weishaput, which was opposed to a religious hierarchy, or the ideas of Schelling and Franz Van Baader, were not able to revive the illuminationist movement in its authentic and traditional sense.

In the contemporary Western world, the works of Henry Corbin have created a great deal of interest in Suhrawardi's school of illumination. Corbin's early training was in Western philosophy with a focus on medieval ontology, and his interest in Islamic philosophy began with Ibn Sīnā. The focal point of his scholarship, however, was the *ishraqi* tradition and the wisdom of ancient Persia. In the words of S.H. Naṣr, "Corbin has without doubt done more than anyone else, outside and even inside Persia to revive the teachings of Suhrawardi."[42]

Like many other teachers of traditional wisdom, Corbin has contributed to the body of Islamic sciences not only through his own writings but by training a number of fine scholars. The following figures were either trained by him directly or influenced by his writings: G. Berger and J. Daniélou, G. Durand and A. Faivre, who belong to the younger generation of the scholars in France. Also, the well known Jewish scholar G. Scholem and biologist A. Portmann are among the important figures who came under his influence.

In particular, Corbin's exposition of "oriental ontology", in particular that of Suhrawardi, stimulated much interest among the philosophical movement in France known as the "young philosophers." The main figure in this movement is Christian Jambet, who took interest in the oriental philosophy of Suhrawardi with emphasis on "oriental logic."[43]

Finally, Corbin's influence in the Arab world, in particular the former French colonies, is significant. A number of Arab scholars were directly influenced by Corbin's writings, such as M. Arkhoun, the Algerian Islamicist. The *ishraqi* school of Suhrawardi, which contained both mystical and rationalistic concepts was well received by both the Eastern and Western regions of the Islamic world. The well established mystical traditions of the Indo-Pakistani sub-continent felt at home with Suhrawardi's esoteric doctrines. Persia and North Africa, centers of rationalistic philosophy, were equally receptive to these elements of Suhrawardi's philosophy of illumination.

Notes

1 For more information on the influence of Sufism and the esoteric doctrine of illumination on Shi'ite Islam see S. H. Naṣr, "The Relationship between Suhrawardi and Philosophy in Persian Culture," *Hamdard Islamicus* 6, no. 4 (Winter 1983): 33–47.

2 For a more complete discussion on Abharī, see H. Corbin, Prolegomena to *Opera* 1, 21, note 29.

3 S.H. Naṣr, "The Spread of the Illuminationist School of Suhrawardi," *Islamic Quarterly* 14 (July-September 1970): 113.

4 Ibid., 114.

5 S.H. Naṣr, "Spiritual Movements, Philosophy and Theology in the Safavid Period," in *The Cambridge History of Iran*, ed. P. Jackson, vol. 6 (Cambridge: Cambridge University Press, 1968– 1991), 672.

6 For more information on this see: *Muntakhabāt-i az āthār-i ḥukamā-yi ilāhī-yi Iran,* ed. S. J. Āshtiyānī (Tehran: Imperial Iranian Academy of Philosophy) 3–61.

7 Mīr Dāmād, *Qabasāt,* (Tehran: Tehran University Press, 1367 A.H.s.), 2–4.

8 *Muntakhabāt-i az āthār-i ḥukamā-yi ilāhī-yi,* Iran, ed. S. J. Āshtiyānī, 9. footnote no.1.

9 For more information on Mīr Dāmād's view of the relationship between time and existence see: Ibid., 40ff.

10 For more information on Tabrīzī and his students see, Lāhījānī, *Sharḥ-i risālat,* with an introduction by J. Humā'ī and S. J. Āshtiyānī.

11 Naṣr, "Spiritual Movements," 689.

12 Ibid., 681.

13 For more information on Mullā Ṣadrā's concept of *wujūd* and *māhiyyah* see: *Muntakhabāti az āthār-i* . . ., 99.ff; and S.J. Āshtiyānī, *Hastī az naẓar-i falsafah wa 'irfān,* 63–95.

14 Āshtiyānī's work, *Hastī az naẓar-i falsafāh wa irfān,* provides an excellent exposition of the two rival schools of Mullā Ṣadrā and Suhrawardi by a traditional master. This work is particularly interesting because there Āshtiyānī provides different interpretations of *aṣālat al-māhiyyah* and *āṣālat al-wujūd.*

15 Ibid., 67.

16 For more information on Mullā Ṣadrā 's criticism of Suhrawardi see his *Sharḥ-i ḥikmat al-ishraq,* 210.

17 Sabziwārī in his poems has stated some of the most profound philosophical issues in the traditional symbolic language of Persian poetry. Most of his poems are *ghazal* and the style is often that of *mathnawī.* For more information see: Sabziwārī, *Dīwān-i ash'ār* (Isfahan: Saqafī press, 1959).

18 Sabziwārī, *Ta'līqāt Sharḥ al-manẓumah,* Nāṣirī Edition (Tehran: Tehran University Press), 7.

19 Sabziwārī's commentary upon the *Asfār* does not include the sections on "essence and accident."

20 *Muntakhabāt-i az āthār-i ḥukamā-yi ilāhī-yi Iran,* p.14.

21 Mīrzā Razavī was a learned scholar and a contemporary of Sabziwārī

who asked Sabziwārī seven questions known as the "*'Ajwibah masā'il Mīrzā Abū'l-Ḥasan Razavī.*" For more information see: *Sabziwārī, Yādbūd-i ṣadumīn sāl-i ḥakīm* (Mashhad University: 1969), 35ff.

22 The word here is "*Kashf wa shuhūd,*" literally meaning "discovery and witnessing." This is another term that is often used to allude to the concept of "knowledge by presence."

23 Sabziwārī, *Yādbūd-i ṣadumīn sāl-i,* 45–49.

24 For a more complete discussion on Shaykhī doctrine and their differences from Suhrawardi, see H. Corbin, *L'Ecole shaikhie en theologie Shi'ite* (Tehran: Imperial Iranian Academy of Philosophy, 1957).

25 Mangol Bayāt, *Mysticism and Dissent* (Syracuse: Syracuse University Press, 1982), 44–45.

26 Āshtiyānī has written numerous commentaries on Mullā Ṣadrā and Suhrawardi, including an anthology on the great *ḥakims* of the last four centuries. His collaboration with H. Corbin and S. H. Naṣr has produced a number of texts on the traditional masters of Islamic philosophy.

27 *The Principles of Epistemology in Islamic Philosophy* is a comparative work on epistemology in which M. Ḥa'irī demonstrates the inadequacies of the existing epistemological theories.

28 For more information on S. H. Naṣr's bibliography see: M. Aminrazavi and Z. Moris, *The Works of Seyyed Hossein Naṣr From 1958 Through April 1993,* (Malaysia, Islamic Academy of Science, 1994).

29 See also Sayyid Athar Abbās Rizvī, *A Socio-Intellectual History of the Isnā 'Ashari Shi'is in India,* (Australia: Ma'rifat Pub., 1986).

30 Ibid., 180.

31 Translated into English by H. Lowe.

32 For a more complete discussion on the history of *ḥikmat* in India see: Rizvī, *Isnā 'Ashari Shi'ism in India;* and Badā'ūnī, *Muntakhab al-tawārīkh,* vol.1, ed. George Ranking (Karachi: Karimsons, 1976–1978), 323–25.

33 H. Ziā'ī, who has edited this book, has also written a valuable introduction to *Anwāriyyah.* There he argues that this work is less significant than Shīrāzī and Shahrazūrī's commentary. Ziā'ī maintains that the significance of *Anwāriyyah* is because Harawi has compared the Indian traditions of wisdom with the *ishraqi* doctrine.

34 Ibid., 15.

35 The influence of Mullā Ṣadrā is still present in India and his works, especially the *Asfār,* are being taught in many traditional *madrasahs.* Suhrawardi's influence, however, is strong among the Zoroastrian community. This is because the *ishraqi* ideas were spread in India by the mysterious 12th century Zoroastrian priest, Āzar Kaywān, who had gone to India from Iran.

36 Suhrawardi, *Opera* 2, 258–259.

37 Ibid.

38 For more information on Shahrazūrī see: M. Mo'īn, *Ta'liqāt-i chahār maqālah,* Lyton Press, 211 and M. Mo'īn "Ḥikmat ishraqi wa farhang-i Iran," in *Majmūa'-yi maqālāt,* vol.1, 436, and in *Kashf al-ẓunūn,* vol.1, 913.

39 S. H. Naṣr, "The Spread of the Illuminationist School of Suhrawardi," *Islamic Quarterly* 14, no. 1 (1970): 118.

40 Ibid., 119.

41 For more information on the presence of *ishraqi* ideas in Aleppo and its influence on the development of Jewish illuminationist thought see the work by Maimonides' great-great grandson which is translated and commented by Paul Fenton in *Deux Traitès de mystique juive,* (Paris: 1987).

42 S.H. Naṣr ed., *Jashn nāmah-yi Henry Corbin,* (Tehran: Imperial Academy of Philosophy, 1977), 100.

43 For more information on the influence of Corbin on the young philosophers see the introduction that Christian Jambet has written to Corbin's introduction of the *ḥikmat al-ishrāq.*

6

CONCLUDING REMARKS

Before concluding this work, it is necessary to respond to the criticism of some scholars who have regarded Suhrawardi's works as having been strongly influenced by nationalistic sentiments. They have gone so far as to accuse him of belonging to the Shu'ūbiyyah,[1] a Persian nationalistic movement of the third century A.H. This intellectual movement was led by a group of Persian poets, philosophers, literary figures and scientists reacting to the Arab oppression of Persians and their sophisticated cultural sensitivities during the Abbasid dynasty. Later referred to as the Shu'ūbiyyah, this movement intended to confront Arab supremacy with the revival of the pre-Islamic Persian culture and religious values. It has been argued that Suhrawardi's *ishraqi* school represents this stream of Persian nationalism for which it provided the philosophical framework. It is true that there are those who accuse the Arabs of inability to fully appreciate speculative thought such as we find in the *al-Bayān wa'l-tabyīn*[2] of Jāḥiẓ or Sa'd ibn Aḥmad, who in his book *Tabaqāt al-umam*[3] argues that philosophical thinking has never been appreciated among the Arabs. The most scathing attack comes from Taqī al-Dīn Aḥmad ibn 'Alī Maqrizī, who wrote in his *al-Khaṭāṭ*[4] that while Arabs might be capable of appreciating philosophical discourse, their genius lies in other domains.

This view, which tends to attribute a relative absence of philosophical tradition among the Arabs compared to the Persians, is rejected by Ibn Khaldūn who attributes the interest or disinterest of a society in philosophical issues to its socio-political and geographical location. There are also those Persians who have defended the philosophical and cultural acumen of the Arabs. For instance, Shahrastānī, the celebrated rationalist, says in his book *al-Milal wa'l-niḥal*,[5] that in fact, the Arabs possess a type of wisdom that is far superior to that of other nations. This type of wisdom manifests itself in numerous narratives, expressions, hyperbolic and metaphorical statements.

The unfortunate fact remains that despite Suhrawardi's praise for the other traditions of wisdom which we have reviewed earlier in this work, he has been accused of being a nationalist even by such famous scholars as Muhammad 'Alī Abū Rayyān, who states in his *Tārīkh al-fikr al-falsafī fi'l-Islam* that Suhrawardi has been one of the Shu'ūbiyyah.[6]

To accuse Suhrawardi of nationalism is to misunderstand him completely. The school of illumination which he advocated argues for the universality of truth to which everyone has equal access, provided they are willing to undergo the process of purification and illumination. Suhrawardi would argue that truth is not an exclusive property of Persians, nor of anyone else, and to argue as such is contrary to the spirit of the *ishraqi* school. In fact, Suhrawardi argues that *ḥikmat* originated from Hermes and through Egypt came to Persia where it became united with the other branch of wisdom of Persian origin. Suhrawardi's use of Zoroastrian symbolism, as well as the symbolism of other traditions, was intended to demonstrate how all these traditions adhere to the same underlying reality.

Suhrawardi could have argued for his philosophy of illumination within the context of Islam alone, and for that matter Zoroastrian tradition only, but he chose to include other traditions precisely to demonstrate the ecumenical and transhistorical nature of *ishraqi* wisdom. This, plus the fact that Suhrawardi wrote most of his treatises in Arabic, demonstrates that such objections are invalid and stem from a misunderstanding of Suhrawardi's philosophy.

*　　　*　　　*

It is difficult to write a conclusion that does justice to the vast corpus of philosophical concepts, theological arguments, mystical assertions and the profoundly esoteric and yet rationally justifiable philosophical school of Suhrawardi. Rarely has such a vast domain of ideas and concepts been synthesized into a philosophical paradigm.

Suhrawardi first discusses intricacies of the spiritual path in numerous mystical narratives in which he uses traditional Sufi symbolism as well as his own metaphors. His message is not an exclusive theory of truth accessible only to the followers of one path or tradition, but proposes to describe that fountain of life whose origin lies within the realm of divine sapience and runs through various civilizations to benefit all those who thirst for wisdom. Suhrawardi's vast synthesis of philosophy and science, myth and ritual, as well as esoteric teachings and his integration of Hermeticism, Pythagorianism and Zoroastrianism has indeed brought about a unified theory of knowledge which has come to be known as the school of illumination. For these reasons, Suhrawardi's writings should be studied by students of comparative philosophy and religion. Not only does Suhrawardi's ontology provide ingenious and original insights for the analysis of the traditional problems of philosophy, but his mystical narratives offer a symbolic and profound view of human nature.

Suhrawardi showed how the wisdom of illumination includes discursive reasoning and asceticism but is not limited to them. He is distinguished from the Muslim thinkers who came before him by his synthesis of philosophy and mysticism, whose integration he considers provides the human condition for the attainment of truth.

Notes

1 Shu'ūbiyyah was a 3/9 movement among Persian intellectuals, poets and artists who opposed the domination of Persians by Arabs. This nationalisitc movement made an attempt to revive Persian language, culture and Zoroastrian religion, which were identified with the golden era of the Persian empire.
2 Jāḥiẓ, *Al-Bayān wa'l-tabyīn*, Cairo, 1984.
3 Ṣā'id ibn Aḥmad, *Ṭabaqat al-umam*, Beirut: Dar al-Ma'ārifah, 1912.
4 Taqī al-Dīn Aḥmad ibn 'Alī Maqrizī, *al-Khaṭāt* (N.P.).
5 Shahrastānī, *al-Milal wa'l-niḥal*, Beirut: Daral-Ma'rifah Press, 1990, 253.
6 Muḥammad 'Alī Abū Rayyān, *Tārīkh al-fikr al-falsafī fi'-Islam* (N.P.), 18.

7

APPENDIX

This is the translation[1] of a treatise called *Sharḥ-i āwāz-i par-i Jibrā'īl* (*A Commentary Upon the Chant of Gabriel's Wing*).[2] The commentary was written in Persian by an unknown author of Persian origin who lived in India in the 14th century.[3] The text was written by the philosopher-mystic, Suhrawardi, in the 12th century and discusses metaphorically some of the medieval philosophical themes such as the hierarchy of the intellects and its relationship with angels, the problem of emanation of multiplicity from unity, form and matter, and finally the relationship between philosophy and the spiritual path.

The present translation is significant because it presents an example of Suhrawardi's writings, in particular one of his most esoteric treatises. This treatise also provides us with an insight into the medieval cosmology, ontology and the macrocosm-microcosm correspondance upon which Suhrawardi so extensively elaborates. Second, the commentary of the author is important since it decodes some of the esoteric symbols and brings out the intricacies and the more hidden and unfamiliar symbols of this work. Thirdly, this commentary is important from a historical point of view not only because it represents a 7/13 text but it also indicates that as early as the 7/13, only two centuries after Suhrawardi's death, his works had traveled from Syria to India. This is an indication that Suhrawardi must have had followers who propagated his philosophy after his death and that his thoughts were well received by the intellectual communities of the lands in between. This may also explain the presence of so many *ishraqi* texts in the libraries of India, in particular in Petna.[4]

TRANSLATION

Commentator: Once[5] I was studying the treatise "*The Chant of Gabriel's Wing*," which is one of the Treatises of the learned discoverer, Shahāb al-Dīn, the martyr; peace be upon him. There are numerous mysteries and signs therein that not everyone can undersand. [Since] those problems were solved for me, I wanted to write a commentary so everyone may understand. May God help me.

Suhrawardi: I once flew from the women's court, and freed myself from some of the bondages of the childhood court.

Commentary: I became detached from impurities[6] of the world of forms implies a father-son relationship with this world, because this is a place of pleasure and natural desires. When he said, "I freed myself from some of the bondages of childhood," he is referring to the external senses. By saying "some of", he refers to the internal senses since the internal senses are the means of understanding and recollecting the universals through the particulars.

S: One night darkness had settled in sky and a darkness that had held the hand of the brother of non-existence had been scattered around the lower world.

C: The non-existence (*'adam*) and annihilation (*fanā*) of the sensible world can be understood by the inner eye. Disappointment came after engagement since absence of engagement is associated with night.

S: After sleep came upon me, disappointment resulted.

C: I became disillusioned with sense perception in that being asleep is indeed being drowned in the material attachments. Once awakened from that sleep, they [the senses] become conscious of the incorporeal world, discover the unseen and master the true reality. As Imam Ali, God's grace be upon him, said: "People die so they may ascend."[7] Therefore, consciousness of the incorporeal world is contingent upon dying from the world of form. The master of the worlds [Muḥammad], peace be upon him, in a famous *ḥadith* has said, "Die a true death before you die a natural death."[8]

If thou die before thy natural death.
Be content that the eternal heaven is yours.

S: I was holding a candle.

C: The candle is the intellect which is the guide and the master of mankind. [It is] the light of guidance that takes man from the depth of subsistence to the height of prosperity as is indicated in various verses of the Quran, *ḥadīth* and the sayings of Imām 'Alī that for the sake of briefness I have not mentioned.

S: I aimed towards the man's abode and searched until dusk.

C: Once I freed myself from the abode of women, which signifies worldly attachments, I then aimed at the mens court which alludes to the incorporeal and the angelic world.[9] It is here that the path towards the incorporeal world begins, since the rising of the morning sun requires divine grace and so is shining of the incorporeal light.

S: The yearning to enter into the *khānaqāh* (Sufi house) of father prevailed.

C: In this *khānaqāh* he looks for his "self" and father as the existential cause of his being, which is the intellect. After this search [he wants] to refer to the father as the cause of his existence. Through entering the *khānaqah*, he seeks esoteric knowledge and contemplates his own ego (*nafs*).

S: The *khānaqah* has two doors, one to the city and the other one to the desert. I went and closed the door that opens to the city and then aimed at the door to the desert.

C: These are the gates of soul and body, just as truth has two doors: one door in the corporeal world and the other one in the incorporeal world. The door that opens to the city represents the world of objects and that which opens to the desert belongs to the world of spirit. When it is said, "I closed the door that opens to the city and went towards the desert," he means he left the sensible world and turned to the spiritual world.

S: Once I looked, I saw ten old masters of sublime beauty sitting in the courtyard.

C: These ten old masters are the ten intellects that are incorporeal substances and free from the impurities of matter. The angels who are the companions of God and intermediaries between the Necessary Being and the human souls were disclosed to me.

S: Their charisma and greatness puzzled me and a sense of wonder came upon me such that I became speechless.

C: They were epitome of beauty and their potential perfection had actualized. By the extent of their charisma and beauty, I was perplexed.

S: With great fear I put my foot forward and went away.

C: I was not worthy yet to unite and converse with them due to the material attachments that remained a veil between us.

S: I intended to greet one master who was in the corner. Due to the humility of his character, he greeted me first and smiled at me such that his wisdom tooth appeared.

C: The old master in the corner is the "Active Intellect" and he is in the corner is because his existence and status comes at the end of all other intellects and he is called the "Final Intellect."[10] It is he who casts form unto the elements and is an intermediary between the Necessary Being and the human souls and in religion is called the "spirit of God" (*Rūh al-qudus*) or "Gabriel." His smile alludes to the discovery of knowledge, and the benefit that one derives from this knowledge is in accordance to one's talent.

S: I asked: "Tell me, where did the noble men come from?" The old master in the corner answered, "We are a group of incorporeal beings who have come from 'the nowhere but prosperous land' (*Nākojā-ābād*)."

C: They have proved their detachment from spaitiality since needing that is an attribute of objects and they are pure spirits, free from substances and heavenly elements. Therefore, "placeless" to which they have alluded, is an attribute or an accident and a category among the ten categories.[11] On "relation", it is said that this is an attribute of things because of its relationship with place.

S: I did not comprehend it and asked, "To which place does this city belong?" He said, "The place to which the index finger cannot point."

C: That which can be demonstrated by the index finger has a point of reference which then must be an object, and as we said they are incorporeal.

S: Thus it became known to me that the old master knows.

C: I came to know of their wisdom through [their knowledge of] the substance of the world.

S: I said "For God's sake, tell me how you spend your time?" He said, "Know that we are tailors and guardians of divine words and that we travel."

C: Through "tailoring," he wants to demonstrate how substances [are imposed] unto forms. It is in accordance with the potentialities of these substances [that they] clothe them as a shirt covers (the body) and the efficient cause is he [the active intellect]. It is this tailoring that brings order to the chain of beings, each one in accordance with its state. Through preserving God's word, sciences and knowledge are emanated from the Necessary Being. It is through wondering that they [intellects] want to spread their grace to all beings.

S: I asked, "Why are those elders who are sitting on that high place, silent?" He replied, "So people like you cannot mingle with them." "I am their tongue," means your intellect is not worthy to be united with theirs. When he said "I am their tongue," he means through my mediation grace is bestowed upon you in accordance with your capacity.

S: I then saw an eleven-layered pot thrown into the desert with some water in it and in the water were some pebbles around which there were a few animals.

C: By the eleven layered pot, he alludes to the world, which has nine heavens and two elements, air and fire, and both are limited by the heavens in as much as they demand the water element. Some pebbles [refers to] the center of the earth and the four elements. He did not say a thirteen layered pot so the substance of water and the center of earth are not within that which limits them completely. And he refers to these eleven layers due to their sphericity, continuity and dominance. When he said a few animals were crawling around the pebbles, he meant the animal species which have a multiplicity of genuses over them such as man, etc. In every genus, there is a multiplicity of types such as Romans, Sudanese, etc. Every type consists of a multiplicity of individuals such as Zayd, Bakr, etc. who reside in the four corners of the earth.

S: On each level of this eleven-layered pot from the upper nine layers, a glowing ball is implanted in them except the second one in which there were many balls, luminous as the path of the Sufis. The first level had no glowing ball.

C: On each of the nine heavens there was implanted a glowing pearl except for the eighth heaven, in which there were many pearls implanted,[12] and the ninth heaven was devoid of pearls, meaning the supreme heaven. The reason they call it the first and second heaven is because it requires the eighth and ninth heaven which is the zodiac. The supreme heaven, whose understanding comes through the inner eye, is dominant over heavenly bodies. That which is the ninth heaven for us is his [the old master] first one, etc.

S: Despite this, the entity was more sphere-shaped than any sphere and on its surface there was no crack or hole.

C: The heavenly spheres were absolutely round and a straight line could not have been [drawn] between them.

S: Those eleven levels were colorless and due to their extreme fineness, what was in them could not be veiled.

C: They were colorless so their concave surface could be distinguished from convex in that there are impurities in the concavity that prohibits vision from occurring. We see all these heavens through the first heaven while they shine from the eighth heaven that is zodiac. Therefore, it became apparent that the absence of a veil among heavens is due to the fineness that exists in their substance, that is their luminosity and colorlessness.

S: The upper nine [heavens] should not be pierced and the two layers below should be peeled with ease.

C: When he said the nine should not be punched he wants no harm or damage inflicted upon the heavens. The learned men have concrete reasons for why the nature of heavenly bodies are irreparable and this short work is inadequate for this discussion. When he says "The levels below are easily worthy to being torn" he alludes to the coming together of the spheres of fire and air, for when can softness accept divisibility?

S: I asked the Master, "What is this entity?" He replied, "In the first one, whose mass is more intense than other levels, the grand Master who is sitting above all has given his order and on the second one, the second master and so on until it reaches me. These companions and nine friends have done this due to their will to create. The following two levels below (that contain) water and a piece of sand are my creation.

C: Know that the higher the level, the more superior [its corresponding] heaven is and the master above this is the first intellect, whose effect is the supreme heaven. The second level is emanated by the second intellect and so on. Therefore, from this it became apparent that these nine heavens are emanated by nine intellects and the lower heaven with water and sand is caused by the active intellect.

Treatment (*tanbīḥ*): Know that the *ḥakīms* have said that pure intellect existed in the beginning and emanated from the Necessary Being and had three characteristics: First, that its essence was its substance, second, that it was a Necessary Being from a causal point of view, third, it is a contingent being from the point of view of its nature. Therefore, due to the principality of its substance, the first intellect came to be that which is called "universal intellect."

Due to its existence, which is caused, the second intellect came to be and from the point of its possibility that is due to its essence, the first heaven came to be which they call "grand heaven", "determinator of direction", "universal body", "sphere of Atlas", "mean longtitude", "nobel throne".

From the second intellect a third intellect and soul and heaven appeared and so on until it reached the last intellect. So, every intellect is the cause of three events, another intellect, soul and heaven which belongs to it except the "active intellect" which is the cause of the four elements which are the instruments of [the coming into existence] of the created order and corruptions.

S: Since their willpower is superior, their creation can not be destroyed, however, that which is my creation can be damaged.

C: The rotation of the heavens is due to their inner yearing such as the substance of the elements which is explained elsewhere.

S: I asked, "How are these masters related to you?" He said, "Know that the master whose prayer rug is on the top, is the master of the second one who is sitting next to him. The same with the second, third and fourth until myself. The ninth master has initiated me, given me the *khirqah*[13] and has taught me.

C: The master who is on the top is the "first intellect," and by referring to the second master as the teacher, he is referring to the existential cause of the second intellect and so on until it reaches the active intellect. And the one who said the ninth master initiated him is saying that the master is the existential cause of his presence.[14]

S: I asked, "Do you have children, property and so on?" He said, "We do not have wives but each of us has a child and a mill and we assigned each child to one mill so he may look after it.

C: Absence of wives is separation from matter, children are heavenly souls and the mill is the ninth heaven and the four substances. Stating that each child was assigned to a mill means each soul was placed in a heavenly body that is exclusive to it.

S: Until we build mills, we never looked at them.

C: The reason for not looking at them is their incorporeal nature.

S: Each of our children is working at a mill or a building. Each sees the mill with one eye and sees the father with another.

C: Meaning that each one influences his own work and due to their [desire] for subsistence they are the cause of themselves and this is in accord with science and their quiddity is influential in the rotation of the heavens. This is the reason its relation to ego (*nafs*)[15] is like that of a son to a father in that intellect is the cause of the existence of the ego since its existence is contingent upon the existence of the intellect and not vice versa. As in a father, also it is the case that the existence of one is contingent upon the existence of the other one and not the reverse. In a father and son it is refelected that [the term] father can be said only when there is a son and son can only be if there is a father.

S: My mill has four levels and my children are many and although they may be intelligent they cannot be counted.

C: The four levels are referred to as the four substances[16] which are emanated from the "active Intellect." Various children represent the material forms that seek to overcome the substances through the generation and the corruption that uncovers one appearance and clothes another. There are many things such as air that disown their own appearances and accept the form of fire and vice versa or water that disowns its own form and accepts the form of air. These various faces of appearance are beyond any limit.

S: Whenever I have a child I send him to my mill and each one is given a period to be in charge of the place. Once they serve their time, they come to me and do not leave me and the new children that are attained go there.

C: These children are the appearances that are to be imposed upon the substances of the world. Limited time means the duration that these appearances remain [imposed] unto the substances. The appearance of each form of a substance from [existing] substances and its duration upon matter is determined in that its subsistence depends on its elevation beyond obstacles and the sum of its conditions. When the necessary condition disappears or a problem occurs, the duration of its life [imposition of form upon matter] comes to an end. When it was said that once their time is terminated they come to me and do not leave me [he meant] it is impossible for that which has perished to return since "that which perishes does not only perish in appearance." This means once a change occurs in a compound (*murakkab*) [substance], each simple (*basīṭ*) [substance] yearns towards its natural state and therefore that form accepts corruption and thereby [wants] to return to its origin and its return is no longer possible. With new children, new appearances follow the corrupted forms through emanation.

S: The other old masters, however, have only one child who is responsible for a mill, and who continuously affirms his mastery of that place.

C: Meaning that the souls that influence the heavens are permanent, contrary to the forms that are corruptible [and from which] new forms result.

S: One of [their] children is stronger than one of [my] children. The help [my] children receive in [their] mill is from their children.

C: That strong child is the "archetypal ego" (*nafs-i kulli*) which is caused by the "first intellect." Just as the first intellect influences other intellects, the first ego influences other egos. When he said "the aids in the mill are my children," he means the souls that are descendants of the Original Soul are effective in the creation of forms.

S: [I said] how does this birth and reproduction in accordance with being a bachelor occur? He said, "Know that my state does not change and I have no mate except a Sudani's maid whom I never look upon. No motion emanates from me except that which is focused in the center of the mill and the black maid's sight lies in the rotation of the heavens. Whenever during the rotation, the eyes of the black maid gaze upon me, from me a child is conceived in her womb without causing any change or motion [in me].[17]

C: Non-existence of his archetype is apparent here. By depicting a black Sudani's maid, [he shows] how matter is separated from form and by attributing blackness to her [he wants to] show "non-existence", meaning matter cannot exist without form. Absence of motion in the old master is necessary since motion is one of the properties of matter. And when he said that his attention was on the rotation of the mill [he] means that he expects the emanation of form from one who bestows form [upon matter] (*wāhib al-ṣuwar*). And when he said whenever in my presence a child is conceived in her womb, [he] means, whenever it [matter] becomes worthy [of receiving a form], from me the giver of form, a form will be bestowed upon that matter.

S: I said, "How is this view and worthiness conceived?" He said, "The purpose of these words is none other than worthiness and ability.

C: He means that these words are worthy of these meanings we have stated. That is, understanding of the intellect with our corporeal self is not conceivable but that such potentiality and worthiness of matter necessitates form.

S: I asked the old master, "How is it that you have descended to this state having claimed that no change or motion occurred within you?"[18] He replied, "Oh, pure hearted, the sun is always in the heavens but if a blind man does not have the consciousness to understand and experience its state, the absence of this ability does not cause the absence of the sun in its position. If the inability of a blind man vanished, he could not complain to the sun, "Why you were not present in the world before and did not benefit me?" The sun has always been moving and change has been in the blind man and not the sun. We are always in the same state; your not seeing us is not a reason that we do not exist and is not an indication that we undergo change in your state.

C: The purpose of all these words is that the grace and benefit which are spiritual essences continuously emanate upon the worthy. There is no jealousy and if one does not benefit from their grace is not because of the absence of their grace but is his inability and lack of attention to the [spiritual] world and his engagement within the world of the sensibles.

S: I asked the old master to teach me the art of tailoring. He smiled and said: "Oh, shadows and your type cannot learn and such beings as you cannot master this. However, you will be taught enough so you may make something from your cloth. And this much he taught me.

C: As I indicated in the beginning of the treatise, "tailoring" consists of imposing form upon matter, and man does not have the ability to comprehend this. By saying, "you will be taught enough so you may construct a building," he is alluding to the science of medicine and body as a theurgy or a building. He said to turn your Sufi dress into a building, and did not say sewing which is the composition of the form and matter since that is not what he can do; it was previously discussed.

S: I asked the master to teach me the word of God. He said: "It is inconceivable for you to learn much about God as long as you live in this city."

C: As long as you are in the world of sensibles you will not know the universals and the truth of all the sciences.

S: The master said, "I will teach you in accordance with your ability." He took my tablet and taught me a strange mantra such that with it I could know every secret I desired.

C: Tablet is the common sense and by "word" he means logic is relative to the world of knowledge (*ḥikmat*).[19] By saying, "I could solve any problems I wanted," he means that any problem he encountered in science, he could resolve using logic as a criterion.

S: The master said: "Anyone who does not come to know of this secret will not know the secrets of the divine word as he [God] necessitated, and he who knows this word attains inner peace."

C: This means that anyone who has not studied logic cannot distinguish between right and wrong since knowledge requires composition of inferences and construction of analogies and inferring conclusions so the unknown becomes known, and all these are clarified through logic.

S: After that I learned the science of letters (*abjad*)[20] and my "tablet" was beautified by it such that I gained power and went beyond matter, and then from divine word many mysteries appeared to me that are beyond any limit or comparison.

C: The science of letters refers to the science of *ḥikmat* and *Abjad* stands with respect to the worldly sciences. The tablet after it has attained the secret, discovers the science and knowledge and they [the old masters] call this the science of transcendence (*ladunīyyah*) through which the hidden secrets in this science reveal themselves and this has no limit.

S: Every time a problem was posed, I offered it to the master and the problem was solved.

C: This means that every time two analogous situations arose in my mind, I relied on the intellectual world so the result of that analogy through the path of grace, from the giver of forms, would emanate upon me.

S: Often we discussed the "blowing of the spirit." The master pointed that it emanates from the holy spirit.

C: The souls of animals and illuminated beings are numerous and are emanated from the active intellect.

S: I asked the master, "How is this order?" He said, "Know that God Almighty has many supreme words and those words are illuminated and the center of some is above that of others."

C: These "words" refer to the intellects, meaning that the essences are luminous intellects which are numerous and are emanated from the Necessary Being, the most high. Some are above others in their dignity and status, though not spatially.

S: The first Light is the supreme word beyond which there is no superior one. The relation between this in luminosity and apparentness with other words is like the sun to other planets.

C: The first Light is the "first intellect", and no status amongst beings is higher than this.

S: The master said, "From the ray of this word, another word was attained."

C: This means the "first intellect" is the cause of the "second intellect" and the second [is cause of] the third and so on until a perfect number which is ten was attained. God said, "Ten is perfect."

S: The word is useless.[21]

C: This means that his grace is continuously descending upon those who are worthy of it.

S: At the end of these words is Gabriel and the soul of men from this world is the last.

C: It is clear that Gabriel is the last intellect in rank and that the souls of men belong to him and this has been illustrated.

S: [the original manuscript is not clear]

C: For instance, once the conception is complete in the womb and [fetus] becomes worthy of [receiving] a human form from the "active intellect" a soul emanates so it may be united with it.

S: I said, "Tell me of Gabriel's wing." He said, "Know that Gabriel has two wings: one is the right wing and that is pure light. That wing is its incorporeal existence and a relation [*iḍafā*] to truth. There is a wing to the left which indicates the darkness such as the dark spots on the moon. It resembles the feet of peacocks and that is the sign of its existence which is juxtaposed to the non-existent. Once you see the relation between its existence and the existence of truth, it does have the attribute of existence. If you look at the worthiness of its essence, it is worthy of non-existence. These two concepts are like two wings; the added (attributes) are due to a grace from the east, and the possibility of self subsistence from the west.

C: We have indicated before that the first Intellect contains three entities and it is because of each of them that something is emanated. Here, by saying the "wing of Gabriel", he means two characteristics. One is "necessary", meaning that if you look at its cause, you will find a necessary being due to the presence of its cause and this was what the master was alluding to when he said: "It is from pure Light and incorporeality which is its relational existence to that truth and it is this necessity that is the attribute of truth. The other attribute is possibility, meaning if you look at its essence it is contingent." The master is alluding to this when he says, "Its sign is darkness such as the dark spots on the moon and that darkness is the sign of contingency." He attributes darkness to contingency since non-existence comes from a contingency and because of this it was said: "If you look at the worthiness of its essence, it is worthy of non-existence." It is these two concepts that are like two wings: the east [wing] is an attribute of truth which is "necessary" and the west [wing] is an attribute of himself and that is contingency and [therefore] non-existence.

S: As God almighty has stated: "The angels were sent [in sets of] twos, threes and fours."[22] The closest number to one is two, then three and four. Indeed that which has two wings is more virtuous than that which has three and four. In the science of reality and visionary discovery there is much to elaborate on this but not everyone can understand it.

C: All this means that if multiplicity would decrease, closeness to the source of unity would increase and once closeness intensifies, so does virtuosity. It is for this reason that he said, "That which has two wings is more virtuous than that which has three and four." When he said, "In the sciences and discoveries, not everyone can understand," he means that the virtuosity of that which has two wings is different than that which has three wings and that which has three wings to that which has four and so on. Indeed, not everyone can understand the truth.

S: The world of ego is the shadow of Gabriel which is emanated from his left wing, and the illuminated souls come from his right wing.

C: This means that the corporeal and corruptible worlds come from his contingent nature since they are perishable, and human souls are emanated from the aspect of its necessity because it is not perishable.

S: The realities which come to mind as it is said, "It was written within their hearts with faith, and we blow unto them from our spirit,"[23] and the voice of the angel [who said] "We called upon him, oh Ibrahim."[24] Other than these are the sound of Gabriel's wing.

C: It has become apparent that Gabriel is the intermediary between the Necessary Being and human souls and it is because of this that revealing the truth through divine voice, is his task.

S: Vengeance and the occurrence of events are also from Gabriel's voice.

C: It thus became known that it is he who influences the world of permanence and corruption and it is here that events occur. Therefore, everything is due to his influence.

S: I asked, "Finally, what does this Gabriel look like?" He said, "Oh, you ignorant one, do you not know that all these are secrets, if taken exoterically, are useless utterances?"

C: He (Gabriel) has a face and voice that cannot be identified; however, he uses [human] language so the masses may understand.

S: I was in the Sufi house when the "good day" occurred; they closed the exterior door and opened the door of the city. The merchant entered and the group of elders disappeared from my sight. Of their absence I remained wondrous.

C: Once worldly engagements prevailed over disengagement and the exterior door, which is the world of spirit, was closed, the city, which represents the material world, became dominant. The merchants who are the bodily functions, meaning the sense perceptions, took over. He alluded to them as merchants since they are the ones who plant the seeds of understanding the particulars so the result can be the universals. When he said, "The elders disappeared from my sight", he means that once drawn into the sensible world, the Intellect is turned away.

Suffering that results from the absence of the observation of the intelligible world and incorporeal essences is necessary.

Notes

1 This translation is based on the version that Mas'ūd Ghāsimī has edited. The article has appeared in: "Sharḥ-i āwāz-i par-i Jibra'īl" in *Ma'ārif*, no.1, (March 1985): 77–99.

2 This work represents one of the masterpieces of Suhrawardi's Persian writings. For a complete version of this mystical narrative see: Suhrawardi, *Opera* 3, 208–223.

3 Not much is known about the author's life except that he must have been affiliated with a spiritual order and has practiced the *ishraqi* doctrine. The author's commentary indicates that he was well versed in the *ishraqi* tradition and its symbolism.

4 One can find a great depository of such texts in India. For example, in Rezā library in Rampur and in Khudabakhsh library in Patna there are a great deal of *ishraqi* texts. Spreng, the German scholar who in the 19th century traveled to India had brought 1966 texts in Arabic, Persian and Hindi back to Germany, many of which are commentaries on *The Philosophy of Illumination. Catalogue of the Biblioetheca orientalis Sprengerianna* (Gillssun: Wilhelm Keller, 1857).

5 The treatise begins with several verses of the Quran which are not translated. The verses are: *Quran*, XI, 96–XXIV, 35; and XXXVI, 56.

6 Suhrawardi and the commentator both use the word *kidr* meaning that which does not allow light to pass through it easily.

7 Ajhalūnī, in the *Kashf al-khifā'*, has attributed this saying to Imām Alī. See: V.2, 312. However, Sha'rānī in his *Ṭabaqāt* has attributed this saying to the famous Sufi, Sahl Ṭustarī.

8 Ibn Ḥājar considered this *Ḥadīth* to be a saying of the Sufi masters and not the prophet himself. See: *Kashf al-khifā'*, v.2, 291.

9 For more information on Suhrawardi's angelology see: G. Webb, The Human/Angelic Relation in the Philosophies of Suhrawardi and Ibn 'Arabī (Ph.D. Diss., Temple Univ., 1989).

10 Suhrawardi believes that the first being God created was the "first intellect" (*al-'aql al-awwal*). His argument is partially based on the Quranic verse that states: "The first intellect then emanates the active intellect which he identifies with the 'giver of form' (*wāhib al-ṣuwar*) or 'luminous old master' (*Pīr-i rūḥānī*)."

11 By the ten categories he is referring to the Aristotelian categories. Suhrawardi reduces these categories to five, which are quantity, quality, essence, relation and motion. Adding motion to the Aristotelian categories is Suhrawardi's original contribution, which later on in Mullā Ṣadrā's philosophy became the basis of the theory of "Transsubstantial Motion" (*al-ḥarikat al-jūwhariyyah*).

12 In the text it is phrased "meaning the eighth heaven", which the editor has judged to be erroneous and should be "supreme heaven."

13 *Khirqah* or the Sufi dress is a long and white cloth often made of rough materials which the spiritual master offers to the novice at the time of initiation.

14 "Presence" is a key concept in the *ishraqi* doctrine and is used in two different contexts. First, it is used within the context of emanation

meaning the world is the result of an emanation, and second it is the theory of knowledge by presence, which lies at the heart of Suhrawardi's theory of knowledge. For more information see Mehdī Ḥā'irī Yazdī, *The Principles of Epistemology in Islamic Philosophy: Knowledge by Presence*, with a forward by S.H. Nasr (New York: SUNY Press, 1992).

15 The word *nafs* here translated as "ego" has a pejorative meaning in Islam which Suhrawardi argues is subservient to intellect in the order of creation but often rebels against it.

16 The four substances are fire, water, earth, wind, which some of the pre-Socratics argued constitute the primordial substance from which the world was created.

17 The material world for Suhrawardi represents non-existence (*'adam*). This non-existence should not be mistaken with non-existing but it should be regarded as the anti-pole to the light of lights. The female character is the world of senses that is identified with the material world. What Suhrawardi is alluding to here is that the divine essence can create the existent objects without change being introduced into his essence.

18 The relationship between change and permanence has been a central issue in Islamic philosophy. God, by nature changeless, has emanated a world that undergoes change. Suhrawardi, in the tradition of Ibn Sīnā, wants to argue that presence of change does not necessitate that the cause of this change must also undergo change.

19 The commentator does not use the word *ḥikmah* in a consistant fashion, sometimes using it to mean knowledge and other times refers to a particular tradition of wisdom as opposed to the peripatetic philosophy.

20 The science of letters is based on a synthesis of Pythagorean mathematics and the belief that each letter of alphabet represents a sacred mathematical number. This field, which in Islam is referred to as *Jafr*, is also prevalent in Judaism and Medieval Christianity.

21 The word here is *ṭāmmāt* which also means a "prodigious event" or a great suffering which will come on the day of judgment. It is not clear in what context Suhrawardi used it.

22 Quran, XXXV: 1.

23 Quran, LVIII: 22.

24 Quran, XXXVII: 104.

Selected Bibliography

Aristotle. *Posterior Analytics.* New York: Random House, 1941.

Averroes. *Tahāfut al-tahāfut.* Translated by S. Van den Bergh. London: Luzac and Co., 1954.

Badā'ūnī. *Muntakhab at-tawārikh.* Vol. 1, Edited by George Ranking. Karachi: Karimsons, 1976–1978.

Bayat, Mangol. *Mysticism and Dissent.* New York: Syracuse University Press, 1982.

Brown, E.G. *A Literary History of Persia,* 4 vols. London: T. Fishter Unwin, 1902–1924; and Cambridge: Cambridge University Press, 1951.

Burckhardt, T. *Alchemie, Sinn und Weltbild.* Olten: Walter-Verlag, 1960.

Bylebly, Michael, "The Wisdom of Illumination: A Study of the Prose Stories of Suhrawardi." Ph.D. Diss, University of Chicago, 1976.

Chittick, W.C. *Jalāl al-Dīn Rūmī. The Path of Love: The Spiritual Teachings of Rumi.* New York: New York State University Press, 1983.

—— "The Works of Seyyed Hossein Naṣr Through his Fortieth Birthday." University of Utah: Middle East Center, Research Monograph 6, 1977.

Corbin, H. *L'archange empourprée.* Paris: Fayand, 1976.

—— *Avicenna and the Visionary Recital.* Texas: Spring Pub., 1980.

—— *Creative Imagination in the Sufism of Ibn 'Arabī.* Princeton: Princeton Press, 1969.

—— *En Islam iranien,* vol. 2. Paris: Gallinard, 1971.

—— *L'Ecole shaikhie en theologie Shi'ite.* Tehran: Imperial Iranian Academy of Philosophy 1957.

—— *Mundus Imaginalis or the Imaginary and the Imaginal.* Translated by Ruth Horine. Ipswich: Golgonooza Press 1976.

—— *The Man of Light in Iranian Sufism.* Boulder and London: Shambala, 1978.

—— *Rawābit-i ḥikmat-i ishrāq wa falsafah dar Iran-i bāstān.*

—— *Racueil de textes inedits concernant l'histoire de la mystique en pays d'Islam.* Paris: 1929.

—— *Spiritual Body and Celestial Earth.* Princeton: Princeton Press, 1978.

Corbin, H., in collaboration with S.H. Naṣr, and O. Yaḥyā. *Histoire de la philosophie islamique.* Paris: Gallimard, 1964.

Dānāseresht, Akbar. *Afkār-i Suhrawardi wa Mullā Ṣadrā.* Tehran: Tehran University Press, 1939.

de Boer, T.J. *The History of Philosophy in Islam*, Paris: P. Geuthner, 1921–1926.

Dīnānī, Ghulām Husayn. *Shua'ī andīsha wa shuhūd dar falsafa-yi Suhrawardi.* Tehran: Ḥikmat Pub., 1985.

Gilson, E. *History of Christian Philosophy in the Middle Ages.* New York: Random House, 1955.

Habibi, N. *Si Risālah az shaykh-i ishrāq.* Tehran: Imperial Academy of Philosophy Press, 1975.

Ḥā'irī, Mehdī. *The Principles of Epistemology in Islamic Philosophy: Knowledge by Presence.* New York: SUNY Press, 1992.

Harawī, Aḥmad ibn. *Anwāriyyah.* Tehran: Amīr Kabīr Press, 1980.

Heidegger, M. *Poetry, Language, Thought.* Translation and Introduction by A. Hofstadter. New York: Harper and Row, 1971.

Hourānī, G., ed. *Essays on Islamic Philosophy and Science.* Albany: SUNY Press, 1975.

Ibn, Abī Uṣaybi'ah. *Tabaqāt al-aṭibbā'.* Edited by A. Muller. Kōnigsberg Press, 1884.

Ibn Sīnā. *Kitāb al-ishārāt wa'l-tanbīhāt.* Edited by M. Shahābī. Tehran: Tehran University Press, 1939.

—— *Manṭiq al-Mashraqīyīn.* Tehran: Ja'farī Tabrīzī Pub. House, 1973.

—— *Risālat Ḥayy ibn Yaqẓān.* Edited by Aḥmad Amīn. Egypt: Dār al-Ma'ārif Pub., 1966.

Imām, Kāẓim S.M. *Falsafah dar Iran-i bāstān wa mabānī-yi ḥikmat-i ishrāq.* Tehran: Nourani Found., 1974.

Iqbal, M. *The Development of Metaphysics in Persia.* London: Luzac, 1908.

Izutsi, T. "The Basic Structure of Metaphysical Thinking in Islam." In *Collected Papers on Islamic Philosophy and Mysticism*, ed. M. Mohaqheqh and H. Landolt. Tehran: Imperial Iranian Academy of Philosophy, 1971.

Izutsu, T. Introduction to *Sharḥ-i manẓumah*, by Sabzawārī, ed. M. Mohaghegh and T. Izutsu. Tehran: 1969.

—— *Metaphysical Structure of Sabzawārī.* New York: Caravan Books, 1977.

Lāhījī, 'Abdu'l Razzāq. *Gawhar murād.* Bombay: 1923.

—— "Risālah nūriyah dar 'Alam-i mithāl." In *Majilla-yi illāhiyāt wa ma'ārif Islamī.* Mashhad: Mashhad University Press, 1972.

Madkour, I. *Fi'l-falsafat al-islāmiyyah.* Cairo: Dār Iḥyā' al-Kutub al-'Arabiyyah, 1947.

Marmura, M., ed. *Islamic Theology and Philosophy.* Albany: SUNY Press, 1984.

Michot, J. *Dieu et la destinée de l'homme-ma'ad* chez *Avicenne.* Peetrs: Louvain Publishers, 1987.

Mīr Dāmād, *Qabasāt*, Tehran: Tehran University Press, 1365 A.H.s.

Mo'īn, M. *Majalla-yi āmūzish wa parwarish.* Tehran: Ministry of Education Press, 1924.

Morewedge, P., ed. *Islamic Philosophical Theology.* Albany: SUNY Press, 1979.

Naṣr, S.H. *An Introduction to Islamic Cosmological Doctrine.* New York, SUNY, 1993.

—— *Cosmography in pre-Islamic and Islamic Persia*, Tehran: Cultural Committee Press (monograph), 1971.
—— *Jashn nāmay-i Henry Corbin*. Tehran: Imperial Iranian Academy of Philosophy, 1977.
—— *Knowledge and the Sacred*. New York: Crossroad, 1981.
—— *Oeuvres Philosophiques et Mystiques*, III. Tehran: Académie Imperiale Iranienne de Philosophie, 1977.
—— *Ṣadr al-Dīn Shīrāzī and His Transcendental Theosophy*. Tehran: 1978.
—— *Science and Civilization in Islam*. Cambridge: Islamic Text Society, 1987.
—— *Three Muslim Sages*. Delmar, N.Y: Caravan Books, 1969.
—— *The Islamic Intellectual Tradition in Persia*. ed. M. Aminrazavi, London: CURZON Press, 1996.
Perry, John. *Personal Identity*. Berkeley: University of Berkeley Press, 1975.
Peters, F.E., *Aristotle and the Arabs: The Aristotelian Tradition in Islam*. New York: New York University Press; and London: University of London, 1968.
Plotinus. *Enneads*. Translated by Stephen Mackenna. New York: Pantheon Books, 1969.
Rahman, F. *Prophecy in Islam: Philosophy and Orthodoxy*. Chicago: University of Chicago Press, 1979.
—— *The Philosophy of Mullā Ṣadrā*. Albany, N.Y.: SUNY Press, 1976.
Rahman, F. *Essence and Existence in Avicenna*. Vol. 4, *Medieval and Renaissance Studies*. London: Warburg Institute, 1958.
Rizvī, Saiyid Athar Abbās. *A Socio-Intellectual History of the Isnā 'Asharī Shī'is in India*, 2 vols. Australia: Ma'rifat Pub. House, 1986.
Sabzawārī. *Asrār al-ḥikam*. Tehran: Tehran University Press.
—— *Dīwān-i ash'ār*. Isfahan: Saqafī Press, 1959.
—— *Sharh-i al-manẓūmah*. Nāṣirī Edition. Tehran: Tehran University Press.
Sajjādī, S.J. *Shahāb al-Dīn Suhrawardi wa sayrī dar falsafah-yi ishrāq*. Tehran: Falsafah Press, 1984.
Shīrāzī, Ṣadr al-Dīn. *Ḥashiyah 'alā sharḥ-i ḥikmat al-ishrāq*. Tehran: Chape Sangī Tehran, 1913.
Ṣalībī, Kamāl. *Tārikh Lubnān*, Beirut: Dār al-Nahar Press, 1967.
Schimmel, Annamarie. *Mystical Dimension of Islam*. Chapel Hill: University of North Carolina Press, 1978.
Schuon, F. *From the Divine to the Human*. Translated by G. Polit and D. Lambert. Bloomington, Ind.: World Wisdom Books, 1986.
—— *Survey of Metaphysics and Esotercism*. Translated by G. Polit. Bloomington, Ind.: World Wisdom Books, 1986.
—— *Understanding Islam*. London: George Allen and Unwin Ltd., 1976.
Sharif, M.M. *A History of Muslim Philosophy*. 2 vols., Wiesbaden: Otto Harrassowitz, 1963–66.
Shahrazūrī, Shams al-Dīn Muḥammad. *Nuzhat al-arwāḥ*. Istanbul: Yeni Cami, 1908.
Shīrāzī, Quṭb al-Dīn. *Sharḥ-i ḥikmat al-ishraq*. Tehran: Tehran University Press, 1951.

Shayegan, D. *La Topographie spirituelle de l'Islam iranien.* Edited by Dariush Shayegan. Paris: Editions de la Différence, 1990.

Suhrawardi. *Kalimat al-taṣawwuf.* In *Si risalah az shaykh-i ishrāq*, edited by Najafqulī Ḥabībī. Tehran: Imperial Iranian Academy of Philosophy, 1977.

Suhrawardi. *Kitāb al-Lamaḥāt.* In *Si risalah az shaykh-i ishrāq*, edited by Najaf qulī Ḥabībī. Tehran: Imperial Iranian Academy of Philosophy, 1977.

Suhrawardi. Le Livre de la sagesse orientale. Translation and notes by H. Corbin. Paris: Verdier, 1986.

Suhrawardi. *Opera Metaphysica et Mystical 1.* Edited and Introduction by Henry Corbin. Tehran: Institut d'Etudes et des Recherches Culturelles, 1993.

Suhrawardi. *Opera Metaphysica et Mystical 2.* Edited and Introduction by Henry Corbin, Tehran: Institut d'Etudes et des Recherches Culturelles, 1993.

Suhrawardi. *Opera Metaphysica et Mystical 3.* Edited and Introduction by Seyyed H. Naṣr. Tehran: Institut d'Etudes et des Recherches Culturelles, 1993.

Ṭabāṭabā'ī, Muḥammad Husayn, *Uṣūl-i falsafah wa rawish-i ri'ālism*, Murtaḍā Muṭahharī, 5 vol., Qum 1350/1972.

Tehrānī, Kāẓim. "Mystical Symbolism in Four Treatises of Suhrawardi." Ph.D. Diss., Columbia University, 1974.

Thackston, W.M. *Mystical and Visionary Treatise of Suhrawardi.* London: Octagon Press, 1982.

Ṭūsī. *Kashf al-murād-sharḥ tajrīd al-i'tiqād*, With a Commentary by Hilli. Edited and Translated by Abu'l-Ḥasan Sha'rānī. Tehran: 1351/1872.

Webb, G. *The Human/Angelic Relation in the Philosophies of Suhrawardi and Ibn 'Arabi.* Ph.D. Diss., Temple Univ., 1989.

Wittgenstine, *Lectures and Conversations on Aesthetic Psychology and Religious Belief*, ed. C. Barratt. Berkeley: University of California, 1969.

Yazdī, Mehdī Ḥā'irī. *The Principles of Epistemology in Islamic Philosophy: Knowledge by Presence.* With a forward by S.H. Naṣr. New York: SUNY Press, 1992.

Ziā'ī, H. *Knowledge and Illumination.* Atlanta: Scholars Press, 1990.

—— "*Suhrawardi's Philosophy of Illumination.*" Ph.D. Diss., Harvard University, 1976.

ARTICLES

Burnet, J., "The Socratic Doctrine of the Soul." *Proceedings of the British Academic* 7 (1915–1916).

Carra de Vaux. "La philosophie illuminative d'après Suhrawardi Maqtūl." *Journal Asiatique* 19 (1902): 63–94.

Corbin, H. "Rawābiṭ-i ḥikmat-i ishrāq wa falsafa-yi Iran-i bāstān." *Majillayah-yi anjuman-i Iran shināsī*, no. 3 (1946): 34ff.

Corbin, H. and Paul Kraus, "Traitée du bruissement de l'aile de Gabriel." *Journal Asiatique* (1935): 1–82.

Lloyd, A.C. "Neoplatonic Logic and Aristolian Logic." *Phronesis* 1, no. 1 (November 1955): 58–72; and in *Phronesis* 1, no. 2 (1956): 146–159.

Evans, Robert. "Henry Corbin and Suhrawardi's Angelology." *Hamdard Islamicus* 11, no. 1 (n.d.): 12–20.
Qāsemī. "Sharḥ-i āwāz-i par-i Jibra'īl." *Ma'ārif*, no. 1 (March 1985): 77–99.
Ḥalamī, M.M. "Āthār al-Suhrawardi al-maqtūl taṣnifuhā wa khaṣā'ṣuhā al-taṣawwufiyyāt wa'l-falsafiyyāt." *Kulīyāt al-ā'dāb* 2 (1951): 145–178.
Jurjī, E.J. "The Ishraqi Revival of al-Suhrawardi." *Journal of the American Oriental Society* 60 (1940): 90–94.
Naṣr, S.H. "The Illuministic Sufis." *Journal of the American Oriental Society* 57 (1973): 99–101.
—— "Mufassir-i 'ālam-i ghurbat wa shahīd-i ṭarīq-i ma'ārifat." *Ma'ārif-i islāmī* 10 (Nov. 1970): p. 8–19.
—— "Nukātī chand dar bāra-yi shaykh-i ishrāq." *Ma'arif-i islāmī, n.s.* 1 (Sep. 1967): 16–18.
—— "The Relationship Between Sufism and Philosophy in Persian Culture," *Hamdard Islamicus* 6, no. 4 (1983): 33–47.
—— "Spiritual Movements, Philosophy and Theology in the Safavid Period." In Vol. 4, *History of Iran.* Edited by R.N. Fry. Cambridge: Cambridge University Press, 1975.
—— "The Spread of the Illuminationist School of Suhrawardi," *Islamic Quarterly* 14 (1970): 111–121.
Zia'i, H. "The Source and Nature of Political Authority in Suhrawardi's Philosophy of Illumination." In *Political Aspects of Islamic Philosophy*, ed. Butterworth. Cambridge: Harvard University Press, 1992.

INDEX

a priori knowledge. *See* knowledge, *a priori*
Abbasid, 146
Abharī, Athir al-Dīn, 122, 123
Abraham, 18
Abū Rayyān, Muhammad 'Alī, 147
accidental: darkness. *See* darkness, accidental; intellects, 87; accidental light. *See* light, accidental
accident (s) (*lavasim*), 97, 99
Active Intellect. *See* Intellect, Active
Agathadaimons, 10
Ahmad-Abad, 138
Ahmad, Sa'd ibn, 146
Ahrīman, 43
Asḥāī, Shaykh Aḥmad, 135
Ahūrmazdā, 43
Akbar, 138
Akhutas (Archytus), 9
'Alawī, Sayyid Aḥmad, 126
alchemy, 18
'Alī (Imam), 151, 152
'Alī wa'l-ḥikmat al-ilāhiyyah (*'Alī and Divine Wisdom*), 136
Alleppo, 1, 3
Āmulī, Sayyaid Ḥaydar, 123, 124
Āmulī, Shaykh Bahā' al-Dīn (Shaykh Bahā'ī), 126
analytical, 141
Anatolia, 1, 122, 139
ancient wisdom (*ḥikmat al-'atīq*), xv
angelic, 45, 85
angelic order, 46, 47, 82; latitudinal (*'araḍī*), 46, 47, 81, 82; longitudinal (*ṭūlī*), 46, 47, 81, 82
angelic world (*'ālam-i qāhriah*), 88, 152
angelology, xix, xx, 25, 43, 45–47, 81, 83, 84
angel (s), xvi, 46, 81, 86, 150, 162
annihilation (*fana*), 73, 151
annihilation of annihilation (*fana dar fana*), 73
Anwāriyyah, 138
Apprehension (*wahm*), 49
Arab, 146
Arab world, 142
Arabic: grammar, 126; poetry, 126; texts, 7; treatises, 147; works, 8, 95
Arabs, 147; domination over Persia, 4
'Archange empourprée, 7, 9
archetypal ego (*nafs-i kullī*), 158
archetypal world (*'ālam mithāl*), 60, 63, 86, 87–89. *See also* *Mundus Imaginalis*
archetype (s) (*al-mujarradāt*), xvi, 37, 42, 46, 83, 88, 90, 125, 158; of humanity (*rabb al-naw 'al-insān*), 82; of species (*Shahriyār*), 84; Platonic, 42, 46; Plato's, 81, 82, 88; supreme (*hurmūzd*), 82; suspending (*muthul mu'allaqah*), 88
architecture, 126, 127

ghāsaq (corporeal), 79
Guwhar murād, 115
Ghazzālī, Aḥmad, 5, 17, 31, 51, 127, 129
al-Ghurbat al-gharbiyyah (*The Occidental Exile*), 6, 50
Gilānī, Mullā Rafī'a, 127
Gilānī, Mullā Shamsā, 126
gitī (Corporeal world), 84. *See also* Corporeal world
gnosis (*ma'rifah*), 8, 65, 113, 124, 134; Shi'a, 131; Shi'ite, 126, 127, 128
Gnostic (s), xv; 5, 21, 123, 129, Muslim gnostics, 139
God's vicegerent (Khalifat Allah). *See* Vicegerent of God
gradations of Being (*tashkik*), 129
Greater Persia, 121, 122–137
Greek philosophy. *See* philosophy, Greek
Greeks, xv, 6, 50, 51, 75, 125
Grossteste, Robert, 141
Growth (*nāmiyyah*), 49

Ḥadīth, 9, 16, 70, 132, 151, 152; Islamic, 129
Ḥā'irī Yazdī, Mehdī, xvii, 104, 106, 110, 136
ḥakim, ishrāqī. *See ishrāqī, ḥakim*
Ḥakims, 100, 128, 135, 137, 138
al-Ḥallāj, Manṣūr, 5, 10, 31, 60
al-Ḥamawī, Yaqūt ibn 'Abdallah, 1
ḥaqq al-yaqīn, 132
al-Harawi, Aḥmad ibn, 13, 138
Hastī az naẓar-i falsafah wa 'irfān (*Existence from a Philosophical and Gnostic View*), 129–30
Hayākil al-nūr (Luminous Bodies), 8, 15, 40, 95, 123; Dawani's comentary on, 137; Lāhīji's commentary on, 127
hay'at-i ẓulamānī, 79
Haykal, 15, 62
Ḥayy ibn Yaqẓān, 6
Healing (Shifā), 44
Hermes, 4, 10, 52, 60, 147
hermeneutics (*ta'wīl*), 88, 124, 127
Hermetic, 8
Hermeticism, xviii, 6, 148
ḥikmah, xix, 51, 65, 137
ḥikmat, 1, 10, 50–54, 78, 116, 126, 127, 128, 130, 136, 147, 159, 160
Ḥikmat al-'arshiyya (*The Wisdom of the Throne*), 129
al-Ḥikmat al-muta'āliyyah fi'l-asfār al-arba'at al-'aqliyyah (*Transcendental Theosophy on The Four Intellectual Journies of the Soul*), see *Asfār*
Ḥillī, 'Allāmah, 122
Hindī, Fāḍil-i. *See* Iṣfahānī, Bahā' al-Dīn
Hinduism, 63
Hindu (s), 51, 127
holy spirit (*ruh al-qudus*), 82
hudhud (hoepoe), 72
Ḥudūth al-'alam, 127
ḥukamā', 1
Hume, 104
Hurakhsh (heavenly sun), 25, 84
Hurqalyā, 84, 88, 135. *See also* archetypal world
huwa, 103

I (*nafs nāṭiqah*), 62
I-ness (*anā'iyyah*), 103
your-self (*anā'iyyātuka*), 112
Ibn 'Arabi, 124, 127, 128, 129, 134, 139
Ibn Kammunah, 122
Ibn Khaldun, 146
Ibn Sab'in, 141
Ibn Sina, xvi, xviii, 5, 6, 7, 8, 9, 10, 14, 17, 24, 31, 41, 43, 44, 45, 47, 48, 50, 81, 85, 123, 124, 125, 126, 127, 128–29, 131, 137, 140, 142
Ibn Sinian, xviii, 5, 31, 41, 78, 80, 83, 85, 127; logic. *See* logic, Ibn Sinian; metaphysics. *See* metaphysics, Ibn Sinian
icons (*sanam*), 82
iḍāfah (relation), 80, 86, 161
ideas (*a'yān al-thābitah*), 46; innate, 100, 101
ignorance (*ashqiyā'*), 49